EARLY BRITAIN—
ROMAN BRITAIN

A MAP OF BRITAIN to illustrate
THE ROMAN OCCUPATION.

London: Published by the Society for Promoting Christian Knowledge.

Edward Conybeare

EARLY BRITAIN—ROMAN BRITAIN

WITH MAP

BIBLIOBAZAAR

EARLY BRITAIN—
ROMAN BRITAIN

PREFACE

A little book on a great subject, especially when that book is one of a "series," is notoriously an object of literary distrust. For the limitations thus imposed upon the writer are such as few men can satisfactorily cope with, and he must needs ask the indulgence of his readers for his painfully-felt shortcomings in dealing with the mass of material which he has to manipulate. And more especially is this the case when the volume which immediately precedes his in the series is such a mine of erudition as the 'Celtic Britain' of Professor Rhys.

In the present work my object has been to give a readable sketch of the historical growth and decay of Roman influence in Britain, illustrated by the archaeology of the period, rather than a mainly archaeological treatise with a bare outline of the history. The chief authorities of which I have made use are thus those original classical sources for the early history of our island, so carefully and ably collected in the 'Monumenta Historica Britannica';[1] which, along with Huebner's 'Corpus Inscriptionum Latinarum[2],' must always be the foundation of every work on Roman Britain. Amongst the many other authorities consulted I must acknowledge my special debt to Mr. Elton's 'Origins of English History'; and yet more to Mr. Haverfield's invaluable publications in the 'Antiquary' and elsewhere, without which to keep abreast of the incessant development of my subject by the antiquarian spade-work now going on all over the land would be an almost hopeless task.

EDWARD CONYBEARE.

* * * * *

BIBLIOGRAPHY

A complete Bibliography of Roman Britain would be wholly beyond the scope of the present work. Much of the most valuable material, indeed, has never been published in book form, and must be sought out in the articles of the 'Antiquary,' 'Hermes,' etc., and the reports of the many local Archaeological Societies. All that is here attempted is to indicate some of the more valuable of the many scores of sources to which my pages are indebted.

To begin with the ancient authorities. These range through upwards of a thousand years; from Herodotus in the 5th century before Christ, to Gildas in the 6th century after. From about 100 A.D. onwards we find that almost every known classical authority makes more or less mention of Britain. A list of over a hundred such authors is given in the 'Monumenta Historica Britannica'; and upwards of fifty are quoted in this present work. Historians, poets, geographers, naturalists, statesmen, ecclesiastics, all give touches which help out our delineation of Roman Britain.

Amongst the historians the most important are—Caesar, who tells his own tale; Tacitus, to whom we owe our main knowledge of the Conquest, with the later stages of which he was contemporary; Dion Cassius, who wrote his history in the next century, the 2nd A.D.;[3] the various Imperial biographers of the 3rd century; the Imperial panegyrists of the 4th, along with Ammianus Marcellinus, who towards the close of that century connects and supplements their stories; Claudian, the poet-historian of the 5th century, whose verses throw a lurid gleam on his own disastrous age, when Roman authority in Britain was at its last gasp; and finally the British writers, Nennius and Gildas, whose "monotonous plaint" shows that authority dead and gone, with the first stirring of our new national life already quickening amid the decay.

Of geographical and general information we gain most from Strabo, in the Augustan age, who tells what earlier and greater geographers than himself had already discovered about our island; Pliny the Elder, who, in the next century, found the ethnology and botany of Britain so valuable for his 'Natural History'; Ptolemy, a generation later yet, who includes an elaborate survey of our island in his stupendous Atlas (as it would now be called) of the world;[4] and the unknown compilers of the 'Itinerary,' the 'Notitia,' and the 'Ravenna Geography.' To these must be added the epigrammatist Martial, who lived at the time of the Conquest, and whose references to British matters throw a precious light on the social connection between Britain and Rome which aids us to trace something of the earliest dawn of Christianity in our land.[5]

* * * * *

ANCIENT AUTHORITIES REFERRED TO IN THIS WORK

NAME.	REFERENCE.	APPROXIMATE DATE, ETC.
Aelian	III. A. 6	A.D. 220. Naturalist.
Appian	IV. D. 1	A.D. 140. Historian.
Aristides	V.E. 4	A.D. 160. Orator.
Aristotle	I.C. 1	B.C. 333. Philosopher.
St. Athanasius	V.B. 1, etc.	A.D. 333. Theologian.
Ausonius	V.B. 7	A.D. 380. Poet.
Caesar	V. etc.	B.C. 55. Historian.
Capitolinus	IV. E. 3	A.D. 290. Imperial Biographer.
Catullus	V.E. 4	B.C. 33. Poet.
St. Chrysostom	V.E. 15, etc.	A.D. 380. Theologian.
Cicero	I.D. 3, etc.	B.C. 55. Orator, etc.
Claudian	vi. etc.	A.D. 400. Poet-Historian.
St. Clement	V.E. 4	A.D. 80. Theologian.
Constantius	V.F. 4	A.D. 480. Ecclesiastical Biographer.
Diodorus Siculus	I.E. 11, etc.	B.C. 44. Geographer.
Dion Cassius	v. etc.	A.D. 150. Historian.
Dioscorides	I.E. 4	A.D. 80. Physician.
Eumenius	V.A. 1	A.D. 310. Imperial Panegyrist.
Eutropius	V.A. 1	A.D. 300. Imperial Panegyrist.
Firmicus	V.B. 2	A.D. 350. Controversialist.
Frontinus	III. A. 1	A.D. 80. Wrote on Tactics.
Fronto	IV. D. 2	A.D. 100. Historian.
Gildas	vi. etc.	A.D. 500. Theologian.
Hegesippus	II. F. 3	A.D. 150. Historian.

Herodian	IV. E. 3	A.D. 220. Historian.
Herodotus	I.C. 3	B.C. 444. Historian, etc.
St. Hilary	V.B. 3	A.D. 350. Theologian.
Horace	III. A. 7	B.C. 25. Poet.
Itinerary	IV. A. 7	A.D. 200.
St. Jerome	V.C. 12	A.D. 400. Theologian.
Josephus	III. F. 1	A.D. 70. Historian.
Juvenal	III. F. 5	A.D. 75. Satirist.
Lampridius	IV. E. 1	A.D. 290. Imperial Biographer.
Lucan	II. E. 1	A.D. 60. Historical Poet.
Mamertinus	V.A. 5	A.D. 280. Panegyrist.
Marcellinus	vi. etc.	A.D. 380. Historian.
Martial	vi. etc.	A.D. 70. Epigrammatist.
Maximus	II. C. 13	A.D. 30. Wrote Memorabilia.
Mela	I.H. 7	A.D. 50. Geographer, etc.
Menologia Graeca	V.E. 5	A.D. 550.
Minucius Felix	I.E. 2	A.D. 210. Geographer.
Nemesianus	IV. C. 15	A.D. 280. Wrote on Hunting.
Nennius	vi. etc.	A.D. 500. Historian.
Notitia	vi. etc.	A.D. 406.
Olympiodorus	V.C. 10	A.D. 425. Historian.
Onomacritus	I.C. 1	B.C. 333. Poet.
Oppian	IV. C. 15	A.D. 140. Wrote on Hunting
Origen	V.E. 13	A.D. 220. Theologian.
Pliny	vi. etc.	A.D. 70. Naturalist.
Plutarch	I.C. 1	A.D. 80. Historian, etc.
Polyaenus	II. E. 8	A.D. 180. Wrote on Tactics.
Procopius	V.D. 5	A.D. 555. Wrote on Geography, etc.
Propertius	III. 1. 7	B.C. 10. Poet.
Prosper	V.F. 4	A.D. 450. Ecclesiastical Historian.
Prudentius	IV. C. 15	A.D. 370. Ecclesiastical Poet.
Ptolemy	v. etc.	A.D. 120. Geographer.
Ravenna Geography	vi. etc.	A.D. 450.

Seneca	III. C. 7	A.D. 60. Philosopher.
Sidonius Apollinaris	V.F. 3	A.D. 475. Letters.
Solinus	I.E. 4, etc.	A.D. 80. Geographer.
Spartianus	IV. D. 2	A.D. 303. Historian.
Strabo	vi. etc.	B.C. 20. Geographer.
Suetonius	I.H. 10	A.D. 110. Imperial Biographer.
Symmachus	IV. C. 15	A.D. 390. Statesman, etc.
Tacitus	v. etc.	A.D. 80. Historian.
Tertullian	V.E. 11	A.D. 180. Theologian.
Theodoret	V.E. 4	A.D. 420. Wrote Commentaries.
Tibullus	III. A. 7	B.C. 20. Poet.
Timaeus	I.D. 2	B.C. 300. Geographer.
Vegetius	V.B. 5	A.D. 380. Historian.
Venantius	V.E. 4	A.D. 580. Wrote Ecclesiastical Poems.
Victor	V.A. 9	A.D. 380. Historian.
Virgil	III. 1. 7	B.C. 30. Poet.
Vitruvius	I.G. 5	A.D. Wrote on Geography, etc.
Vobiscus	IV. C. 17	A.D. 290. Historian.
Xiphilinus	vi. etc.	A.D. 1200. Abridged Dio Cassius.
Zosimus	V.C. 11	A.D. 400. Historian.

* * * * *

LATER AUTHORITIES

The constant accession of new material, especially from the unceasing spade-work always going on in every quarter of the island, makes modern books on Roman Britain tend to become obsolete, sometimes with startling rapidity. But even when not quite up to date, a well-written book is almost always very far from worthless, and much may be learnt from any in the following list:—

BABCOCK	'The Two Last Centuries of Roman Britain' (1891).
BARNES	'Ancient Britain' (1858).
BROWNE, BISHOP	'The Church before Augustine' (1895).
BRUCE	'Handbook to the Roman Wall' (1895).
CAMDEN	'Britannia' (1587).
COOTE	'Romans in Britain' (1878).
DAWKINS	'Early Man in Britain' (1880).
	'The Place of the Welsh in English History' (1889).
DILL	'Roman Society' (1899).
ELTON	'Origins of English History' (1890).
EVANS, SIR J.	'British Coins' (1869).
	'Bronze Implements' (1881).
	'Stone Implements' (1897).
FREEMAN	'Historical Essays' (1879).
	'English Towns' (1883).
	'Tyrants of Britain' (1886).
FROUDE	'Julius Caesar' (1879).
GUEST	'Origines Celticae' (1883).

HADDAN AND STUBBS	'Concilia' (1869).
	'Remains' (1876).
HARDY	'Monumenta Historica Britannica' (1848).
HAVERFIELD	'Roman World' (1899), etc.
HODGKIN	'Italy and her Invaders' (1892), etc.
HOGARTH (ed.)	'Authority and Archaeology' (1899).
HORSLEY	'Britannia Romana' (1732).
HUEBNER	'Inscriptiones Britannicae Romanae' (1873).
	'Inscriptiones Britannicae'
	'Christianae' (1876), etc.
KEMBLE	'Saxons in England' (1876).
KENRICK	'Phoenicia' (1855).
	'Papers on History' (1864).
LEWIN	'Invasion of Britain' (1862).
LUBBOCK, SIR J.	'Origin of Civilization' (1889).
LYALL	'Natural Religion' (1891).
LYELL	'Antiquity of Man' (1873).
MAINE, SIR H.	'Early History of Institutions' (1876).
MAITLAND	'Domesday Studies' (1897).
MARQUARDT	'Römische Staatsverwaltung' (1873).
MOMMSEN	'Provinces of the Roman Empire' (1865).
NEILSON	'Per Lineam Valli' (1892).
PEARSON	'Historical Atlas of Britain' (1870).
RHYS	'Celtic Britain' (1882).
	'Celtic Heathendom' (1888).
	'Welsh People' (1900).
ROLLESTON	'British Barrows' (1877).
	'Prehistoric Fauna' (1880).
SCARTH	'Roman Britain' (1885).
SMITH, C.R.	'Collectanea' (1848), etc.
TOZER	'History of Ancient Geography' (1897).

TRAILL AND MANN	'Social England' (1901).
USHER, BP.	'British Ecclesiastical Antiquity' (1639).
VINE	'Caesar in Kent' (1899).
WRIGHT	'Celt, Roman and Saxon' (1875).

CHRONOLOGICAL TABLE

DATE	EVENTS.	EMPEROR.
B.C.		
350 (?)	Pytheas discovers Britain [I.D. 1]	
100 (?)	Divitiacus Overlord of Britain (?) [II. B. 4]	
	Gauls settle on Thames and Humber (?) [I.F. 4]	
	Posidonius visits Britain [I.D. 3]	
	Birth of Julius Caesar [II. A. 6]	
58	Caesar conquers Gaul [II. A. 9]	
56	Sea-fight with Veneti and Britons [II. B. 3]	
55	First invasion of Britain [II. C., D.]	
	Cassivellaunus Overlord of Britain (?) [II. F. 3]	
	Mandubratius, exiled Prince of Trinobantes, appeals to Caesar (?) [II. E. 10]	
54	Second Invasion of Britain [II. E., F., G.]	
52	Revolt of Gaul. Commius, Prince of Arras, flies to Britain and reigns in South-east [III. A. 1]	
44	Caesar slain [II. G. 9]	
32	Battle of Actium [III. A. 6]	Augustus.

	About this time the sons of Commius reign in Kent, etc., Addeomarus over Iceni, and Tasciovan at Verulam [III. A. 1]	
A.D.	About this time the Commian princes are overthrown [III. A. 2]	
	Cymbeline, son of Tasciovan, becomes Overlord of Britain [III. A. 4]. Commians appeal to Augustus [III. A. 5]	
14	Death of Augustus	Tiberius.
29	Consulship of the Gemini. The Crucifixion (?)	
37	Death of Tiberius	Caligula.
40 (?)	Cymbeline banishes Adminius, who appeals to Rome [III. A. 5] Caligula threatens invasion [III. A. 6]	
41	Caligula poisoned [III. A. 9] Death of Cymbeline (?). His son Caradoc succeeds	Claudius.
43	Antedrigus and Vericus contend for Icenian throne: Vericus appeals to Rome [III. A. 9]	
44	Claudius subdues Britain [III. B.] Cogidubnus, King in South-east, made Roman Legate [III. C. 8]	
45	Triumph of Claudius [III. C. 1, 2]	
47	Ovation of Aulus Plautius, conqueror of Britain. [III. C. 2]	
48	Vespasian and Titus crush British	

guerrillas [III. C. 3]

50   Britain made "Imperial" Province.
Ostorius Pro-praetor
[III. C. 9]
Icenian revolt crushed [III. D.
1-6].
Camelodune a colony [III. D. 8]

51   Silurian revolt under Caradoc
[III. D. 7, 8]

52   Caradoc captive [III. D. 9]

53   Uriconium and Caerleon founded
[III. D. 12]

54   Death of Ostorius [III. D. 11]

55   Didius Gallus Pro-praetor. Last
Silurian effort [III. D. 13]
Death of Claudius [III. D. 13]   Nero.

56 (?)   Aulus Plautius marries Pomponia
Graecina [V.E. 10]

61   Suetonius Paulinus Pro-praetor
[III. E. 7]
Massacre of Druids in Mona
[III. E. 8, 9]
Boadicean revolt [III. E. 2-13].
St. Peter in Britain (?) [V.E. 5]

62   Turpiliannus Pro-praetor. "Peace"
in Britain [III. E. 13]

63 (?)   Claudia Rufina Marries Pudens
[V.E. 9]

64   Burning of Rome. First Persecution.
St. Paul in Britain (?)
[V.E. 4]

65   Aristobulus Bishop in Britain (?)
[V.E. 5]

68	Death of Nero (June 10)	Galba.
	Galba slain (Dec. 16)	Civil War between
69	Otho slain (April 20)	Otho and Vitellius.
	Vitellius slain (Dec. 20)	
	British army under Agricola	Vespasian.
	pronounces for Vespasian	
	[III. F. 1]	
70	Cerealis Pro-praetor. Brigantes	
	subdued by Agricola [III. F. 1]	
	Destruction of Jerusalem	
	[IV. C. 5]	
75	Frontinus Pro-praetor. Silurians	
	subdued by Agricola [III. F. 2]	
78	Agricola Pro-praetor. Ordovices	
	and Mona subdued [III. F. 3]	
79	Agricola Latinizes Britain [III.	Titus.
	F. 4]. Vespasian dies	
80	Agricola's first Caledonian campaign	
	[III. F. 5].	
81	Agricola's rampart from Forth to	Domitian.
	Clyde [III. F. 7]. Titus dies	
82	Agricola invades Ireland (?) [III.	
	F. 5]	
83	Agricola advances into Northern	
	Caledonia [III. F. 5]	
	First circumnavigation of Britain	
	[III. F. 7]	
84	Agricola defeats Galgacus [III.	
	F. 6], resigns and dies [III. F. 7]	
95	Second persecution. Flavia Domitilla	
	[V.E. 11]	
96	Domitian slain	Nerva.
98	Nerva dies	Trajan.

117	Trajan dies	Hadrian.
120	Hadrian visits Britain and builds Wall [IV. D. 1]	
	Britain divided into "Upper" and "Lower" [IV. D. 3]	
	First "Britannia" coinage [IV. D. 4]	
138	Hadrian dies	Antoninus Pius.
139	Lollius Urbicus, Legate in Britain, replaces Agricola's rampart by turf wall from Forth to Clyde [IV. D. 5]	
140	Britain made Pro-consular [IV. E. 5]	
161	Antoninus dies	Marcus Aurelius.
180	British Church organized by Pope Eleutherius (?) [V.E. 12]	
	Marcus Aurelius dies	Commodus.
181	Caledonian invasion driven back by Ulpius Marcellus [IV. E. 1]	
184	Commodus "Britannicus" [IV. E. 1]	
185	British army mutinies against reforms of Perennis [IV. E. 1]	
187	Pertinax quells mutineers [IV. E. 3]	
192	Pertinax superseded by Junius Severus [IV. E. 3]	
	Death of Commodus	Interregnum.
193	Pertinax slain by Julianus and Albinus. Julianus slain	Pertinax; Julianus; Albinus; Severus.
	Severus proclaimed. Albinus Emperor in Britain [IV. E. 3]	
197	British army defeated at Lyons. Albinus slain [IV. E. 3]	Severus.
201	Vinius Lupus, Pro-praetor, buys off Caledonians [IV. E. 4]	
208	Caledonian invasion. Severus comes to	

	Britain [IV. E. 5]	
209	Severus overruns Caledonia [IV. E. 5]	
210	Severus completes Hadrian's Wall [IV. E. 6]	
211	Severus dies at York [IV. G. 2]	Caracalla. Geta.
212	Geta murdered [IV. G. 2]	Caracalla.
215 (?)	Roman citizenship extended to British provincials [IV. G. 2]	
(?)	Itinerary of Antonius [IV. A. 7]	
217	Caracalla slain	Macrinus.
218	Macrinus slain	Helagabalus.
222	Helagabalus slain	Alexander Severus.
235	Alexander Severus slain	Maximin.
238	Maximin slain	Gordian.
244	Gordian slain	Philip.
249	Philip slain	Decius.
251	Decius slain	Gallus.
254	Gallus slain	Valerian. {Gallienus.
258	Postumus proclaimed Emperor in Britain [V.A. 1]	
260	Valerian slain	Gallienus.
265	Victorinus associated with Postumus [V.A. 1]	
268	Gallienus slain	Tetricus.
269	Tetricus slain	Claudius Gothicus.
270	Claudius Gothicus dies	Aurelian.
273 (?)	Constantius Chlorus marries Helen, a British lady [V.A. 6]	
274	Constantine the Great born at York [V.A. 6]	

275	Aurelian slain	Tacitus.
276	Tacitus slain	Florianus.
	Florianus slain	Probus.
277	Vandal prisoners deported to Britain [V.A. 1]	
282	Probus slain	Carus.
283	Carus dies	Numerian.
284	Numerian dies	Carinus.
285	Carinus dies	Diocletian.
		Maximian.
286	Carausius, first "Count of the Saxon Shore," becomes Emperor in Britain [V.A. 3]	
292	Constantine and Galerius "Caesars" [V.A. 5]	
294	Carausius murdered by Allectus [V.A. 4]	
296	Constantius slays Allectus and recovers Britain [V.A. 7, 8] Britain divided into four "Diocletian" Provinces [V.A. 9]	
303	Tenth Persecution. Martyrdom of St. Alban [V.A. 11]	
305	Diocletian and Maximian abdicate [V.A. 12]	Constantius. Galerius.
306	Constantius dies at York [V.A. 13]. Constantine, Galerius, Maxentius, Licinius, etc., contend for Empire [V.A. 14]	Interregnum.
312	Constantine with British Army wins at Milvian Bridge, and embraces Christianity [V.A. 14]	Constantine.
314	Council of Arles [V.E. 14]	

325	Council of Nicaea [V.B. 1]	
		Constantine II.
337	Constantine dies	Constantius II.
		Constans.
340	Constantine II. dies	
343	Constans and Constantius II. visit Britain [V.B. 1]	
350	Constans slain. Usurpation of Magnentius in Britain [V.B. 3]	Constantius II.
353	Magnentius dies [V.B. 3]	
358	Britain under Julian. Exportation of corn [V.B. 4]	
360	Council of Ariminum [V.E. 14]	
361	Death of Constantius [V.B. 6]	Julian.
362	Lupicinus, Legate in Britain, repels first attacks of Picts and Scots [V.B. 5]	
363	Julian dies	Valentinian. Valens.
365	Saxons, Picts, and Scots ravage shores of Britain [V.B. 7]	
		Valentinian.
366	Gratian associated in Empire	Valens.
		Gratian.
367	Great barbarian raid on Britain Roman commanders slain [V.B. 7]	
368	Theodosius, Governor of Britain, expels Picts and Scots [V.B. 7]	
369	Theodosius recovers Valentia [V.B. 7]	
374	Saxons invade Britain [V.B. 8]	

Year	Event	Emperors
375	Valentinian dies	Valens. Gratian. {Valentinian II. Gratian.
378	Valens slain. Theodosius associated in Empire	Valentinian II. Theodosius.
383	Gratian slain. British Army proclaims Maximus and conquer Gaul [V.C. 1]	Valentinian II. Theodosius.
387	British Army under Maximus take Rome [V.C. 1]	
388	Maximus slain. First British settlement in Armorica (?) [V.C. 1]	
392	Valentinian II. slain. Penal laws against Heathenism	Theodosius.
394	Ninias made Bishop of Picts by Pope Siricius (?) [V.F. 1]	
395	Death of Theodosius	Arcadius. Honorius.
396	Stilicho sends a Legion to protect Britain (?) [V.C. 1]	
402	Theodosius II. associated in Empire	Arcadius. Honorius. Theodosius II.
406	Stilicho recalls Legion to meet Radagaisus [V.C. 2] 'Notitia' composed (?) [V.C. 3-9] German tribes flood Gaul [V.C. 2]	
407	British Army proclaim Constantine III. and reconquer Gaul [V.C. 10]	
408	Arcadius dies. Constantine III.	Honorius.

	recognized as "Augustus"	Theodosius II.
		Constantine III.
410	Visigoths under Alaric take Rome [V.C. 11]	
411	Constantine III. slain	Honorius.
		Theodosius II.
413 (?)	Pelagian heresy arises in Britain [V.F. 3]	
415 (?)	Rescript of Honorius to the Cities of Britain [V.C. 11]	
423	Death of Honorius	Theodosius II.
425	Valentinian III., son of Galla Placidia, Emperor of West [V.D. 3]	Theodosius II. Valentinian III.
429 (?)	SS. Germanus and Lupus sent to Britain by Pope Celestine (?) [V.F. 4]	
432 (?)	St. Patrick sent to Ireland by Pope Celestine [V.F. 2]	
435 (?)	Roman Legion sent to aid Britons (?)	
436 (?)	Roman forces finally withdrawn (?)	
446	Vain appeal of Britons to Actius (?) [V.D. 2]	
447 (?)	The Alleluia Battle [V.F. 4]	
449 (?)	Hengist and Horsa settle in Thanet (?) [V.D. 3]	
450 (?)	English defeat Picts at Stamford(?) [V.B. 2]	
	Theodosius II. dies	Valentinian III.
455 (?)	Battle of Aylesford begins English conquest of Britain (?) [V.D. 2]	

* * * * *

CONTENTS

THE END OF ROMAN BRITAIN
A.D. 211-455

* * * * *

CHAPTER I

PRE-ROMAN BRITAIN

SECTION A.

Palaeolithic Age—Extinct fauna—River-bed men—Flint implements—Burnt stones—Worked bones—Glacial climate.

A. 1.—All history, as Professor Freeman so well points out, centres round the great name of Rome. For, of all the great divisions of the human race, it is the Aryan family which has come to the front. Assimilating, developing, and giving vastly wider scope to the highest forms of thought and religion originated by other families, notably the Semitic, the various Aryan nationalities form, and have formed for ages, the vanguard of civilization. These nationalities are now practically co-extensive with Christendom; and on them has been laid by Divine Providence "the white man's burden"—the task of raising the rest of mankind along with themselves to an ever higher level—social, material, intellectual, and spiritual.

A. 2.—Aryan history is thus, for all practical purposes, the history of mankind. And a mere glance at Aryan history shows how entirely its great central feature is the period during which all the leading forces of Aryanism were grouped and fused together under the world-wide Empire of Rome. In that Empire all the streams of our Ancient History find their end, and from that Empire all those of Modern History take their beginning. "All roads," says the proverb, "lead to Rome;" and this is emphatically true of the lines of historical research; for as we tread them we are conscious at every step of the *Romani Nominis umbra*, the all-pervading influence of "the mighty name of Rome."

A. 3.—And above all is this true of the history of Western Europe in general and of our own island in particular. For Britain, History (meaning thereby the more or less trustworthy record of political and social development) does not even begin till its destinies were drawn within the sphere of Roman influence. It is with Julius Caesar, that great writer (and yet greater maker) of History, that, for us, this record commences.

A. 4.—But before dealing with "Britain's tale" as connected with "Caesar's fate," it will be well to note briefly what earlier information ancient documents and remains can afford us with regard to our island and its inhabitants. With the earliest dwellers upon its soil of whom traces remain we are, indeed, scarcely concerned. For in the far-off days of the "River-bed" men (five thousand or five hundred thousand years ago, according as we accept the physicist's or the geologist's estimate of the age of our planet) Britain was not yet an island. Neither the Channel nor the North Sea as yet cut it off from the Continent when those primaeval savages herded beside the banks of its streams, along with elephant and hippopotamus, bison and elk, bear and hyaena; amid whose remains we find their roughly-chipped flint axes and arrow-heads, the fire-marked stones which they used in boiling their water, and the sawn or broken bases of the antlers which for some unknown purpose[6] they were in the habit of cutting up—perhaps, like the Lapps of to-day, to anchor their sledges withal in the snow. For the great Glacial Epoch, which had covered half the Northern Hemisphere with its mighty ice-sheet, was still, in their day, lingering on, and their environment was probably that of Northern Siberia to-day. Some archaeologists, indeed, hold that they are to this day represented by the Esquimaux races; but this theory cannot be considered in any way proved.

A. 5.—Whether, indeed, they were "men" at all, in any real sense of the word, may well be questioned. For of the many attempts which philosophers in all ages have made to define the word "man," the only one which is truly defensible is that which differentiates him from other animals, not by his physical or intellectual, but by his spiritual superiority. Many other creatures are as well adapted in bodily conformation for their environment, and the lowest savages are intellectually at a far lower level of development than the highest insects; but none stand in the same relation to the Unseen. "Man," as has been well said, "is the one animal that can pray." And there is nothing amongst the remains of these "river-bed men" to show us that they either did pray, or could. Intelligence, such as is now found only in human beings, they undoubtedly had. But whether they had the capacity for Religion must be left an unsolved problem. In this connection, however, it may be noted that Tacitus, in describing the lowest savages of his Germania [c. 46], "with no horses, no homes, no weapons, skin-clad, nesting on the bare ground, men and women alike, barely kept alive by herbs and such flesh as their bone-tipped arrows can win them," makes it his climax that they are "beneath the need of prayer;"—adding that this spiritual condition is, "beyond all others, that least attainable by man."

SECTION B.

Neolithic Age— "Ugrians"—Polished flints—Jadite—Gold ornaments— Cromlechs—Forts—Bronze Age—Copper and tin—Stonehenge.

B. 1.—Whatever they were, they vanish from our ken utterly, these Palaeolithic savages, and are followed, after what lapse of time we know not, by the users of polished flint weapons, the tribes of the Neolithic period. And with them we find ourselves in touch with the existing development of our island. For an island it already was, and with substantially the same area and shores and physical features as we have them still. Our rivers ran in the same valleys, our hills rose with the same contour, in those far-off days as now. And while the place of flint in the armoury of Britain was taken first by bronze and then by iron, these changes were made by no sudden breaks, but so gradually that it is impossible to say when one period ended and the next began.

B.2.—It is almost certain, however, that the Neolithic men were not of Aryan blood. They are commonly spoken of by the name of *Ugrians,*[7] the "ogres"[8] of our folk-lore; which has also handed down, in the spiteful Brownie of the wood and the crafty Pixie of the cavern, dimly-remembered traditions of their physical and mental characteristics. Indeed it is not impossible that their blood may still be found in the remoter corners of our land, whither they were pushed back by the higher civilization of the Aryan invaders, before whom they disappeared by a process in which "miscegenation" may well have played no small part. But disappear they did, leaving behind them no more traces than their flint arrow-heads and axes (a few of these being of jadite, which must have come from China or thereabouts), together with their oblong sepulchral barrows, from some of which the earth has weathered away, so that the massive stones imbedded in it as the last home of the deceased stand exposed as a "dolmen" or "cromlech." But an appreciable number of the earthworks which stud our hill-tops, and are popularly called "Roman" or "British" camps, really belong to this older race. Such are "Cony Castle" in Dorset, and the fortifications along the Axe in Devon.

B. 3.—During the neolithic stage of their development the Ugrians were acquainted with but one metal, gold, and some of their stone weapons and implements are thus ornamented. For gold, being at once the most beautiful, the most incorruptible, the most easily recognizable, and the most easily worked of metals, is everywhere found as used by man long before any other. But before the Ugrian races vanish they had learnt to use bronze, which shows them to have discovered the properties not only of gold, but of both tin and copper. All three metals were doubtless obtained from the streams of the West. They had also become proficients, as their sepulchral urns show, in the manufacture of pottery. They could weave, moreover, both linen and woollen being known, and had passed far beyond the mere savage.

B. 4.—The race, indeed, which could erect Avebury and Stonehenge, as we may safely say was done by this people,[9] must have possessed engineering skill of a very high order, and no little accuracy of astronomical observation. For the mighty "Sarsen" stones have all been brought from a distance,[10] and the whole vast circles are built on a definite astronomical plan; while so careful is the orientation that, at the summer solstice, the disc of the rising sun, as seen from the "altar" of Stonehenge, appears to be poised exactly on the summit of one of the chief megaliths (now known as "The Friar's Heel"). From this it would seem that the builders were Sun-worshippers; and amongst the earliest reports of Britain current in the Greek world we find the fame of the "great round temple" dedicated to Apollo. But no Latin author mentions it; so that it is doubtful whether it was ever used by the Aryan, or at least by the Brythonic, immigrants. These brought their own worship and their own civilization with them, and all that was highest in Ugrian civilization and worship faded before them, such Ugrians as remained having degenerated to a far lower level when first we meet with them in history.

SECTION C.

Aryan immigrants—Gael and Briton—Earliest classical nomenclature—British Isles—Albion—Ierne—Cassiterides—Phoenician tin trade viâ Cadiz.

C. 1.—How or when the first swarms of the Aryan migration reached Britain is quite unknown.[11] But they undoubtedly belonged to the Celtic branch of that family, and to the Gaelic (Gadhelic or Goidelic) section of the branch, which still holds the Highlands of Scotland and forms the bulk of the population of Ireland. By the 4th century B.C. this section was already beginning to be pressed northwards and westwards by the kindred Britons (or Brythons) who followed on their heels; for Aristotle (or a disciple of his) knows our islands as "the Britannic[12] Isles." That the Britons were in his day but new comers may be argued from the fact that he speaks of Great Britain by the name of *Albion*, a Gaelic designation subsequently driven northwards along with those who used it. In its later form *Albyn* it long remained as loosely equivalent to North Britain, and as *Albany* it still survives in a like connection. Ireland Aristotle calls *Ierne*, the later Ivernia or Hibernia; a word also found in the Argonautic poems ascribed to the mythical Orpheus, and composed probably by Onomacritus about 350 B.C., wherein the Argo is warned against approaching "the Iernian islands, the home of dark and noisome mischief." This is the passage familiar to the readers of Kingsley's 'Heroes.'[13]

C. 2.—Aristotle's work does no more than mention our islands, as being, like Ceylon, not pelagic, but oceanic. To early classical antiquity, it must be remembered, the Ocean was no mere sea, but a vast and mysterious river encircling the whole land surface of the earth. Its mighty waves, its tides, its furious currents, all made it an object of superstitious horror. To embark upon it was the height of presumption; and even so late as the time of Claudius we shall find the Roman soldiers feeling that to do so, even for the passage of the Channel, was "to leave the habitable world."

C. 3.—But while the ancients dreaded the Ocean, they knew also that its islands alone were the source of one of the most precious and rarest of their metals. Before iron came into general use (and the difficulty of smelting it has everywhere made it the last metal to do so), tin had a value all its own. It was the only known substance capable of making, along with copper, an alloy hard enough for cutting purposes—the "bronze" which has given its name to one entire Age of human development. It was thus all but a necessary of life, and was eagerly sought for as amongst the choicest objects of traffic.

C. 4.—The Phoenicians, the merchant princes of the dawn of history, succeeded, with true mercantile instinct, in securing a monopoly of this trade, by being the first to make their way to the only spots in the world where tin is found native, the Malay region in the East, Northern Spain and Cornwall in the West. That tin was known amongst the Greeks by its Sanscrit name *Kastira*[14] κασσιτερ'ς [kassiteros], shows that the Eastern source was the earliest to be tapped. But the Western was that whence the supply flowed throughout the whole of the classical ages; and, as the stream-tin of the Asturian mountains seems to have been early exhausted, the name *Cassiterides*, the Tin Lands, came to signify exclusively the western peninsula of Britain. Herodotus, in the 5th century B.C., knew this name, but, as he frankly confesses, nothing but the name.[15] For the whereabouts of this El Dorado, and the way to it, was a trade secret most carefully kept by the Phoenician merchants of Cadiz, who alone held the clue. So jealous were they of it that long afterwards, when the alternative route through Gaul had already drawn away much of its profitableness, we read of a Phoenician captain purposely wrecking his ship lest a Roman vessel in sight should follow to the port, and being indemnified by the state for his loss.

SECTION D.

Discoveries of Pytheas—Greek tin trade viâ Marseilles—Trade routes—Ingots—Coracles—Earliest British coins—Lead-mining.

D. 1.—But contemporary with Aristotle lived the great geographer Pytheas; whose works, unfortunately, we know only by the fragmentary references to them in later, and frequently hostile, authors, such as Strabo, who dwell largely on his mistakes, and charge him with misrepresentation. In fact, however, he seems to have been both an accurate and truthful observer, and a discoverer of the very first order. Starting from his native city Massilia (Marseilles), he passed through the Straits of Gibraltar and traced the coast-line of Europe to Denmark (visiting Britain on his way), and perhaps even on into the Baltic.[16] The shore of Norway (which he called, as the natives still call it, Norgé) he followed till within the Arctic Circle, as his mention of the midnight sun shows, and then struck across to Scotland; returning, apparently by the Irish Sea, to Bordeaux and so home overland. This truly wonderful voyage he made at the public charge, with a view to opening new trade routes, and it seems to have thoroughly answered its purpose. Henceforward the Phoenician monopoly was broken, and a constant stream of traffic in the precious tin passed between Britain and Marseilles.[17]

D. 2.—The route was kept as secret as possible; Polybius tells us that the Massiliots, when interrogated by one of the Scipios, professed entire ignorance of Britain; but Pytheas (as quoted by his contemporary Timaeus, as well as by later writers) states that the metal was brought by coasters to a tidal island, *Ictis*, whence it was shipped for Gaul. This island was six days' sail from the tin diggings, and can scarcely be any but Thanet. St. Michael's Mount, now the only tidal island on the south coast, was anciently part of the mainland; a fact testified to by the forest remains still seen around it. Nor could it be six days' sail from the tin mines. The Isle of Wight, again, to which the name Ictis or Vectis would seem to point, can never have been tidal at this date. But Thanet undoubtedly was so in mediaeval times, and may well have been so for ages, while its nearness to the Continent would recommend it to the Gallic merchants. Indeed Pytheas himself probably selected it on this account for his new emporium.

D. 3.—In his day, as we have seen, the tin reached this destination by sea; but in the time of the later traveller Posidonius[18] it came in wagons, probably by that track along the North Downs now known as the "Pilgrims' Way." The chalk furnished a dry and open road, much easier than the swamps and forests of the lower ground. Further west the route seems to have been *viâ* Launceston, Exeter, Honiton, Ilchester, Salisbury, Winchester, and Alton; an ancient track often traceable, and to be seen almost in its original condition near "Alfred's Tower," in Somerset, where it is known as "The Hardway." And this long land transit argues a considerable degree of political solidarity throughout the south of the island. The tale of Posidonius is confirmed by Caesar's statement that tin reached Kent "from the interior," *i.e.* by land. It was obtained at first from the streams of Dartmoor and Cornwall, where abundant traces of ancient washings are visible, and afterwards by mining, as now. And when smelted it was made up into those peculiar ingots which still meet the eye in Cornwall, and whose shape seems never to have varied from the earliest times. Posidonius, who visited Cornwall, compares them to knuckle-bones[19] αστρηαγαλοι [astrhagaloi]

D. 4.—The vessels which thus coasted from the Land's End to the South Foreland are described as on the pattern of coracles, a very light frame-work covered with hides. It seems almost incredible that sea-going craft could have been thus constructed; yet not only is there overwhelming testimony to the fact throughout the whole history of Roman Britain, but such boats are still in use on the wild rollers which beat upon the west coast of Ireland, and are found able to live in seas which would be fatal to anything more rigidly built. For the surf boats in use at Madras a similar principle is adopted, not a nail entering into their construction. They can thus face breakers which would crush an ordinary boat to pieces. This method of ship-building was common all along the northern coast of Europe for ages.[20] Nor were these coracles only used for coasting. As time went on, the Britons boldly struck straight across from Cornwall to the Continent, and both the Seine and the Loire became inlets for tin into Gaul, thus lessening the long land journey—not less than thirty days—which was required, as Polybius tells us, to convey it from the Straits of Dover to the Rhone. (This journey, it may be noted, was made not in wagons, as through Britain, but on pack-horses.)

D. 5.—Thus it reached Marseilles; and that the trade was founded by the Massiliot Pytheas is borne testimony to by the early British coins, which are all modelled on the classical currency of his age. The medium in universal circulation then, current everywhere, like the English sovereign now, was the Macedonian stater, newly introduced by Philip, a gold coin weighing 133 grains, bearing on the one side the laureated head of Apollo, on the other a figure of Victory in a chariot. Of this all known Gallic and British coins (before the Roman era) are more or less accurate copies. The earliest as yet found in Britain do not date, according to Sir John Evans, our great authority on this subject,[21] from before the 2nd century B.C. They are all dished coins, rudely struck, and rapidly growing ruder as time goes on. The head early becomes a mere congeries of dots and lines, but one horse of the chariot team remains recognizable to quite the end of the series.

D. 6.—These coins have been found in very large numbers, and of various types, according to the locality in which they were struck. They occur as far north as Edinburgh; but all seem to have been issued by one or other of the tribes in the south and east of the island, who learnt the idea of minting from the Gauls. Whence the gold of which the coins are made came from is a question not yet wholly solved: surface gold was very probably still obtainable at that date from the streams of Wales and Cornwall. But it was long before any other metal was used in the British mints. Not till after the invasion of Julius Caesar do we find any coins of silver or bronze issued, though he testifies to their existence. The use of silver shows a marked advance in metallurgy, and is probably connected with the simultaneous development of the lead-mining in the Mendip Hills, of which about this time we first begin to find traces.

SECTION E.

Pytheas trustworthy—His notes on Britain—Agricultural tribes—Barns—Manures—Dene Holes—Mead—Beer—Parched corn—Pottery—Mill-stones—Villages—Cattle—Pastoral tribes—Savage tribes—Cannibalism—Polyandry—Beasts of chase—Forest trees—British clothing and arms—Sussex iron.

E. 1.—The trustworthiness of Pytheas is further confirmed by the astronomical observations which he records. He notices, for example, that the longest day in Britain contains "nineteen equinoctial hours." Amongst the ancients, it must be remembered, an "hour," in common parlance, signified merely the twelfth part, on any given day, of the time between sunrise and sunset, and thus varied according to the season. But the standard hour for astronomical purposes was the twelfth part of the equinoctial day, when the sun rises 6 a.m. and sets 6 p.m., and therefore corresponded with our own. Now the longest day at Greenwich is actually not quite seventeen hours, but in the north of Britain it comes near enough to the assertion of Pytheas to bear out his tale. We are therefore justified in giving credence to his account of what he saw in our country, the earliest that we possess. He tells us that, in some parts at least, the inhabitants were far from being mere savages. They were corn-growers (wheat, barley, and millet being amongst their crops), and also cultivated "roots," fruit trees, and other vegetables. What specially struck him was that, "for lack of clear sunshine[22]," they threshed out their corn, not in open threshing-floors, as in Mediterranean lands, but in barns.

E. 2.—From other sources we know that these old British farmers were sufficiently scientific agriculturalists to have invented *wheeled* ploughs,[23] and to use a variety of manures; various kinds of mast, loam, and chalk in particular. This treatment of the soil was, according to Pliny, a British invention[24] (though the Greeks of Megara had also tried it), and he thinks it worth his while to give a long description of the different clays in use and the methods of their application. That most generally employed was chalk dug out from pits some hundred feet in depth, narrow at the mouth, but widening towards the bottom. [*Petitur ex alto, in centenos pedes actis plerumque puteis, ore angustatis; intus spatiante vena.*]

E. 3.—Here we have an exact picture of those mysterious excavations some of which still survive to puzzle antiquaries under the name of *Dene Holes*. They are found in various localities; Kent, Surrey, and Essex being the richest. In Hangman's Wood, near Grays, in Essex, a small copse some four acres in extent, there are no fewer than seventy-two Dene Holes, as close together as possible, their entrance shafts being not above twenty yards apart. These shafts run vertically downwards, till the floor of the pit is from eighty to a hundred feet below the surface of the ground. At the bottom the shaft widens out into a vaulted chamber some thirty feet across, from which radiate four, five, or even six lateral crypts, whose dimensions are usually about thirty feet in length, by twelve in width and height. When the shafts are closely clustered, the lateral crypts of one will extend to within a few feet of those belonging to its neighbours, but in no case do they communicate with them (though the recent excavations of archaeologists have thus connected whole groups of Dene Holes). Many theories have been elaborated to account for their existence, but the data are conclusive against their having been either habitations, tombs, store-rooms, or hiding-places; and, in 1898, Mr. Charles Dawson, F.S.A., pointed out that, in Sussex, chalk and limestone are still quarried by means of identically such pits. The chalk so procured is found a far more efficacious dressing for the soil than that which occurs on the surface, and moreover is more cheaply got than by carting from even a mile's distance. At the present day, as soon as a pit is exhausted (that is as soon as the diggers dare make their chambers no larger for fear of a downfall), another is sunk hard by, and the first filled up with the *débris* from the second. In the case of the Dene Holes, this *débris* must have been required for some other purpose; and to this fact alone we owe their preservation. It is probable that the celebrated cave at Royston in Hertfordshire was originally dug for this purpose, though afterwards used as a hermitage.

E. 4.—Pytheas is also our authority for saying that bee-keeping was known to the Britons of his day;[25] a drink made of wheat and honey being one of their intoxicants. This method of preparing mead (or metheglin) is current to this day among our peasantry. Another drink was made from barley, and this, he tells us, they called κονϱμι [kourmi], the word still used in Erse for beer, under the form *cuirm*. Dioscorides the physician, who records this (and who may perhaps have tried our national beverage, as he lived shortly after the Claudian conquest of Britain), pronounces it "head-achy, unwholesome, and injurious to the nerves": κεφαλαλγές ἐστι καὶ κακόχυμον, καὶ τοῦ νεύρου βλαπτικόν [kephalalges esti kai kakhochymon, kai tou neurou].

E. 5.—Not all the tribes of Britain, however, were at this level of civilization. Threshing in barns was only practised by those highest in development, the true Britons of the south and east. The Gaelic tribes beyond them, so far as they were agricultural at all, stored the newly-plucked ears of corn in their underground dwellings, day by day taking out and dressing κατεργαζομένους [katergazomenous] what was needed for each meal. The method here referred to is doubtless that described as still in use at the end of the 17th century in the Hebrides.[26] "A woman, sitting down, takes a handful of corn, holding it by the stalks in her left hand, and then sets fire to the ears, which are presently in a flame. She has a stick in her right hand, which she manages very dexterously, beating off the grains at the very instant when the husk is quite burnt . . . The corn may be thus dressed, winnowed, ground, and baked, within an hour of reaping."

When kept, it may usually have been stored, like that of Robinson Crusoe, in baskets;[27] for basket-making was a peculiarly British industry, and Posidonius found "British baskets" in use on the Continent. But probably it was also hoarded—again in Crusoe fashion—in the large jars of coarse pottery which are occasionally found on British sites. These, and the smaller British vessels, are sometimes elaborately ornamented with devices of no small artistic merit. But all are hand-made, the potter's wheel being unknown in pre-Roman days.

E. 6.—Nor does the grinding of corn, even in hand-mills, seem to have been universal till the Roman era, the earlier British method being to bruise the grain in a mortar.[28] Without the resources of civilization it is not easy to deal with stones hard enough for satisfactory millstones. We find that the Romans, when they came, mostly selected for this use the Hertfordshire "pudding-stone," a conglomerate of the Eocene period crammed with rolled flint pebbles, sometimes also bringing over Niederendig lava from the Rhine valley, and burr-stone from the Paris basin for their querns.

E. 7.—These tribes are described as living in cheap εὐτελεῖς [euteleis], dwellings, constructed of reeds or logs, yet spoken of as subterranean.[29] Light has been thrown on this apparent contradiction by the excavation in 1889 of the site of a British village at Barrington in Cambridgeshire. Within a space of about sixty yards each way, bounded by a fosse some six feet wide and four deep, were a collection of roughly circular pits, distributed in no recognizable system, from twelve to twenty feet in diameter and from two to four in depth. They were excavated in the chalky soil, and from each a small drainage channel ran for a yard or two down the gentle slope on which the settlement stood. Obviously a superstructure of thatch and wattle would convert these pits into quite passable wigwams, corresponding to the description of Pytheas. This whole village was covered by several feet of top-soil in which were found numerous interments of Anglo-Saxon date. It had seemingly perished by fire, a layer of incinerated matter lying at the bottom of each pit.

E. 8.—The domestic cattle of the Britons were a diminutive breed, smaller than the existing Alderney, with abnormally developed foreheads (whence their scientific name *Bos Longifrons*). Their remains, the skulls especially, are found in every part of the land, with no trace, in pre-Roman times, of any other breed. The gigantic wild ox of the British forests

(*Bos Primigenius*) seems never to have been tamed by the Celtic tribes, who, very possibly, like the Romans after them, may have brought their own cattle with them into the island. According to Professor Rolleston the small size of the breed is due to the large consumption of milk by the breeders. (He notes that the cattle of Burmah and Hindostan are identically the same stock, and that in Burmah, where comparatively little milk is used, they are of large size. In Hindostan, on the contrary, where milk forms the staple food of the population, the whole breed is stunted, no calf having, for ages, been allowed its due supply of nutriment.) The Professor also holds that these small oxen, together with the goat, sheep, horse, dog, and swine (of the Asiatic breed), were introduced into Britain by the Ugrian races in the Neolithic Age; and that the pre-Roman Britons had no domestic fowls except geese.[30]

E. 9.—If these considerations are of weight they would point to an excessive dependence on milk even amongst the agricultural tribes of Britain. And there were others, as we know, who had not got beyond the pastoral stage of human development. These, as Strabo declares, had no idea of husbandry, "nor even sense enough to make cheese, though milk they have in plenty."[31] And some of the non-Aryan hordes seem to have been mere brutal savages, practising cannibalism and having wives in common. Both practices are mentioned by the latest as well as the earliest of our classical authorities. Jerome says that in Gaul he himself saw Attacotti (the primitive inhabitants of Galloway) devouring human flesh, and refers to their sexual relations, which more probably imply some system of polyandry, such as still prevails in Thibet, than mere promiscuous intercourse. Traces of this system long remained in the rule of "Mutter-recht," which amongst several of the more remote septs traced inheritance invariably through the mother and not the father.

E. 10.—These savages knew neither corn nor cattle. Like the "Children of the Mist" in the pages of Walter Scott,[32] their boast was "to own no lord, receive no land, take no hire, give no stipend, build no hut, enclose no pasture, sow no grain; to take the deer of the forest for their flocks and herds," and to eke out this source of supply by preying upon their less barbarous neighbours "who value flocks and herds above honour and freedom." Lack of game, however, can seldom have driven them to this; for the forests of ancient Britain seem to have swarmed with animal life. Red deer, roebuck, wild oxen, and wild swine were in every brake, beaver and waterfowl in every stream; while wolf, bear, and wild-cat shared with man in taking toll of their lives. The trees of these forests, it may be mentioned, were (as in some portions of Epping Forest now) almost wholly oak, ash, holly, and yew; the beech, chestnut, elm, and even the fir, being probably introduced in later ages.

E. 11.—Of the British tribes, however, almost none, even amongst these wild woodlanders, were the naked savages, clothed only in blue paint, that they are commonly imagined to have been. On the contrary, they could both weave and spin; and the tartan, with its variegated colours, is described by Caesar's contemporary, Diodorus Siculus, as their distinctive dress, just as one might speak of Highlanders at the present day.[33] Pliny mentions that all the colours used were obtained from native herbs and lichens,[34] as is still the case in the Hebrides, where sea-weed dyes are mostly used. Woad was used for tattooing the flesh with blue patterns, and a decoction of beechen ashes for dyeing the hair red if necessary, whenever that colour was fashionable.[35] The upper classes wore collars and bracelets of gold, and necklaces of glass and amber beads.

E. 12.—This last item suggests an interesting question as to whence came the vast quantities of amber thus used. None is now found upon our shores, except a very occasional fragment on the East Anglian beaches. But the British barrows bear abundant testimony to its having been in prehistoric times the commonest of all materials for ornamental purposes—far commoner than in any other country. Beads are found by the myriad—a single Wiltshire grave furnished a thousand—mostly of a discoid shape, and about an inch in diameter. Larger plates occasionally appear, and in one case (in Sussex) a cup formed from a solid block of exceptional size. If all this came from the Baltic, the main existing source of our amber,[36] it argues a considerable trade, of which we find no mention in any extant authority. Pytheas witnesses to the amber of the Baltic, and says nothing, so far as we know, of British amber. But, according to Pliny,[37] his contemporary Solinus speaks of it as a British product; and at the Christian era it was apparently a British export.[38] The supply of amber as a jetsom is easily exhausted in any given district; miles of Baltic coast rich in it within mediaeval times are now quite barren; and the same thing has probably taken place in Britain. The rapid wearing away of our amber-bearing Norfolk shore is not unlikely to have been the cause of this change; the submarine fir-groves of the ancient littoral, with their resinous exudations, having become silted over far out at sea.[39] The old British amber sometimes contained flies. Dioscorides[40] applies to it the epithet πτερυγοφόρον [pterugophoron] ["fly-bearing"].

E. 13.—The chiefs were armed with large brightly-painted shields,[41] plumed (and sometimes crested) helmets, and cuirasses of leather, bronze, or chain-mail. The national weapons of offence were darts, pikes (sometimes with prongs—the origin of Britannia's trident), and broadswords; bows and arrows being more rarely used. Both Diodorus Siculus [v. 30] and Strabo [iv. 197] describe this equipment, and specimens of all the articles have, at one place or another, been found in British interments.[42] The arms are often richly worked and ornamented, sometimes inlaid with enamel, sometimes decorated with studs of red coral from the Mediterranean.[43] The shields, being of wood, have perished, but their circular bosses of iron still remain. The chariots, which formed so special a feature of British militarism, were also of wood, painted, like the shields, and occasionally ironclad.[44] The iron may have been from the Sussex fields. We know that in Caesar's day rings of this metal were one of the forms of British currency, so that before his time the Britons must have attained to the smelting of this most intractable of metals.

SECTION F.

F. 1.—Our earliest records point to the existence among the Celtic tribes in Britain of the two physical types still to be found amongst them; the tall, fair, red-haired, blue-eyed Gael, whom his clansmen denominate "Roy" (the Red), and the dark complexion, hair and eyes, usually associated with shorter stature, which go with the designation "Dhu" (the Black). Rob Roy and Roderick Dhu are familiar illustrations of this nomenclature. In classical times these types were much less intermingled than now, and were characteristic of separate races. The former prevailed almost exclusively amongst the true Britons of the south and east, and the Gaelic septs of the north, while the latter was found throughout the west, in Devon, Cornwall, and Wales. The Silurians, of Glamorgan, are specially noted as examples of this "black" physique, and a connection has been imagined between them and the Basques of Iberia, an idea originating with Strabo.

F. 2.—That a good deal of non-Aryan blood was, and is, to be found in both regions is fairly certain; but any closer correlation must be held at any rate not proven. For though Strabo asserts that the Silurians differ not only in looks but in language from the Britons, while in both resembling the Iberians, it is probable that he derives his information from Pytheas four centuries earlier. At that date non-Aryan speech may very possibly still have lingered on in the West, but there is no trace whatever to be found of anything of the sort in the nomenclature of the district during or since the Roman occupation. All is unmitigated Celtic. We may, however, possibly find a confirmation of Strabo's view in the word *Logris* applied to Southern Britain by the Celtic bards of the Arturian cycle. The word is said to be akin to *Liger* (Loire), and tradition traced the origin of the Loegrians to the southern banks of that river, which were undoubtedly held by Iberian (Basque) peoples at least to the date when Pytheas visited those parts. The name, indeed, seems to be connected with that of the Ligurians, a kindred non-Aryan community, surviving, in historical times, only amongst the Maritime Alps.

F. 3.—It is probable that the status of each clan was continually shifting; and what little we know of their names and locations, their rise and their fall, presents an even more kaleidoscopic phantasmagoria than the mediaeval history of the Scotch Highlands, or the principalities of Wales, or the ever-changing septs of ancient Ireland. Tribes absorbed or destroyed by conquering tribes, tribes confederating with others under a fresh name, this or that chief becoming a new eponymous hero,—such is the ceaseless spectacle of unrest of which the history of ancient Britain gives us glimpses.

F. 4.—By the time that these glimpses become anything like continuous, things were further complicated by two additional elements of disturbance. One of these was the continuous influx of new settlers from Gaul, which was going on throughout the 1st century B.C. Caesar tells us that the tribes of Kent, Sussex, and Essex were all of the Belgic stock, and we shall see that the higher politics of his day were much influenced by the fact that one and the same tribal chief claimed territorial rights in Gaul and Britain at once; just like so many of our mediaeval barons. The other was the coincidence that just at this period the British tribes began to be affected by the turbulent stage of constitutional development connected, in Greece and Rome, with the abolition of royalty.

F. 5.—The primitive Aryan community (so far, at least, as the western branch of the race is concerned) everywhere presents to us the threefold element of King, Lords, and Commons. The King is supreme, he reigns by right of birth (though not according to strict primogeniture), and he not only reigns but governs. Theoretically he is absolute, but practically can do little without taking counsel with his Lords, the aristocracy of the tribe, originally an aristocracy of birth, but constantly tending to become one of wealth. The Commons gather to ratify the decrees of their betters, with a theoretical right to dissent (though not to discuss), a right which they seldom or never at once care and dare to exercise.

F. 6.—In course of time we see that everywhere the supremacy of the Kings became more and more distasteful to the Aristocracy, and was everywhere set aside, sometimes by a process of quiet depletion of the Royal prerogative, sometimes by a revolution; the change being, in the former case, often informal, with the name, and sometimes even the succession, of the eviscerated office still lingering on. The executive then passed to the Lords, and the state became an oligarchical Republic, such as we see in Rome after the expulsion of the Tarquins. Next came the rise of the Lower Orders, who insisted with ever-increasing urgency on claiming a share in the direction of politics, and in every case with ultimate success. Almost invariably the leaders who headed this uprising of the masses grasped for themselves in the end the supreme power, and as irresponsible "Dictators," "Tyrants," or "Emperors" took the place of the old constitutional Kings.

F. 7.—Such was the cycle of events both in Rome and in the Greek commonwealths; though in the latter it ran its course within a few generations, whilst amongst the law-abiding Romans it was a matter of centuries. And the pages of Caesar bear abundant testimony to the fact that in his day the Gallic tribes were all in the state of turmoil which mostly attended the "*Regifugium*" period of development. Some were still under their old Kings; some, like the Nervii, had developed a Senatorial government; in some the Commons had set up "Tyrants" of their own. It was this general unrest which contributed in no small degree to the Roman conquest of Gaul. And the same state of things seems to have been begun in Britain also. The earliest inscribed British coins bear, some of them the names of Kings and Princes, others those of peoples, others again designations which seem to point to Tyrants. To the first class belong those of Commius, Tincommius, Tasciovan, Cunobelin, etc.; to the second those of the Iceni and the Cassi; to the last the northern mintage of Volisius, a potentate of the Parisii, who calls himself Domnoverus, which, according to Professor Rhys,[45] literally signifies "Demagogue."

SECTION G.

Clans at Julian invasion—Permanent natural boundaries—Population—Celtic settlements— "Duns"—Maiden Castle.

G. 1.—The earliest of these inscribed coins, however, take us no further back than the Julian invasion; and it is to Caesar's Commentaries that we are indebted for the first recorded names of any British tribes. It is no part of his design to give any regular list of the clans or their territories; he merely makes incidental mention of such as he had to do with. Thus we learn of the four nameless clans who occupied Kent (a region which has kept its territorial name unchanged from the days of Pytheas), and also of the Atrebates, Cateuchlani, Trinobantes, Cenimagni, Segontiaci, Ancalites, Bibroci, and Cassi.

G. 2.—To the localities held by these tribes Caesar bears no direct evidence; but from his narrative, as well as from local remains and later references, we know that the Trinobantes possessed Essex, and the Cenimagni (i.e. "the Great Iceni" as they were still called,[46] though their power was on the wane), East Anglia; while the Cateuchlani, already beginning to be known as the Cassivellauni (or Cattivellauni), presumably from their heroic chieftain Caswallon (or Cadwallon),[47] corresponded roughly to the later South Mercians, between the Thames and the Nene. The Segontiaci, Ancalites, Bibroci, and Cassi were less considerable, and must evidently have been situated on the marches between their larger neighbours. The name of the Cassi may still, perhaps, cling to their old home, in the *Cashio* Hundred and *Cassiobury*, near Watford; while conjecture finds traces of the Ancalites in *Henley*, and of the Bibroci in *Bray*, on either side of the Thames.

G. 3.—The Atrebates, who play a not unimportant part (as will be seen in the next chapter) in Caesar's connection with Britain, were apparently in possession of the whole southern bank of the Thames, from its source right down to London—the river then, as in Anglo-Saxon times, being a tribal boundary throughout its entire length. This would make the Bibroci a sub-tribe of the Atrebatian Name, and also the Segontiaci, if Henry of Huntingdon (writing in the 12th century with access to various sources of information now lost) is right in identifying Silchester, the Roman *Calleva*, with their local stronghold Caer Segent.

G. 4.—But the whole attempt to locate accurately any but the chiefest tribes found by the Romans in Britain is too conjectural to be worth the infinite labour that has been expended upon the subject by antiquaries. All we can say with certainty is that forest and fen must have cut up the land into a limited number of fairly recognizable districts, each so far naturally separated from the rest as to have been probably a separate or quasi-separate political entity also. Thus, not only was the Thames a line of demarcation, only passable at a few points, from its estuary nearly to the Severn Sea, but the southern regions cut off by it were parted by Nature into five main districts. Sussex was hemmed in by the great forest of Anderida, and that of Selwood continued the line from Southampton to Bristol. Kent was isolated by the Romney marshes and the wild country about Tunbridge, while the western peninsula was a peninsula indeed when the sea ran up to beyond Glastonbury. In this region, then, the later Wessex, we find five main tribes; the men of Kent, the Regni south of the Weald, the Atrebates along the Thames, the Belgae on the Wiltshire Avon, and the Damnonii of Devon and Cornwall, with (perhaps) a sub-tribe of their Name, the Durotriges, in Dorsetshire.

G. 5.—Like the south, the eastern, western, and northern districts of England were cut off from the centre by natural barriers. The Fens of Cambridgeshire and the marshes of the Lea valley, together with the dense forest along the "East Anglian" range, enclosed the east in a ring fence; within which yet another belt of woodland divided the Trinobantes of Essex from the Iceni of Norfolk and Suffolk. The Severn and the Dee isolated what is now Wales, a region falling naturally into two sub-divisions; South Wales being held by the Silurians and their Demetian subjects, North Wales by the Ordovices. The lands north of the Humber, again, were barred off from the south by barriers stretching from sea to sea; the Humber itself on the one hand, the Mersey estuary on the other, thrusting up marshes to the very foot of the wild Pennine moorlands between. And the whole of this vast region seems to have been under the Brigantes, who held the great plain of York, and exercised more or less of a hegemony over the Parisians of the East Riding, the Segontii of Lancashire, and the Otadini, Damnonii, and Selgovae between the Tyne and the Forth. Finally, the Midlands, parcelled up by the forests of Sherwood, Needwood, Charnwood, and Arden, into quarters, found space for the Dobuni in the Severn valley (to the west of the Cateuchlani), for the Coritani east of the Trent, and for their westward neighbours the Cornavii.[48]

G. 6.—All these tribes are given in Ptolemy's geography, but only a few, such as the Iceni, the Silurians, and the Brigantes, meet us in actual history; whilst, of them all, the Damnonian name alone reappears after the fall of the Roman dominion. Thus the accepted allotment of tribal territory is largely conjectural. North of the Forth all is conjecture pure and simple, so far as the location of the various Caledonian sub-clans is concerned. We only know that there were about a dozen of them; the Cornavii, Carini, Carnonacae, Cerones, Decantae, Epidii, Horestae, Lugi, Novantae, Smertae, Taexali, Vacomagi, and Vernicomes. Some of these may be alternative names.

G. 7.—The practical importance of the above-mentioned natural divisions of the island is testified to by the abiding character of the corresponding political divisions. The resemblance which at once strikes the eye between the map of Roman and Saxon Britain is no mere coincidence. Physical considerations brought about the boundaries between the Roman "provinces" and the Anglo-Saxon principalities alike. Thus a glance will show that Britannia Prima, Britannia Secunda, Maxima Caesariensis, and Flavia Caesariensis correspond to the later Wessex, Wales, Northumbria, and Mercia (with its dependency East Anglia).[49] And even the sub-divisions remained approximately the same. In Anglo-Saxon times, for example, the Midlands were still divided into the same four tribal territories; the North Mercians holding that of the British Cornavii, the South Mercians that of the Dobuni, the Middle Angles that of the Coritani, and the South Angles that of the Cateuchlani. So also the Icenian kingdom, with its old boundaries, became that of the East Angles, and the Trinobantian that of the East Saxons.

G. 8.—What the entire population of Britain may have numbered at the Roman Conquest is, again, purely a matter of guess-work. But it may well have been not very different in amount from what it was at the Norman Conquest, when the entries in Domesday roughly show that the whole of England (south of the Humber) was inhabited about as thickly as the Lake District at the present day, and contained some two million souls. The primary hills, and the secondary plateaux, where now we find the richest corn lands of the whole country, were in pre-Roman times covered with virgin forest. But in the river valleys above the level of the floods were to be found stretches of good open plough land, and the chalk downs supplied excellent grazing. Where both were combined, as in the valleys of the Avon and Wily near Salisbury, and that of the Frome near Dorchester, we have the ideal site for a Celtic settlement. In such places we accordingly find the most conspicuous traces of the prehistoric Briton; the round barrows which mark the burial-places of his chiefs, and the vast earthworks with which he crowned the most defensible *dun*, or height, in his territory.

G. 9.—These fortified British *duns* are to be seen all over England. Sometimes they have become Roman or mediaeval towns, as at Old

Sarum; sometimes they are still centres of population, as at London, Lincoln, and Exeter; and sometimes, as at Bath and Dorchester, they remain still as left by their original constructors. For they were designed to be usually untenanted; not places to dwell in, but camps of refuge, whither the neighbouring farmers and their cattle might flee when in danger from a hostile raid. The lack of water in many of them shows that they could never have been permanently occupied either in war or peace.[50] Perhaps the best remaining example is Maiden[51] Castle, which dominates Dorchester, being at once the largest and the most untouched by later ages. Here three huge concentric ramparts, nearly three miles in circuit, gird in a space of about fifty acres on a gentle swell of the chalk ridge above the modern town by the river. A single tortuous entrance, defended by an outwork, gives access to the levelled interior. All, save the oaken palisades which once topped each round of the barrier, remains as it was when first constructed, looking down, now as then, on the spot where the population for whose benefit it was made dwelt in time of peace. For English Dorchester is the British town whose name the Romans, when they raised the square ramparts which still encircle it, transliterated into Durnovaria. Durnovaria in turn became, on Anglo-Saxon lips, Dornwara-ceaster, Dorn-ceaster, and finally Dorchester.

G. 10.—We have already, on physical grounds, assigned these Durotriges to the Damnonian Name. There were certainly fewer natural obstacles between them and the men of Devon to the west than between them and the Belgae to the northward. Caesar, however, distinctly states that the Belgic power extended to the coast line, so the Britons of the Frome valley may have been conquered by them. Or the Durotriges may be a Belgic tribe after all. For, as we have pointed out, our evidence is of the scantiest, and there is every reason to suppose that the era of the Roman invasion was one of incessant political confusion in the land.

SECTION H.

Religious state of Britain—Illustrated by Hindooism—Totemists—Polytheists—Druids—Bards—Seers—Druidic Deities—Mistletoe—Sacred herbs— "Ovum Anguinum"—Suppression of Druidism—Druidism and Christianity.

H. 1.—The religious state of the country seems to have been in no less confusion than its political condition. The surviving "Ugrian" inhabitants appear to have sunk into mere totemists and fetish worshippers, like the aboriginal races of India; while the Celtic tribes were at a loose and early stage of polytheism, with a Pantheon filled by every possible device, by the adoration of every kind of natural phenomenon, the sky, the sun, the moon, the stars, the winds and clouds, the earth and sea, rivers, wells, sacred trees, by the creation of tribal divinities, gods and goddesses of war, commerce, healing, and all the congeries of mutually tolerant devotions which we see in the Brahmanism of to-day. And, as in Brahmanism, all these devotions were under the shadow of a sacerdotal and prophetic caste, wielding vast influence, and teaching, esoterically at least, a far more spiritual religion.

H. 2.—These were the Druids, whose practices and tenets fortunately excited such attention at Rome that we know more about them by far than we could collect concerning either Jews or Christians from classical authors. And though most of our authorities refer to Druidism as practised in Gaul, yet we have the authority of Caesar for Britain being the special home and sanctuary of the faith, to which the Gallic Druids referred as the standard for their practices.[52] We may safely, therefore, take the pictures given us by him and others, as supplying a representation of what took place in our land ere the Romans entered it.

H. 3.—The earliest testimony is that of Julius Caesar himself, in his well-known sketch of contemporary Druidism ('De Bello Gallico,' vi. 14-20). He tells us that the Druids were the ministers of religion, the sacrificial priesthood of the nation, the authorized expounders of the Divine will. All education and jurisprudence was in their hands, and their sentences of excommunication were universally enforced. The Gallic Druids were under the dominion of a Primate, who presided at the annual Chapter of the Order, and was chosen by it; a disputed election occasionally ending in an appeal to arms. As a rule, however, Druids were supposed not to shed blood, they were free from all obligation to military service, and from all taxation of every kind. These privileges enabled them to recruit their ranks—for they were not an hereditary caste—from the pick of the national youth, in spite of the severe discipline of the Druidical novitiate. So great was the mass of sacred literature required to be committed to memory that a training of twenty years was sometimes needed. All had to be learnt orally, for the matter was too sacred to be written down, though the Druids were well acquainted with writing, and used the Greek alphabet,[53] if not the Greek language,[54] for secular purposes. Caesar's own view is that this refusal to allow the inditing of their sacred books was due to two causes: first, the fear lest the secrets of the Order should thus leak out, and, secondly, the dread lest reading should weaken memory, "as, in fact, it generally does." Even so, amongst the Brahmans there are, to this day, many who can not only repeat from end to end the gigantic mass of Vedic literature, but who know by heart also with absolute accuracy the huge and complicated works of the Sanscrit grammarians.

H. 4.—Caesar further tells us that the Druids taught the doctrine of transmigration of souls, and that their course of education included astronomy, geography, physics, and theology. The attributes of their chief God corresponded, in his view, with those of the Roman Mercury. Of the minor divinities, one, like Apollo, was the patron of healing; a second, like Minerva, presided over craft-work; a third, like Jupiter, was King of Heaven, and a fourth, like Mars, was the War-god.[55] Their calendar was constructed on the principle that each night belongs to the day before it (not to that after it, as was the theory amongst the Mediterranean nations), and they reckoned all periods of time by nights, not days, as we still do in the word "fortnight." For this practice they gave the mystical reason that the Celtic races were the Children of Darkness. At periods of national or private distress, human sacrifices were in vogue amongst them, sometimes on a vast scale. "They have images [*simulacra*] of huge size, whose limbs when enclosed [*contexta*] with wattles, they fill with living men. The wattles are fired and the men perish amid the hedge of flame [*circumventi flamma exanimantur homines*]." It is usually supposed that these *simulacra* were hollow idols of basket-work. But such would require to be constructed on an incredible scale for their limbs to be filled with men; and it is much more probable that they were spaces traced out upon the ground (like the Giant on the hill above Cerne Abbas in Dorset), and hedged in with the wattles to be fired.

H. 5.—From the historian Diodorus Siculus, whose life overlapped Caesar's, we learn that Druid was a native British name. "There are certain philosophers and theologians held in great honour whom they call Druids."[56] Whether this designation is actually of Celtic derivation is, however, uncertain. Pliny thought it was from the Greek affected by the Druids and connected with their oak-tree worship. Professor Rhys mentions that the earliest use of the word in extant Welsh literature is in the Book of Taliesin, under the form *Derwyddon*,[57] and that in Irish is to be found the cognate form *Drui*. But these are as likely to be derived from the Greek δρουΐδες [drouides], as this from them. Diodorus adds that they have mighty influence, and preside at all sacred rites, "as possessing special knowledge of the Gods, yea, and being of one speech ὁμοφώνων [homophônôn] with them." This points to some archaic or foreign language, possibly Greek, being used in the Druidical ritual. Their influence, he goes on to say, always makes for peace: "Oft-times, when hosts be arrayed, and either side charging the one against the other, yea, when swords are out and spears couched for the onset, will these men rush between and stay the warriors, charming them to rest κατεπᾴσαντες [katepasantes], like so many wild beasts."

H. 6.—With the Druids Diodorus associates two other religiously influential classes amongst the Britons, the Bards (βάρδοι) [bardoi] and the Seers (μάντεις) [manteis]. The former present the familiar features of the cosmopolitan minstrel. They sing to harps (ὀργάνων ταῖς λύραις ὁμοίων) [organôn tais lurais homoiôn], both fame and disfame. The latter seem to have corresponded with the witch-doctors of the Kaffir tribes, deriving auguries from the dying struggles of their victims (frequently human), just as the Basuto medicine-men tortured oxen to death to prognosticate the issue of the war between Great Britain and the Boers in South Africa. Strabo, in the next generation, also mentions together these three classes, Bards, Seers, οὐάτεις [Ouateis] = Vates and Druids. The latter study natural science and ethics (πρὸς τῇ φυσιολογίᾳ καὶ τὴν ἠθικὴν φιλοσοφιαν) [pros tê phusiologia kai tên êthikên philosophian askousin]. They teach the immortality of the soul, and believe the Universe to be eternal, "yet, at the last, fire and water shall prevail."

H. 7.—Pomponius Mela, who wrote shortly before the Claudian conquest of Britain, says that the Druids profess to know the shape and size of the world, the movements of the stars, and the will of the Gods. They teach many secrets in caves and woods, but only to the nobles of the land. Of this esoteric instruction one doctrine alone has been permitted to leak out to the common people—that of the immortality of the soul—and this only because that doctrine was calculated to make them the braver in battle. In accordance with it, food and the like was buried with the dead, for the use of the soul. Even a man's debts were supposed to pass with him to the shades.

H. 8.—Our picture of the Druids is completed by Pliny,[58] writing shortly after the Claudian conquest. Approaching the subject as a naturalist he does not mention their psychological tenets, but gives various highly interesting pieces of information as to their superstitions with regard to natural objects, especially plants. "The Druids," he says, "(so they call their Magi) hold nothing so sacred as the mistletoe and that tree whereon it groweth, if only this be an oak. Oak-groves, indeed, they choose for their own sake, neither do they celebrate any sacred rite without oak-leaves, so that they appear to be called Druids from the Greek word for this tree. Whatsoever mistletoe, then, groweth on such a tree they hold it for a heaven-sent sign, and count that tree as chosen by their God himself. Yet but very rarely is it so found, and, when found, is sought with no small observance; above all on the sixth day of the moon (which to this folk is the beginning of months and years alike),[59] and after the thirtieth year of its age, because it is by then in full vigour of strength, nor has its half-tide yet come. Hailing it, in their own tongue, as 'Heal-all,' they make ready beneath the tree, with all due rites, feast and sacrifice. Then are brought up two bulls of spotless white, whose horns have never ere this known the yoke. The priest, in white vestments, climbeth the tree, and with a golden sickle reapeth the sacred bough, which is caught as it falls in a white robe [*sagum*]. Then, and not till then, slay they the victims, praying that their God will prosper this his gift to those on whom he hath bestowed the same."

H. 9.—A drink made from mistletoe, or possibly the mere insertion of the branch into drinking water, was held by the Druids, Pliny adds, as an antidote to every kind of poison. Other herbs had like remedial properties in their eyes. The fumes of burning "*selago*"[60] were thus held good for affections of the eyesight, only, however, when the plant was plucked with due ceremonies. The gatherer must be all in white, with bare and washen feet, and must hallow himself, ere starting on his quest, with a devotional partaking of bread and wine [*sacro facto . . . pane vinoque*]. He must by no means cut the sacred stem with a knife, but pluck it, and that not with bare fingers, but through the folds of his tunic, his right hand being protruded for this purpose beneath his left, "in thievish wise" [*velut a furante*]. Another herb, "*samolum*," which grew in marshy places, was of avail in all diseases both of man and beast. It had to be gathered with the left hand, and fasting, nor might the gatherer on any account look back till he reached some runlet [*canali*] in which he crushed his prize and drank.

H. 10.—Pliny's picture has the interest of having been drawn almost at the final disappearance of Druidism from the Roman world. For some reason it was supposed to be, like Christianity, peculiarly opposed to the genius of Roman civilization, and never came to be numbered amongst the *religiones licitae* of the Empire. Augustus forbade the practice of it to Roman citizens,[61] Tiberius wholly suppressed it in Gaul,[62] and, in conquering Britain, Claudius crushed it with a hand of iron. Few pictures in the early history of Britain are more familiar than the final extirpation of the last of the Druids, when their sacred island of Mona (Anglesey) was stormed by the Roman legionaries, and priests and priestesses perished *en masse* in the flames of their own altars.[63] Their desperate resistance was doubtless due to the fact that Rome was the declared and mortal enemy of their faith. So baneful, indeed, did Druidism come to be considered, that to hold even with the least of its superstitions was treated at Rome as a capital offence. Pliny tells us of a Roman knight, of Gallic birth, who was put to death by Claudius for no other reason than that of being in possession of a certain stone called by the Druids a "snake's egg," and supposed to bring good luck in law-suits.[64]

H. 11.—This stone Pliny himself had seen, and describes it (in his chapter on the use of eggs) as being like a medium-sized apple, having a cartilaginous shell covered with small processes like the discs on the arms of an octopus. This can scarcely have been, as most commentators suppose, the shell of an echinus (with which Pliny was well acquainted), even if fossil. His description rather seems to point to some fossil covered with *ostrea sigillina*, such as are common in British green-sands. He adds an account of the Druidical view of its production, how it is the solidified poison of a number of serpents who put their heads together to eject it, and how, even when set in gold, it will float, and that against a stream. This "egg," it will be seen, was from Gaul. The British variant of the superstition was that the snakes thus formed a ring of poison matter, larger or smaller according to the number engaged, which solidified into a gem known as *Glain naidr*, "Adder's glass."[65] The small rings of green or blue glass, too thick for wear, which are not uncommonly found in British burial-places, are supposed to represent this gem. So also, possibly, are the much larger rings of roughly-baked clay which occur throughout the Roman period. For superstitions die hard, and Gough assures us that even in 1789 such "adder-beads" or "snake-stones" were considered "lucky" in Wales and Cornwall, and were still ascribed to the same source as by the Druids of old.

H. 12.—After its suppression by Claudius, Druidism still lingered on in Britain beyond the Roman pale, and amid the outlaws of the Armorican forests in Gaul, but in a much lower form. The least worthy representatives of the Brahmanic caste in India are those found in the least civilized regions, whose tendency is to become little better than sorcerers.[66] And in like manner it is as sorcerers that the later Druids of Scotland and Ireland meet us in their legendary encounters with St. Patrick and St. Columba. They are called "The School of Simon the Druid" (*i.e.* Simon Magus), and a 9th-century commentary designates Jannes and Jambres as "Druids." But the word did not wholly lose its higher associations. It is applied to the Wise Men in an early Welsh hymn on the Epiphany; and in another, ascribed to Columba himself, the saint goes so far as to say, "Christ, the Son of God, is my *Druid*."[67]

* * * * *

CHAPTER II

THE JULIAN INVASION, B.C. 55, 54

SECTION A.

Caesar and Britain—Breakdown of Roman Republican institutions—Corruption abroad and at home—Rise of Caesar—Conquest of Gaul.

A. 1.—If the connection of Britain with Rome is the pivot on which the whole history of our island turns, it is no less true that the first connection of Rome with Britain is the pivot whereon all Roman history depends. For its commencement marks the furthest point reached in his career of conquest by the man without whom Roman history must needs have come to a shameful and disastrous end—Julius Caesar.

A. 2.—The old Roman constitution and the old Roman character had alike proved wholly unequal to meet the strain thrown upon them by the acquisition of the world-wide empire which they had gained for their city. Under the stress of the long feud between its Patrician and Plebeian elements that constitution had developed into an instrument for the regulation of public affairs, admirably adapted for a City-state, where each magistrate performs his office under his neighbour's eye and over his own constituents; constantly amenable both to public opinion and to the checks provided by law. But it never contemplated Pro-consuls bearing sway over the unenfranchised populations of distant Provinces, whence news filtered through to Rome but slowly, and where such legal checks as a man had to reckon with were in the hands of a Court far more ready to sympathize with the oppression of non-voters than to resent it.

A. 3.—And these officials had deteriorated from the old Roman rectitude, as the Spartan harmosts deteriorated under conditions exactly similar in the days of the Lacedaemonian supremacy over Hellas. And, in both cases, the whole national character was dragged down by the degradation of what we may call the Colonial executive. Like the Spartan, the Roman of "the brave days of old" was often stern, and even brutal, towards his enemies. But he was a devoted patriot, he was true to his plighted faith, and above all he was free from all taint of pecuniary corruption. The earlier history of both nations is full of legends illustrating these points, which, whether individually true or not, bear abundant testimony to the national ideal. But with irresponsible power, Roman and Spartan alike, while remaining as brutally indifferent as ever to the sufferings of others, lost all that was best in his own ethical equipment. Instead of patriotism we find unblushing self-interest as the motive of every action; in place of good faith, the most shameless dishonesty; and, for the old contempt of ill-gotten gains, a corruption so fathomless and all-pervading as fairly to stagger us. The tale of the doings of Verres in a district so near Rome as Sicily shows us a depth of mire and degeneration to which no constitution could sink and live.

A. 4.—Nor could the Roman constitution survive it. From the Provinces the taint spread with fatal rapidity to the City itself. The thirst for lucre became the leading force in the State; for its sake the Classes more and more trampled down the Masses; and entrance to the Classes was a matter no longer of birth, but of money alone. And all history testifies that the State which becomes a plutocracy is doomed indeed. Of all possible forms of government—autocracy, oligarchy, democracy— that is the lowest, that most surely bears within itself the seeds of its own inevitable ruin.

A. 5.—So it was with the Roman Republic. As soon as this stage was reached it began to "stew in its own juice" with appalling rapidity. Reformers, like the Gracchi, were crushed; and the commonwealth went to pieces under the shocks and counter-shocks of demagogues like Clodius, conspirators like Catiline, and military adventurers such as Marius and Sulla—for whose statue the Senate could find no more constitutional title than "The Lucky General" [*Sullae Imperatori Felici*] Well-meaning individuals, such as Cicero and Pompey, were still to be found, and even came to the front, but they all alike proved unequal to the crisis; which, in fact, threw up one man, and one only, of force to become a real maker of history—Caius Julius Caesar, the first Roman invader of Britain.

A. 6.—Caesar was at the time of this invasion (55 B.C.) some forty-five years old; but he had not long become a real power in the political arena. Sprung from the bluest blood of Rome—the Julian House tracing their origin to the mythical Iulus, son of Aeneas, and thus claiming descent from the Goddess Venus—we might have expected to find him enrolled amongst the aristocratic conservatives, the champions of the *régime* of Sulla. But though a mere boy at the date of the strife between the partisans of Sulla and Marius (B.C. 88-78), Caesar was already clear-sighted enough to perceive that in the "Classes" of that day there was no help for the tempest-tossed commonwealth. Accordingly he threw in his lot with the revolutionary Marian movement, broke off a wealthy matrimonial engagement arranged for him by his parents to become the son-in-law of Cinna, and in the very thick of the Sullan proscriptions, braved the Dictator by openly glorying in his connection with the defeated reformers. How he escaped with his life, even at the intercession, if it was indeed made, of the Vestals, is a mystery; for Sulla (who had little regard for religious, or any other, scruples) was deliberately extirpating every soul whom he thought dangerous to the plutocracy, and is said to have pronounced "that boy" as "more to be dreaded than many a Marius." He did, however, escape; but till the vanquished party recovered in some degree from this ruthless massacre of their leaders, he could take no prominent part in politics. The minor offices of Quaestor, Aedile, and Praetor he filled with credit, and meanwhile seemed to be giving himself up to shine in Society, which was not, in Rome, then at its best; and his reputation for intrigue, his skill at the gaming-table, and his fashionable swagger were the envy of all the young bloods of the day.

A. 7.—The Catiline conspiracy (B.C. 63), and the irregular executions that followed its suppression, at length gave him his opportunity. While the Senate was hailing Cicero as "the Father of his country" for the stern promptitude which enabled him, as Consul, to say "*Vixere*" ["They *have* lived"] in answer to the question as to the doom of the conspirators, Caesar had electrified the assembly by his denunciation of the view that, in whatsoever extremity, the blood of Roman citizens might be shed by a Roman Consul, secretly and without legal warrant. Henceforward he took his place as the special leader on whom popular feeling at Rome more and more pinned its hopes. As Pontifex Maximus he gained (B.C. 63) a shadowy but far from unreal religious influence; as Pro-praetor he solidified the Roman dominion in Spain (where he had already been Quaestor); and on his return (B.C. 60) reconciled Crassus, the head of the moneyed interest, with Pompey, the darling of the Army, and by their united influence was raised next year to the Consulship.

A. 8.—A Roman Consul invariably, after the expiration of his year of office, was sent as Pro-consul to take charge of one of the Provinces, practically having a good deal of personal say as to which should be assigned to him. Caesar thus chose for his proconsular government the district of Gaul then under Roman dominion, *i.e.* the valley of the Po, and that of the Rhone. In making this choice Caesar was actuated by the fact that in Gaul he was more likely than anywhere else to come in for active service. Unquiet neighbours on the frontier, Germans and Helvetians, were threatening invasion, and would have to be repelled. And this would give the Pro-consul the chance of doing what Caesar specially desired, of raising and training an army which he might make as devoted to himself as were Pompey's veterans to their brilliant chieftain—the hero "as beautiful as he was brave, as good as he was beautiful." Without such a force Caesar foresaw that all his efforts to redress the abuses of the State would be in vain. As Consul he had carried certain small instalments of reform; but they had made him more hated than ever by the classes at whose corruption they were aimed, and might any day be overthrown. And neither Pompey nor Crassus were in any way to be depended upon for his plans in this direction.

A. 9.—Events proved kinder to him than he could have hoped. His ill-wishers at Rome actually aided his preparations for war; for Caesar had not yet gained any special military reputation, while the barbarians whom he was to meet had a very high one, and might reasonably be expected to destroy him. And the Helvetian peril proved of such magnitude that he had every excuse for making a much larger levy than there was any previous prospect of his securing. On the surpassing genius with which he manipulated the weapon thus put into his hand there is no need to dwell. Suffice it to say that in spite of overwhelming superiority in numbers, courage yet more signal, a stronger individual physique, and arms as effective, his foes one after another vanished before him. Helvetians, Germans, Belgians, were not merely conquered, but literally annihilated, as often as they ventured to meet him, and in less than three years the whole of Gaul was at his feet.

SECTION B.

Sea-fight with Veneti and Britons—Pretexts for invading Britain—British dominion of Divitiacus—Gallic tribes in Britain—Atrebates—Commius.

B. 1.—One of the last tribes to be subdued (in B.C. 56) was that which, as the chief seafaring race of Gaul, had the most intimate relations with Britain, the Veneti, or men of Vannes, who dwelt in what is now Brittany.[68] These enterprising mariners had developed a form of vessel fitted to cope with the stormy Chops of the Channel on lines exactly opposite to those of the British "curraghs."[69] Instead of being so light as to rise to every lift of the waves, and with frames so flexible as to bend rather than break under their every stress, the Venetian ships were of the most massive construction, built wholly of the stoutest oak planking, and with timbers upwards of a foot in thickness. All were bolted together with iron pins "as thick as a man's thumb." Forecastle and poop were alike lofty, with a lower waist for the use of sweeps if needful. But this was only exceptional, sails being the usual motive power. And these were constructed chiefly with a view to strength. Instead of canvas, they were formed of untanned hides. And instead of hempen cables the Veneti were so far ahead of their time as to use iron chains with their anchors; an invention which perished with them, not to come in again till the 19th century. Their broad beam and shallow keel enabled these ships to lie more conveniently in the tidal inlets on either side of the Channel.[70]

B. 2.—Thus equipped, the Veneti had tapped the tin trade at its source, and established emporia at Falmouth, Plymouth, and Exmouth; on the sites of which ancient ingots, Gallic coins of gold, and other relics of their period have lately been discovered. Thence they conveyed their freight to the Seine, the Loire, and even the Garonne. The great Damnonian clan, which held the whole of Devon and Cornwall, were in close alliance with them, and sent auxiliaries to aid in their final struggle against Caesar. Indeed they may possibly have drawn allies from a yet wider area, if, as Mr. Elton conjectures, the prehistoric boats which have at various times been found in the silt at Glasgow may be connected with their influence.[71]

B. 3.—Caesar describes his struggle with the Veneti and their British allies as one of the most arduous in his Gallic campaigns. The Roman war galleys depended largely upon ramming in their sea-fights, but the Venetian ships were so solidly built as to defy this method of attack. At the same time their lofty prows and sterns enabled them to deliver a plunging fire of missiles on the Roman decks, and even to command the wooden turrets which Caesar had added to his bulwarks. They invariably fought under sail, and manoeuvred so skilfully that boarding was impossible. In the end, after several unsuccessful skirmishes, Caesar armed his marines with long billhooks, instructing them to strike at the halyards of the Gallic vessels as they swept past. (These must have been fastened outboard.) The device succeeded. One after another, in a great battle off Quiberon, of which the Roman land force were spectators, the huge leathern mainsails dropped on to the decks, doubtless "covering the ship as with a pall," as in the like misfortune to the Elizabethan *Revenge* in her heroic defence against the Spanish fleet, and hopelessly crippling the vessel, whether for sailing or rowing. The Romans were at last able to board, and the whole Venetian fleet fell into their hands. The strongholds on the coast were now stormed, and the entire population either slaughtered or sold into slavery, as an object lesson to the rest of the confederacy of the fate in store for those who dared to stand out against the Genius of Rome.

B. 4.—Caesar had now got a very pretty excuse for extending his operations to Britain, and, as his object was to pose at Rome as "a Maker of Empire," he eagerly grasped at the chance. Something of a handle, moreover, was afforded him by yet another connection between the two sides of the Channel. Many people were still alive who remembered the days when Divitiacus, King of the Suessiones (at Soissons), had been the great potentate of Northern Gaul. In Caesar's time this glory was of the past, and the Suessiones had sunk to a minor position amongst the Gallic clans. But within the last half-century the sway of their monarch had been acknowledged not only over great part of Gaul, but in Britain also. Caesar's words, indeed, would almost seem to point to the island as a whole having been in some sense under him: *Etiam Britanniae imperium obtinuit.*[72]

B. 5.—And traces of his rule still existed in the occupation of British districts by colonists from two tribes, which, as his nearest neighbours, must certainly have formed part of any North Gallic confederacy under him—the Atrebates and the Parisii. The former had their continental seat in Picardy; the latter, as their name tells us, on the Seine. Their insular settlements were along the southern bank of the Thames and the northern bank of the Humber respectively. How far the two sets of Parisians held together politically does not appear; but the Atrebates, whether in Britain or Gaul, acknowledged the claim of a single magnate, named Commius, to be their paramount Chieftain.[73] In this capacity he had led his followers against Caesar in the great Belgic confederacy of B.C. 58, and on its collapse, instead of holding out to the last like the Nervii, had made a timely submission. If convenient, this submission might be represented as including that of his British dominions; especially as we gather that a contingent from over-sea may have actually fought under his banner against the Roman eagles. Nay, it is possible that the old claims of the ruler of Soissons over Britain may have been revived, now that that ruler was Julius Caesar. It is even conceivable that his complaint of British assistance having been given to the enemy "in all our Gallic wars" may point to his having heard some form of the legend, whose echoes we meet with in Welsh Triads, that the Gauls who sacked Rome three centuries earlier numbered Britons amongst their ranks.

SECTION C.

Defeat of Germans—Bridge over Rhine—Caesar's army—Dread of ocean—Fleet at Boulogne—Commius sent to Britain—Channel crossed—Attempt on Dover— Landing at Deal—Legionary sentiment—British army dispersed.

C. 1.—For making use of these pretexts, however, Caesar had to wait a while. It was needful to bring home to both supporters and opponents his brilliant success by showing himself in Rome, during the idle season when his men were in winter quarters. And when he got back to his Province with the spring of A.D. 55, his first attention had to be given to the Rhine frontier, whence a formidable German invasion was threatening. With his usual skill and war-craft—which, on this occasion, in the eyes of his Roman ill-wishers, seemed indistinguishable from treachery—he annihilated the Teutonic horde which had dared to cross the river; and then, by a miracle of engineering skill, bridged the broad and rapid stream, and made such a demonstration in Germany itself as to check the national trek westward for half a millennium.

C. 2.—By this time, as this wonderful feat shows, the Army of Gaul had become one of those perfect instruments into which only truly great commanders can weld their forces. Like the Army of the Peninsula, in the words of Wellington, "it could go anywhere and do anything." The men who, when first enlisted, had trembled before the Gauls, and absolutely shed tears at the prospect of encountering Germans, now, under the magic of Caesar's genius, had learnt to dread nothing. Often surprised, always outnumbered, sometimes contending against tenfold odds, the legionaries never faltered. Each individual soldier seems to have learnt to do instinctively the right thing in every emergency, and every man worshipped his general. For every man could see that it was Caesar and Caesar alone to whom every victory was due. The very training of the engineers, the very devices, such as that of the Rhine bridge, by which such mighty results were achieved, were all due to him. Never before had any Roman leader, not even Pompey "the Great," awakened such devotion amongst his followers.

C. 3.—Caesar therefore experienced no such difficulty as we shall find besetting the Roman commanders of the next century, in persuading his men to follow him "beyond the world,"[74] and to dare the venture, hitherto unheard of in the annals of Rome, of crossing the ocean itself. We must remember that this crossing was looked upon by the Romans as something very different from the transits hither and thither upon the Mediterranean Sea with which they were familiar. The Ocean to them was an object of mysterious horror. Untold possibilities of destruction might lurk in its tides and billows. Whence those tides came and how far those billows rolled was known to no man. To dare its passage might well be to court Heaven knew what of supernatural vengeance.

C. 4.—But Caesar's men were ready to brave all things while he led them. So, after having despatched his German business, he determined to employ the short remainder of the summer in a *reconnaissance en force* across the Channel, with a view to subsequent invasion of Britain. He had already made inquiries of all whom he could find connected with the Britanno-Gallic trade as to the size and military resources of the island. But they proved unwilling witnesses, and he could not even get out of them what they must perfectly well have known, the position of the best harbours on the southern shores.

C. 5.—His first act, therefore, was to send out a galley under Volusenus "to pry along the coast," and meanwhile to order the fleet which he had built against the Veneti to rendezvous at Boulogne. Besides these war-galleys (*naves longae*) he got together eighty transports, enough for two legions, besides eighteen more for the cavalry.[75] These last were detained by a contrary wind at "a further harbour," eight miles distant—probably Ambleteuse at the mouth of the Canche.[76]

C. 6.—All these preparations, though they seem to have been carried out with extreme celerity, lasted long enough to alarm the Britons. Several clans sent over envoys, to promise submission if only Caesar would refrain from invading the country. This, however, did not suit Caesar's purpose. Such diplomatic advantages would be far less impressive in the eyes of the Roman "gallery" to which he was playing than his actual presence in Britain. So he merely told the envoys that it would be all the better for them if he found them in so excellent and submissive a frame of mind on his arrival at their shores, and sent them back, along with Commius, who was to bring in his own clan, the Atrebates, and as many more as he could influence. And the Britons on their part, though ready to make a nominal submission to "the mighty name of Rome," were resolved not to tolerate an actual invasion without a fight for it. In every clan the war party came to the front, all negotiations were abruptly broken off, Commius was thrown into chains, and a hastily-summoned levy lined the coast about Dover, where the enemy were expected to make their first attempt to land.

C. 7.—Dover, in fact, was the port that Caesar made for. It was, at this date, the obvious harbour for such a fleet as his. All along the coast of Kent the sea has, for many centuries, been constantly retreating. Partly by the silting-up of river-mouths, partly by the great drift of shingle from west to east which is so striking a feature of our whole southern shore, fresh land has everywhere been forming. Places like Rye and Winchelsea, which were well-known havens of the Cinque Ports even to late mediaeval times, are now far inland. And though Dover is still our great south-eastern harbour, this is due entirely to the artificial extensions which have replaced the naturally enclosed tidal area for which Caesar made. There is abundant evidence that in his day the site of the present town was the bed of an estuary winding for a mile or more inland between steep chalk cliffs,[77] not yet denuded into slopes, whence the beach on either side was absolutely commanded.

C. 8.—Caesar saw at a glance that a landing here was impossible to such a force as he had with him. He had sailed from Boulogne "in the third watch"—with the earliest dawn, that is to say—and by 10 a.m. his leading vessels, with himself on board, were close under Shakespeare's Cliff. There he saw the British army in position waiting for him, crowning the heights above the estuary, and ready to overwhelm his landing-parties with a plunging fire of missiles. He anchored for a space till the rest of his fleet came up, and meanwhile called a council of war of his leading officers to deliberate on the best way of proceeding in the difficulty. It was decided to make for the open shore to the northwards (perhaps for Richborough,[78] the next secure roadstead of those days), and at three in the afternoon the trumpet sounded, the anchors were weighed, and the fleet coasted onwards with the flowing tide.[79]

C. 9.—The British army also struck camp, and kept pace by land with the invaders' progress. First came the cavalry and chariot-men, the mounted infantry of the day; then followed the main body, who in the British as in every army, ancient or modern, fought on foot. We can picture the scene, the bright harvest afternoon—(according to the calculations of Napoleon, in his 'Life of Caesar,' it was St. Bartholomew's Day)—the calm sea, the long Roman galleys with their rows of sweeps, the heavier and broader transports with their great mainsails rounding out to the gentle breeze, and on cliff and beach the British ranks in their waving tartans—each clan, probably, distinguished by its own pattern—the bright armour of the chieftains, the thick array of weapons, and in front the mounted contingent hurrying onwards to give the foe a warm greeting ere he could set foot on shore.

C. 10.—Thus did invaders and defenders move on, for some seven miles, passing, as Dio Cassius notes, beneath the lofty cliffs of the South Foreland,[80] till these died down into the flat shore and open beach of Deal. By this time it must have been nearly five o'clock, and if Caesar was to land at all that day it must be done at once. Anchor was again cast; but so flat was the shore that the transports, which drew at least four feet of water, could not come within some distance of it. Between the legionaries and the land stretched yards of sea, shoulder-deep to begin with, and concealing who could say what treacherous holes and quicksands beneath its surface. And their wading had to be done under heavy fire; for the British cavalry and chariots had already come up, and occupied every yard of the beach, greeting with a shower of missiles every motion of the Romans to disembark. This was more than even Caesar's soldiers were quite prepared to face. The men, small shame to them, hesitated, and did not spring overboard with the desired alacrity. Caesar's galleys, however, were of lighter draught, and with them he made a demonstration on the right flank (the *latus apertum* of ancient warfare, the shield being on every man's *left* arm) of the British; who, under a severe fire of slings, arrows, and catapults, drew back, though only a little, to take up a new formation, and their fire, in turn, was for the moment silenced. And that moment was seized for a gallant feat of arms which shows how every rank of Caesar's army was animated by Caesar's spirit.

C. II.—The ensign of every Roman legion was the Roman Eagle, perched upon the head of the standard-pole, and regarded with all, and more than all, the feeling which our own regiments have for their regimental colours. As with them, the staff which bore the Eagle of the Legion also bore inscriptions commemorating the honours and victories the legion had won, and to lose it to the foe was an even greater disgrace than with us. For a Roman legion was a much larger unit than a modern regiment, and corresponded rather to a Division; indeed, in the completeness of its separate organization, it might almost be called an Army Corps. Six thousand was its normal force in infantry, and it had its own squadrons of cavalry attached, its own engineer corps, its own baggage train, and its own artillery of catapults and balistae.[81] There was thus even more legionary feeling in the Roman army than there is regimental feeling in our own.

C. 12.—At this time, however, this feeling, so potent in its effects subsequently, was a new development. Caesar himself would seem to have been the first to see how great an incentive such divisional sentiment might prove, and to have done all he could to encourage it. He had singled out one particular legion, the Tenth, as his own special favourite, and made its soldiers feel themselves the objects of his special regard. And this it was which now saved the day for him. The colour-sergeant of that legion, seeing the momentary opening given by the flanking movement of the galleys, after a solemn prayer that this might be well for his legion, plunged into the sea, ensign in hand. "Over with you, comrades," he cried, "if you would not see your Eagle taken by the enemy." With a universal shout of "Never, never" the legion followed; the example spread from ship to ship, and the whole Roman army was splashing and struggling towards the shore of Britain.

C. 13.—At the same time this was no easy task. As every bather knows, it is not an absolutely straightforward matter for even an unencumbered man to effect a landing upon a shingle beach, if ever so little swell is on. And the Roman soldier had to keep his footing, and use his arms moreover for fighting, with some half-hundredweight of accoutrements about him. To form rank was, of course, out of the question. The men forced their way onward, singly and in little groups, often having to stand back to back in rallying-squares, as soon as they came within hand-stroke of the enemy.[82] And this was before they reached dry land. For the British cavalry and chariots dashed into the water to meet them, making full use of the advantage which horsemen have under such circumstances, able to ply the full swing of their arms unembarrassed by the waves, not lifted off their feet or rolled over by the swell, and delivering their blows from above on foes already in difficulties. And on their side, they copied the flanking movement of the Romans, and wheeled round a detachment to fire upon the *latus apertum* of such invaders as succeeded in reaching shallower water.

C. 14.—Thus the fight, in Caesar's words, was an exceedingly sharp one. It was not decided till he sent in the boats of his galleys, and any other light craft he had, to mingle with the combatants. These could doubtless get right alongside the British chariots; and now the advantage of position came to be the other way. A troop of irregular horsemen up to their girths in water is no match for a boat's crew of disciplined infantry. Moreover the tide was flowing,[83] and driving the Britons back moment by moment. For a while they yet resisted bravely, but discipline had the last word. Yard by yard the Romans won their way, till at length they set foot ashore, formed up on the beach in that open order[84] which made the unique strength of the Legions, and delivered their irresistible charge. The Britons did not wait for the shock. Their infantry was, probably, already in retreat, covered by the cavalry and chariots, who now in their turn gave rein to their ponies and retired at a gallop.

C. 15.—Caesar saw them go, and bitterly felt that his luck had failed him. Had he but cavalry, this retreat might have been turned into a rout. But his eighteen transports had failed to arrive, and his drenched and exhausted infantry were in no case for effective pursuit of a foe so superior in mobility. Moreover the sun must have been now fast sinking, and all speed had to be made to get the camp fortified before nightfall. But the Roman soldier was an adept at entrenching himself. A rampart was hastily thrown up, the galleys beached at the top of the tide and run up high and dry beyond the reach of the surf, the transports swung to their anchors where the ebb would not leave them grounded, the quarters of the various cohorts assigned them, the sentries and patrols duly set; and under the summer moon, these first of the Roman invaders lay down for their first night on British soil.

SECTION D.

Wreck of fleet—Fresh British levy—Fight in corn-field—British chariots—Attack on camp—Romans driven into sea.

D. 1.—Meanwhile the defeated Britons had made off, probably to their camp above Dover, where their leaders' first act, on rallying, was to send their prisoner, Commius, under a flag of truce to Caesar, with a promise of unconditional submission. That his landing had been opposed, was, they declared, no fault of theirs; it was all the witlessness of their ignorant followers, who had insisted on fighting. Would he overlook it? Yes; Caesar was ready to show this clemency; but, after conduct so very like treachery, considering their embassy to him in Gaul, he must insist on hostages, and plenty of them. A few were accordingly sent in, and the rest promised in a few days, being the quota due from more distant clans. The British forces were disbanded; indeed, as it was harvest time, they could scarcely have been kept embodied anyhow; and a great gathering of chieftains was held at which it was resolved that all alike should acknowledge the suzerainty of Rome.

D. 2.—This assembly seems to have been held on the morrow of the battle or the day after, so that it can only have been attended by the local Kentish chiefs, unless we are to suppose (as may well have been the case), that the Army of Dover comprised levies and captains from other parts of Britain. But whatever it was, before the resolution could be carried into effect an unlooked-for accident changed the whole situation.

D. 3.—On the fourth day after the Roman landing, the south-westerly wind which had carried Caesar across shifted a few points to the southward. The eighteen cavalry transports were thus enabled to leave Ambleteuse harbour, and were seen approaching before a gentle breeze. The wind, however, continued to back against the sun, and, as usual, to freshen in doing so. Thus, before they could make the land, it was blowing hard from the eastward, and there was nothing for them but to bear up. Some succeeded in getting back to the shelter of the Gallic shore, others scudded before the gale and got carried far to the west, probably rounding-to under the lee of Beachy Head, where they anchored. For this, however, there was far too much sea running. Wave after wave dashed over the bows, they were in imminent danger of swamping, and, when the tide turned at nightfall, they got under weigh and shaped the best course they could to the southern shore of the Channel.

D. 4.—And this same tide that thus carried away his reinforcements all but wrecked Caesar's whole fleet at Deal. His mariners had strangely forgotten that with the full moon the spring tides would come on; a phenomenon which had been long ago remarked by Pytheas,[85] and with which they themselves must have been perfectly familiar on the Gallic coast. And this tide was not only a spring, but was driven by a gale blowing straight on shore. Thus the sleeping soldiers were aroused by the spray dashing over them, and awoke to find the breakers pounding into their galleys on the beach; while, of the transports, some dragged their anchors and were driven on shore to become total wrecks, some cut their cables, and beat, as best they might, out to sea, and all, when the tide and wind alike went down, were found next morning in wretched plight. Not an anchor or cable, says Caesar, was left amongst them, so that it was impossible for them to keep their station off the shore by the camp.

D. 5.—The army, not unnaturally, was in dismay. They were merely on a reconnaissance, without any supply of provisions, without even their usual baggage; perhaps without tents, certainly without any means of repairing the damage to the fleet. Get back to Gaul for the winter they must under pain of starvation, and where were the ships to take them?

D. 6.—The Britons, on the other hand, felt that their foes were now delivered into their hands. Instead of the submission they were arranging, the Council of the Chiefs resolved to make the most of the opportunity, and teach the world by a great example that Britain was not a safe place to invade. Nor need this cost many British lives. They had only to refuse the Romans food; what little could be got by foraging would soon be exhausted; then would come the winter, and the starving invaders would fall an easy prey. The annihilation of the entire expedition would damp Roman ambitions against Britain for many a long day. A solemn oath bound one and all to this plan, and every chief secretly began to levy his clansmen afresh.

D. 7.—Naturally, hostages ceased to be sent in; but it did not need this symptom to show Caesar in how tight a place he now was. His only chance was to strain every nerve to get his ships refitted; and by breaking up those most damaged, and ordering what materials were available from the Continent, he did in a week or two succeed in rendering some sixty out of his eighty vessels just seaworthy.

D. 8.—And while this work was in progress, another event showed how imperative was his need and how precarious his situation. He had, in fact, been guilty of a serious military blunder in going with a mere flying column into Britain as he had gone into Germany. The Channel was not the Rhine, and ships were exposed to risks from which his bridge had been entirely exempt. Nothing but a crushing defeat would cut him off from retiring by that; but the Ocean was not to be so bridled.

D. 9.—It was, as we have said, the season of harvest, and the corn was not yet cut, though the men of Kent were busily at work in the fields. With regard to the crops nearest the camp, the legionaries spared them the trouble of reaping, by commandeering the corn themselves, the area of their operations having, of course, to be continually extended. Harvesters numbered by the thousand make quick work; and in a day or two the whole district was cleared, either by Roman or Briton. Caesar's scouts could only bring him word of one unreaped field, bordered by thick woodland, a mile or two from the camp, and hidden from it by a low swell of the ground. Mr. Vine, in his able monograph 'Caesar in Kent,' thinks that the spot may still be identified, on the way between Deal and Dover, where, by this time, a considerable British force was once more gathered. So entirely was the whole country on the patriot side, that no suspicion of all this reached the Romans, and still less did they dream that the unreaped corn-field was an elaborate trap, and that the woodlands beside it were filled, or ready for filling, by masses of the enemy. The Seventh legion, which was that day on duty, sent out a strong fatigue party to seize the prize; who, on reaching the field, grounded shields and spears, took off, probably, their helmets and tunics, and set to work at cutting down the corn, presumably with their swords.

D. 10.—Not long afterwards the camp guard reported to Caesar that a strange cloud of dust was rising beyond the ridge over which the legion had disappeared. Seeing at once that something was amiss, he hastily bade the two cohorts (about a thousand men) of the guard to set off with him instantly, while the other legion, the Tenth, was to relieve them, and follow with all the rest of their force as speedily as possible. Pushing on with all celerity, he soon could tell by the shouts of his soldiers and the yells of the enemy that his men were hard pressed; and, on crowning the ridge, saw the remnant of the legion huddled together in a half-armed mass, with the British chariots sweeping round them, each chariot-crew[86] as it came up springing down to deliver a destructive volley of missiles, then on board and away to replenish their magazine and charge in once more.

D. 11.—Even at this moment Caesar found time to note and admire the supreme skill which the enemy showed in this, to him, novel mode of fighting. Their driving was like that of the best field artillery of our day; no ground could stop them; up and down slopes, between and over obstacles, they kept their horses absolutely in hand; and, out of sheer bravado, would now and again exhibit such feats of trick-driving as to run along the pole, and stand on the yoke, while at full speed. Such skill, as he truly observed, could not have been acquired without constant drill, both of men and horses; and his military genius grasped at once the immense advantages given by these tactics, combining "the mobility of cavalry with the stability of infantry."

D. 12.—We may notice that Caesar says not a word of the scythe-blades with which popular imagination pictures the wheels of the British chariots to have been armed. Such devices were in use amongst the Persians, and figure at Cunaxa and Arbela. But there the chariots were themselves projectiles, as it were, to break the hostile ranks; and even for this purpose the scythes proved quite ineffective, while they must have made the whole equipment exceedingly unhandy. In the 'De Re Militari' (an illustrated treatise of the 5th century A.D. annexed to the 'Notitia') scythed chariots are shown. But the scythes always have chains attached, to pull them up out of the way in ordinary manoeuvres. The Britons of this date, whose chariots were only to bring their crews up to the foe and carry them off again, had, we may be sure, no such cumbrous and awkward arrangement.[87]

D. 13.—On this scene of wild onset Caesar arrived in the nick of time [*tempore opportunissimo*]. The Seventh, surprised and demoralized, were on the point of breaking, when his appearance on the ridge caused the assailants to draw back. The Tenth came up and formed; their comrades, possibly regaining some of their arms, rallied behind them, and the Britons did not venture to press their advantage home. But neither did Caesar feel in any case to retaliate the attack [*alienum esse tempus arbitratus*], and led his troops back with all convenient speed. The Britons, we may well believe, represented the affair as a glorious victory for the patriot arms.[88] They employed several days of bad weather which followed in spreading the tidings, and calling on all lovers of freedom or of spoil to join in one great effort for crushing the presumptuous invader.

D. 14.—The news spread like wild-fire, and the Romans found themselves threatened in their very camp (whence they had taken care not to stir since their check) by a mighty host both of horse and footmen. Caesar was compelled to fight, the legions were drawn up with their backs to the rampart, that the hostile cavalry might not take them in rear, and, after a long hand-to-hand struggle, the Roman charge once more proved irresistible. The Britons turned their backs and fled; this time cut up, in their retreat, by a small body of thirty Gallic horsemen whom Commius had brought over as his escort, and who had shared his captivity and release. So weak a force could, of course, inflict no serious loss upon the enemy, but, before returning to the camp, they made a destructive raid through the neighbouring farms and villages, "wasting all with fire and sword far and wide."

D. 15.—That same day came fresh envoys to treat for peace. They were now required to furnish twice as many hostages as before; but Caesar could not wait to receive them. They must be sent after him to the Continent. His position had become utterly untenable; the equinoctial gales might any day begin; and he was only too glad to find wind and weather serve that very night for his re-embarkation. Under cover of the darkness he huddled his troops on board; and next morning the triumphant Britons beheld the invaders' fleet far on their flight across the Narrow Seas.

SECTION E.

Caesar worsted—New fleet built—Caesar at Rome—Cicero—Expedition of 54 B.C.—Unopposed Landing—Pro-Roman Britons—Trinobantes—Mandubratius—British army surprised—"Old England's Hole."

E. 1.—Caesar too had, on his side, gained what he wanted, though at a risk quite disproportionate to the advantage. So much prestige had he lost that on his disembarkation his force was set upon by the very Gauls whom he had so signally beaten two years before. Their attack was crushed with little difficulty and great slaughter; but that it should have been made at all shows that he was supposed to be returning as a beaten man. However, he now knew enough about Britain and the Britons to estimate what force would be needful for a real invasion, and energetically set to work to prepare it. To make such an invasion, and to succeed in it, had now become absolutely necessary for his whole future. At any cost the events of the year 55 must be "wiped off the slate;" the more so as, out of all the British clans, two only sent in their promised hostages. Caesar's dispatches home, we may be sure, were admirably written, and so represented matters as to gain him a *supplicatio*, or solemn thanksgiving, of twenty days from the Senate. But the unpleasant truth was sure to leak out unless it was overlaid by something better. It did indeed so far leak out that Lucan[89] was able to write: *Territa quaesitis ostendit terga Britannis.*

> "He sought the Britons; then, in panic dread,
> Turned his brave back, and from his victory fled."

E. 2.—Before setting off, therefore, for his usual winter visit to Rome, he set all his legionaries to work in their winter quarters, at building ships ready to carry out his plans next spring. He himself furnished the drawings, after a design of his own, like our own Alfred a thousand years later.[90] They were to be of somewhat lower free-board than was customary, and of broader beam, for Caesar had noted that the choppy waves of the Channel had not the long run of Mediterranean or Atlantic rollers. All, moreover, were to be provided with sweeps; for he did not intend again to be at the mercy of the wind. And with such zeal and skill did the soldiers carry out his instructions, by aid of the material which he ordered from the dockyards of Spain, that before the winter was over they had constructed no fewer than six hundred of these new vessels, besides eighty fresh war-galleys.

E. 3.—Caesar meanwhile was also at his winter's work amid the turmoil of Roman politics. His "westward ho!" movement was causing all the stir he hoped for. We can see in Cicero's correspondence with Atticus, with Trebatius, and with his own brother Quintus (who was attached in some capacity to Caesar's second expedition), how full Rome was of gossip and surmise as to the outcome of this daring adventure. "Take care," he says to Trebatius, "you who are always preaching caution; mind you don't get caught by the British chariot-men."[91] "You will find, I hear, absolutely nothing in Britain—no gold, no silver. I advise you to capture a chariot and drive straight home. Anyhow get yourself into Caesar's good books."[92]

E. 4.—To be in Caesar's good books was, in fact, Cicero's own great ambition at this time. Despite his constitutional zeal, he felt "the Dynasts," as he called the Triumvirate, the only really strong force in politics, and was ready to go to considerable lengths in courting their favour—Caesar's in particular. He not only withdrew all opposition to the additional five years of command in Gaul which the subservient Senate had unconstitutionally decreed to the "dynast," but induced his brother Quintus to volunteer for service in the coming invasion of Britain. Through Quintus he invited Caesar's criticisms on his own very poor verses, and wrote a letter, obviously meant to be shown, expressing boundless gratification at a favourable notice: "If *he* thinks well of my poetry, I shall know it is no mere one-horse concern, but a real four-in-hand." "Caesar tells me he never read better Greek. But why does he write ῥαθυμώτερα [rhathumôtera] ['rather careless'] against one passage? He really does. Do find out why."

E. 5.—This gentle criticism seems to have somewhat damped Cicero's ardour for Caesar and his British glories. His every subsequent mention of the expedition is to belittle it. In the spring he had written to Trebatius: "So our dear Caesar really thinks well of you as a counsel. You will be glad indeed to have gone with him to Britain. There at least you will never meet your match."[93] But in the summer it is: "I certainly don't blame you for showing yourself so little of a sight-seer [*non nimis* φιλοθέωρον [philotheôron]] in this British matter."[94] "I am truly glad you never went there. You have missed the trouble, and I the bore of listening to your tales about it all."[95] To Atticus he writes: "We are all awaiting the issue of this British war. We hear the approaches [*aditus*] of the island are fortified with stupendous ramparts [*mirificis molibus*]. Anyhow we know that not one scruple [*scrupulum*] of money exists there, nor any other plunder except slaves—and none of them either literary or artistic."[96] "I heard (on Oct. 24) from Caesar and from my brother Quintus that all is over in Britain. No booty . . . They wrote on September 26, just embarking."

E. 6.—Both Caesar and Quintus seem to have been excellent correspondents, and between them let Cicero hear from Britain almost every week during their stay in the island, the letters taking on an average about a month to reach him. He speaks of receiving on September 27 one written by Caesar on September 1; and on September 13 one from Quintus ("your fourth")[97] written August 10. And apparently they were very good letters, for which Cicero was duly grateful. "What pleasant letters," he says to Quintus, "you do write . . . I see you have an extraordinary turn for writing (ὑπόθεσιν) [hypothesin] *scribendi egregiam*. Tell me all about it, the places, the people, the customs, the clans, the fighting. What are they all like? And what is your general like?"[98] "Give me Britain, that I may paint it in your colours with my own brush [*penicillo*]."[99] This last sentence refers to a heroic poem on "The Glories of Caesar," which Cicero seems to have meditated but never brought into being. Nor do we know anything of the contents of his British correspondence, except that it contains some speculations about our tide-ways; for, in his 'De Natura Deorum,'[100] Cicero pooh-poohs the idea that such natural phenomena argue the existence of a God: "Quid? Aestus maritimi . . . Britannici . . . sine Deo fieri nonne possunt?"

E. 7.—Neither can we say what he meant by the "stupendous ramparts" against Caesar's access to our island. The Dover cliffs have been suggested, and the Goodwin Sands; but it seems much more probable that the Britons were believed to have artificially fortified the most accessible landing-places. Perhaps they may have actually done so, but if they did it was to no purpose; for this time Caesar disembarked his army quite unopposed. On his return from Rome he had bidden his newly-built fleet, along with what was left of the old one, rendezvous at Boulogne; whence, after long delay through a continuous north-westerly breeze [*Corus*], he was at length enabled to set sail with no fewer than eight hundred vessels. Never throughout history has so large a navy threatened our shores. The most numerous of the Danish expeditions contained less than four hundred ships, William the Conqueror's less than seven hundred;[101] the Spanish Armada not two hundred.

E. 8.—Caesar was resolved this time to be in sufficient strength, and no longer despised his enemies. He brought with him five out of his eight legions, some thirty thousand infantry, that is, and two thousand horse. The rest remained under his most trusted lieutenant, Labienus, to police Gaul and keep open his communications with Rome. According to Polyaenus[102] (A.D. 180), he even brought over with him a fighting elephant, to terrify the natives and their horses. There is nothing impossible about the story; though it is not likely Caesar would have forgotten to mention so striking a feature of his campaign. One particular animal we may be sure he had with him, his own famous charger with the cloven hoof, which had been bred in his own stud, and would suffer on its back none but himself. On it, as the rumour went, it had been prophesied by the family seer that he should ever ride to victory.

E. 9.—It was, as the Emperor Napoleon has calculated, on July 21 that, at sun-set this mighty armament put out before a gentle south-west air, which died away at midnight, leaving them becalmed on a waveless sea. When morning dawned Britain lay on their left, and they were drifting up the straits with the tide. By and by it turned, oars were got out, and every vessel made for the spot which the events of the previous year had shown to be the best landing-place.[103] Thanks to Caesar's foresight the transports as well as the galleys could now be thus propelled, and such was the ardour of the soldiers that both classes of ships kept pace with one another, in spite of their different build. The transports, of course, contained men enough to take turns at the sweeps, while the galley oarsmen could not be relieved. By noon they reached Britain, and found not a soul to resist their landing. There had been, as Caesar learnt from "prisoners," a large force gathered for that purpose, but the terrific multitude of his ships had proved quite too demoralizing, and the patriot army had retired to "higher ground," to which the prisoners were able to direct the invader.

E. 10.—There is obviously something strange about this tale. There was no fighting, the shore was deserted, yet somehow prisoners were taken, and prisoners singularly well informed as to the defenders' strategy. The story reads very much as if these useful individuals were really deserters, or, as the Britons would call it, traitors. We know that in one British tribe, at least, there was a pro-Roman party. Not long before this there had fled to Caesar in Gaul, Mandubratius, the fugitive prince of the Trinobantes, who dwelt in Essex. His father Immanuentius had been slain in battle by Cassivellaunus, or Caswallon[104] (the king of their westward neighbours the Cateuchlani), now the most powerful chieftain in Britain, and he himself driven into exile.

E. 11.—This episode seems to have formed part of a general native rising against the over-sea suzerainty of Divitiacus, which had brought Caswallon to the front as the national champion. It was Caswallon who was now in command against Caesar, and if, as is very probable, there was any Trinobantian contingent in his army, they may well have furnished these "prisoners." For Caesar had brought Mandubratius with him for the express purpose of influencing the Trinobantes, who were in fact thus induced in a few weeks to set an example of submission to Rome, as soon as their fear of Caswallon was removed. And meanwhile nothing is more likely than that a certain number of ardent loyalists should leave the usurper's ranks and hasten to greet their hereditary sovereign, so soon as ever he landed. The later British accounts develop the transaction into an act of wholesale treachery; Mandubratius (whose name they discover to mean *The Black Traitor*) deserting, in the thick of a fight, to Caesar, at the head of twenty thousand clansmen,—an absurd exaggeration which may yet have the above-mentioned kernel of truth.

E. 12.—But whoever these "prisoners" were, their information was so important, and in Caesar's view so trustworthy, that he proceeded to act upon it that very night. Before even entrenching his camp, leaving only ten cohorts and three hundred horse to guard the vessels, most of which were at anchor on the smooth sea, he set off at the head of his army "in the third watch," and after a forced march of twelve miles, probably along the British trackway afterwards called Watling Street, found himself at daybreak in touch with the enemy. The British forces were stationed on a ridge of rising ground, at the foot of which flowed a small stream. Napoleon considers this stream to have been the Lesser Stour (now a paltry rivulet, dry in summer, but anciently much larger), and the hill to have been Barham Down, the camping-ground of so many armies throughout British history.

E. 13.—The battle began with a down-hill charge of the British cavalry and chariots against the Roman horse who were sent forward to seize the passage of the stream. Beaten back they retreated to its banks, which were now, doubtless, lined by their infantry. And here the real struggle took place. The unhappy Britons, however, were hopelessly outclassed, and very probably outnumbered, by Caesar's twenty-four thousand legionaries and seventeen hundred horsemen. They gave way, some dispersing in confusion, but the best of their troops retiring in good order to a stronghold in the neighbouring woods, "well fortified both by nature and art," which was a legacy from some local quarrel. Now they had strengthened it with an abattis of felled trees, which was resolutely defended, while skirmishers in open order harassed the assailants from the neighbouring forest [*rari propugnabant e silvis*]. It was necessary for the Seventh legion to throw up trenches, and finally to form a "tortoise" with their shields, as in the assault on a regularly fortified town, before the position could be carried. Then, at last, the Britons were driven from the wood, and cut up in their flight over the open down beyond. The spot where they made this last stand is still, in local legend, associated with the vague memory of some patriot defeat, and known by the name of "Old England's Hole." Traces of the rampart, and of the assailants' trenches, are yet visible.[105]

SECTION F.

Fleet again wrecked—Britons rally under Caswallon—Battle of Barham Down— Britons fly to London—Origin of London—Patriot army dispersed.

F. 1.—It was Caesar's intention to give the broken enemy no chance of rallying. In spite of the dire fatigue of his men (who had now been without sleep for two nights, and spent the two succeeding days in hard rowing and hard fighting), he sent forward the least exhausted to press the pursuit. But before the columns thus detailed had got out of sight a message from the camp at Richborough changed his purpose. The mishap of the previous year had been repeated. Once more the gentle breeze had changed to a gale, and the fleet which he had left so smoothly riding at anchor was lying battered and broken on the beach. His own presence was urgently needed on the scene of the misfortune, and it would have been madness to let the campaign go on without him. So the pursuers, horse and foot, were hastily recalled, and, doubtless, were glad enough to encamp, like their comrades, on the ground so lately won, where they took their well-earned repose.

F. 2.—But for Caesar there could be no rest. Without the loss of a moment he rode back to the landing-place, where he found the state of things fully as bad as had been reported to him. Forty ships were hopelessly shattered; but by dint of strenuous efforts he succeeded in saving the rest. All were now drawn on shore, and tinkered up by artificers from the legions, while instructions were sent over to Labienus for the building of a fresh fleet in Gaul. The naval station, too, was this time thoroughly fortified.

F. 3.—Ten days sufficed for the work; but meanwhile much of the fruit of the previous victory had been lost. The Britons, finding the pursuit checked, and learning the reason, had rallied their scattered force; and when Caesar returned to his camp at Barham Down he found before it a larger patriot army than ever, with Caswallon (who is now named for the first time) at its head. This hero, who, as we have said, may have been brought to the front through the series of inter-tribal wars which had ruined the foreign supremacy of Divitiacus in Britain, was by this time acclaimed his successor in a dignity corresponding in some degree to the mythical Pendragonship of Welsh legend.[106] His own immediate dominions included at least the future districts of South Anglia and Essex, and his banner was followed by something very like a national levy from the whole of Britain south of the Forth. When we read of the extraordinary solidarity which animated, over a much larger area, the equally separate clans of Gaul in their rising against the Roman yoke a year later, there is nothing incredible, or even improbable, in the Britons having developed something of a like solidarity in their resistance to its being laid upon their necks. Burmann's 'Anthology' contains an epigram which bears witness to the existence amongst us even at that date of the sentiment, "Britons never shall be slaves." Our island is described as *"Libera non hostem non passa Britannia regem."*[107]

F. 4.—Even on his march from the new naval camp to Barham Down Caesar was harassed by incessant attacks from flying parties of Caswallon's chariots and horsemen, who would sweep up, deliver their blow, and retire, only to take grim advantage of the slightest imprudence on the part of the Roman cavalry in pursuit. And when, with a perceptible number of casualties, the Down was reached, a stronger attack was delivered on the outposts set to guard the working parties who were entrenching the position, and the fighting became very sharp indeed. The outposts were driven in, even though reinforced by two cohorts—each the First of its Legion, and thus consisting of picked men, like the old Grenadier companies of our own regiments. Though these twelve hundred regulars, the very flower of the Roman army, awaited the attack in such a formation that the front cohort was closely supported by the rear, the Britons pushed their assault home, and had "the extreme audacity" to charge clean through the ranks of both, re-form behind, and charge back again, with great loss to the Romans (whose leader, Quintus Labienus Durus, the Tribune, or Divisional General in command of one of the legions, was slain), and but little to themselves. Not till several more cohorts were dispatched to the rescue did they at length retire.

F. 5.—This brilliant little affair speaks well both for the discipline and the spirit of the patriot army; and Caesar ungrudgingly recognizes both. He points out how far superior the British warriors were to his own men, both in individual and tactical mobility. The legionaries dare not break their ranks to pursue, under pain of being cut off by their nimble enemies before they could re-form; and even the cavalry found it no safe matter to press British chariots too far or too closely. At any moment the crews might spring to earth, and the pursuing horsemen find themselves confronted, or even surrounded, by infantry in position. Moreover, the morale of the British army was so good that it could fight in quite small units, each of which, by the skilful dispositions of Caswallon, was within easy reach of one of his series of "stations" (*i.e.* block-houses) disposed along the line of march, where it could rest while the garrison turned out to take its turn in the combat.

F. 6.—Against such an enemy it was obviously Caesar's interest to bring on, as speedily as possible, a general action, in which he might deliver a crushing blow. And, happily for him, their success had rendered the Britons over-confident, so that they were even deluded enough to imagine that they could face the full Roman force in open field. Both sides, therefore, were eager to bring about the same result. Next morning the small British squads which were hovering around showed ostentatious reluctance to come to close quarters, so as to draw the Romans out of their lines. Caesar gladly met their views, and sent forward all his cavalry and three legions, who, on their part, ostentatiously broke rank and began to forage. This was the opportunity the Britons wanted—and Caesar wanted also. From every side, in front, flank, and rear, the former "flew upon" their enemies, so suddenly and so vigorously that ere the legions, prepared as they were for the onset, could form, the very standards were all but taken.

F. 7.—But this time it was with legions and not with cohorts that the enemy had to do. Their first desperate charge spent itself before doing any serious damage to the masses of disciplined valour confronting them, and the Romans, once in formation, were able to deliver a counter-charge which proved quite irresistible. On every side the Britons broke and fled; the main stream of fugitives unwisely keeping together, so that the pursuers, cavalry and infantry alike, were able to press the pursuit vigorously. No chance was given for a rally; amid the confusion the chariot-crews could not even spring to earth as usual; and the slaughter was such as to daunt the stoutest patriot. The spell of Caswallon's luck was broken, and his auxiliaries from other clans with one accord deserted him and dispersed homewards. Never again throughout all history did the Britons gather a national levy against Rome.

F. 8.—This break-up of the patriot confederacy seems, however, to have been not merely the spontaneous disintegration of a routed army, but a deliberately adopted resolution of the chiefs. Caesar speaks of "their counsel." And this brings us to an interesting consideration. Where did they take this counsel, and why did the fleeing hosts follow one line of flight? And how was the line of the Roman advance so accurately calculated upon by Caswallon that he was able to place his "stations" along it beforehand? The answer is that there was an obvious objective for which the Romans would be sure to make; indeed there was almost certainly an obvious track along which they would be sure to march. There is every reason to believe that most of the later Roman roads were originally British trackways, broad green ribands of turf winding through the land (such as the Icknield Way is still in many parts of its course), and following the lines most convenient for trade.

F. 9.—But, if this is so, then that convergence of these lines on London, which is as marked a feature of the map of Roman Britain as it is of our railway maps now, must have already been noticeable. And the only possible reason for this must be found in the fact that already London was a noted passage over the Thames. That an island in mid-stream was the original *raison d'être* of London Bridge is apparent from the mass of buildings which is shown in every ancient picture of that structure clustering between the two central spans. This island must have been a very striking feature in primaeval days, coming, as it did, miles below any other eyot on the river, and must always have suggested and furnished a comparatively easy crossing-place. Possibly even a bridge of some sort may have existed in 54 B.C.; anyhow this crossing would have been alike the objective of the invading, and the *point d'appui* of the defending army. And the line both of the Roman advance and of the British retreat would be along the track afterwards known as the Kentish Watling Street. For here again the late British legends which tell us of councils of war held in London against Caesar, and fatal resolutions adopted there, with every detail of proposer and discussion, are probably founded, with gross exaggeration, upon a real kernel of historic truth. It was actually on London that the Britons retired, and from London that the gathering of the clans broke up, each to its own.

SECTION G.

Passage of Thames—Submission of clans—Storm of Verulam—Last patriot effort in Kent—Submission of Caswallon—Romans leave Britain—"Caesar Divus."

G. 1.—Caswallon, however, and his immediate realm still remained to be dealt with. His first act, on resolving upon continued resistance, would of course be to make the passage of the London tide-way impossible for the Roman army; and Caesar, like William the Conqueror after him, had to search up-stream for a crossing-place. He did not, however, like William, have to make his way so far as Wallingford before finding one. Deserters told him of a ford, though a difficult one, practicable for infantry, not many miles distant. The traditional spot, near Walton-on-Thames, anciently called Coway Stakes, may very probably be the real place. Both name and stakes, however, have probably, in spite of the guesses of antiquaries, no connection with Caesar and his passage, but more prosaically indicate that here was a passage for cattle (Coway = Cow Way) marked out by crossing stakes.

G. 2.—The forces of Caswallon were accompanying the Roman march on the northern bank of the stream, and when Caesar came to the ford he found them already in position [*instructas*] to dispute his passage behind a *chevaux de frise* of sharpened stakes, more of which, he was told, were concealed by the water. If the Britons had shown their wonted resolution this position must have been impregnable. But Caswallon's men were disheartened and shaken by the slaughter on the Kentish Downs and the desertion of their allies. Caesar rightly calculated that a bold demonstration would complete their demoralization. So it proved. The sight of the Roman cavalry plunging into the steam, and the legionaries eagerly pressing on neck-deep in water, proved altogether too much for their nerves. With one accord, and without a blow, they broke and fled.[108]

G. 3.—Nor did Caswallon think it wise again to gather them. He had no further hope of facing Caesar in pitched battle, and contented himself with keeping in touch with the enemy with a flying column of chariot-men some two thousand strong. His practice was to keep his men a little off the road—there was still, be it noted, a *road* along which the Romans were marching—and drive off the flocks and herds into the woods before the Roman advance. He made no attempt to attack the legions, but if any foragers were bold enough to follow up the booty thus reft from them, he was upon them in a moment. Such serious loss was thus inflicted that Caesar had to forbid any such excursions, and to content himself with laying waste the fields and farms in immediate proximity to his route.

G. 4.—He was now in Caswallon's own country, and his presence there encouraged the Trinobantian loyalists openly to throw off allegiance to their conqueror and raise Mandubratius to his father's throne under the protection of Rome; sending to Caesar at the same time provisions for his men, and forty hostages whom he demanded of them. Caesar in return gave strict orders to his soldiers against plundering or raiding in their territory. This mingled firmness and clemency made so favourable an impression that the submission of the Trinobantes was followed by that of various adjoining clans, small and great, from the Iceni of East Anglia to the little riverside septs of the Bibroci and Ancalites, whose names may or may not be echoed in the modern Bray and Henley. The Cassi (of Cassiobury) not only submitted, but guided the Romans to Caswallon's own neighbouring stronghold in the forests near St. Alban's. It was found to be a position of considerable natural strength (probably on the site of the later Verulam), and well fortified; but all the heart was out of the Cateuchlanians. When the assailing columns approached to storm the place on two sides at once, they hesitated, broke, and flung themselves over the ramparts on the other sides in headlong flight. Caesar, however, was able to head them, and his troops killed and captured large numbers, besides getting possession of all the flocks and herds, which, as usual, had been gathered for refuge within the stockade.

G. 5.—Caswallon himself, however, escaped, and now made one last bid for victory. So great was still the influence of his prestige that, broken as he was, he was able to prevail upon the clans of Kent to make a sudden and desperate onset upon the Naval Station at Richborough. All four of the chieftains beneath whose sway the county was divided (Cingetorix, Canilius, Taximagulus, and Segonax) rose with one accord at his summons. The attack, however, proved a mere flash in the pan. Even before it was delivered, the garrison sallied out vigorously, captured one of the British leaders, Lugotorix, slaughtered the assailants wholesale, and crushed the whole movement without the loss of a man. This final defeat of his last hopes broke even Caswallon's sturdy heart. His followers slain, his lands wasted, his allies in revolt, he bowed to the inevitable. Even now, however, he did not surrender unconditionally, but besought Caesar's *protégé*, the Atrebatian chieftain Commius, to negotiate terms with the conqueror.

G. 6.—To Caesar this was no small relief. The autumn was coming on, and Caswallon's guerrilla warfare might easily eat up all the remainder of the summer, when he must needs be left alone, conquered or unconquered, that the Roman army might get back to its winter quarters on the Continent; more especially as ominous signs in Gaul already predicted the fearful tempest of revolt which, that winter, was to burst. Easy conditions were therefore imposed. Caswallon pledged himself, as Lord Paramount, that Britain should pay an annual tribute to the Roman treasury, and, as Chief of the Cateuchlani, that he would leave Mandubratius on the Trinobantian throne. Hostages were given, and the Roman forces returned with all convenient speed to the coast; this time, presumably, crossing the Thames in the regular way at London.

G. 7.—After a short wait, in vain expectation of the sixty ships which Labienus had built in Gaul and which could not beat across the Channel, Caesar crowded his troops and the hordes of British captives on board as best he could, and being favoured by the weather, found himself and them safe across, having worked out his great purpose, and leaving a nominally conquered and tributary Britain behind him. This, as we have seen from Cicero's letter, was on September 26, B.C. 54.

G. 8.—We have seen, too, that Cicero's cue was to belittle the business. But this was far from being the view taken by the Roman "in the street." To him Caesar's exploit was like those of the gods and heroes of old; Hercules and Bacchus had done less, for neither had passed the Ocean.

The popular feeling of exultation in this new glory added to Roman fame may be summed up in the words of the Anthologist already quoted:

Libera non hostem, non passa Britannia regem,
Aeternum nostro quae procul orbe jacet;
Felix adversis, et sorte oppressa secunda,
Communis nobis et tibi Caesar erit.

["Free Britain, neither foe nor king that bears,
That from our world lies far and far away,
Lucky to lose, crushed by a happy doom,
Henceforth, O Caesar, ours—and yours—will be."]

G. 9.—Caesar never set foot in Britain again, though he once saved himself from imminent destruction by utilizing his British experiences and passing his troops over a river in coracles of British build.[109] He went his way to the desperate fighting, first of the great Gallic revolt, then of the Civil War (with his own Labienus for the most ferocious of his opponents), till he found himself the undisputed master of the Roman world. But when he fell, upon the Ides of March B.C. 44, it was mainly through the superhuman reputation won by his invasion of Britain that he received the hitherto unheard of distinction of a popular apotheosis, and handed down to his successors for many a generation the title not only of Caesar, but of "Divus."

* * * * *

CHAPTER III

THE ROMAN CONQUEST, B.C. 54—A.D. 85

SECTION A.

Britain after Julius Caesar—House of Commius—Inscribed coins—House of Cymbeline—Tasciovan—Commians overthrown—Vain appeal to Augustus—Ancyran Tablet—Romano-British trade—Lead-mining—British fashions in Rome—Adminius banished by Cymbeline—Appeal to Caligula—Futile demonstration—Icenian civil war—Vericus banished—Appeal to Claudius—Invasion prepared.

A. 1.—With the departure of Caesar from its shores our knowledge of the affairs of Britain becomes only less fragmentary than before he reached them. We do not even learn how far the tribute he had imposed continued to be paid. Most probably during the confusion of the Gallic revolt and the Civil Wars it ceased altogether. In that confusion Commius finally lost his continental principality of Arras, and had to fly for his life into his British dominions. He only saved himself, indeed, by an ingenious stratagem. When he reached the shore of Gaul he found his ship aground in the tide-way. Nevertheless, by hoisting all sail, he deceived the pursuing Romans into thinking themselves too late till the rising tide permitted him really to put to sea.[110] The effect of the extinction of Atrebatian power in Gaul was doubtless to consolidate it in Britain, as when our

English sovereigns lost their hold on Normandy and Anjou, for we find that Commius reigned at least over the eastern counties of Wessex, and transmitted his power to his sons, Verica, Eppillus, and Tincommius, who seem to have shared the kingdom between them. Tincommius, however, may possibly be, as Professor Rhys suggests, merely a title, signifying the *Tanist* (or Heir) of Commius. In this case it would be that of Verica, who was king after his father.[111]

A. 2.—The evidence for this is that in the district mentioned British coins are found bearing these names. For now appears the first inscribed British coinage; the inscriptions being all in Latin, a sign of the abiding influence of the work of Caesar. And it is by that light mainly that we know the little we do know of British history for the next century. The coins are very numerous, and preserve for us the names of no fewer than thirty several rulers (or states). They are mostly of gold (though both silver and bronze also occur), and are found over the greater part of the island, the southern and the eastern counties being the richest. The inscriptions indicate, as has already been mentioned,[112] a state of great political confusion throughout the country. But they also bear testimony not only to the dynasty of Commius, but to the rise of a much stronger power north of the Thames.

A. 3.—That power was the House of Cunobelin, or Cinobellinus[113] (Shakespeare's Cymbeline), who figures in the pages of Suetonius as King of all Britain, insomuch that his fugitive son, Adminius, posed before Caligula as the rightful sovereign of the whole island. His coins were undoubtedly current everywhere south of Trent and east of Severn, if not beyond those rivers. They are found in large numbers, and of most varied devices, all showing the influence of classical art. A head (probably his own portrait) is often on the obverse, and on the reverse Apollo playing the lyre, or a Centaur, or a Victory, or Medusa, or Pegasus, or Hercules. Other types show a warrior on horse or foot, or a lion,[114] or a bull, or a wolf, or a wild boar; others again a vine-leaf, or an ear of bearded wheat. On a very few is found the horse, surviving from the old

Macedonian mintage.[115] And all bear his own name, sometimes in full, CVNOBELINVS REX, oftener abbreviated in various ways.

A. 4.—But the coins do more than testify to the widespread power of Cymbeline himself. They show us that he inherited much of it from his father. This prince, whose name was Tasciovan, is often associated with his son in the inscriptions, and the son is often described as TASCIIOVANI F. (*Filius*) or TASCIOVANTIS. There are besides a large number of coins belonging to Tasciovan alone. And these tell us where he reigned. They are struck (where the mint is recorded) either at Segontium[116] or at Verulam. The latter is pretty certainly the town which had sprung up on the site of Caswallon's stronghold, so that we may reasonably conclude that Tasciovan was the successor of the patriot hero on the Cateuchlanian throne—very probably his son. But Cymbeline's coins are struck at the *Trinobantian* capital, Camelodune,[117] which we know to have been the royal city of his son Caratac (or Caradoc) at the Claudian conquest.

A. 5.—It would seem, therefore, that, Caesar's mandate to the contrary notwithstanding, Caswallon's clan, who were now called (perhaps from his name), Cattivellauni, had again conquered the Trinobantes, deposing, and probably slaying, Mandubratius.[118] This would be under Tasciovan, who gave the land to his son Cymbeline, and, at a later date, must have subdued the Atrebatian power in the south. The sons of Commius were, as is shown by Sir John Evans, contemporary with Tasciovan. But, by and by, we find Epaticcus, *his* son, and Adminius, apparently his grandson, reigning in their realm, the latter taking Kent, the former the western districts. The previous Kentish monarch was named Dumnovellanus, and appears as DAMNO BELLA on the Ancyran Tablet. This wonderful record of the glories of Augustus mentions, *inter alia*, that certain British kings, of whom this prince was one, fled to his protection. The tablet is, unhappily, mutilated at the point where their names occur, but that of another begins with TIM— probably, as Sir John Evans suggests, Tin-Commius. Adminius also was afterwards exiled by his own father, Cymbeline, and in like manner appealed to Caesar—Caligula—in 40 A.D.

A. 6.—Nothing came of either appeal. Augustus did indeed, according to Dio Cassius, meditate completing his "father's" work, and (in B.C. 34) entered Gaul with a view to invading Britain. But the political troubles which were to culminate at Actium called him back, and he contented himself with laying a small duty on the trade between Britain and Gaul. Tin, as before, formed the staple export of our island, and other metals seem now to have been added—iron from Sussex and lead from Somerset. Doubtless also the pearls from our native oysters (of which Caesar had already dedicated a breastplate to his ancestral Venus) found their way to Rome, though of far less value than the Oriental jewel, being of a less pure white.[119] Besides these we read of "ivory bracelets and necklets, amber and glass ornaments, and such-like rubbish,"[120] which doubtless found a sale amongst the *virtuosi* of Rome, as like products of savage industry from Africa or Polynesia find a sale amongst our *virtuosi* nowadays. Meanwhile, Roman dignity was saved by considering these duties to be in lieu of the unpaid tribute imposed by Caesar, and the island was declared by courtly writers to be already in practical subjection. "Some of the chiefs (δυνάσται) [dunastai] have gained the friendship of Augustus, and dedicated offerings in the Capitol . . . The island would not be worth holding, and could never pay the expenses of a garrison."[121]

A. 7.—At the same time the Romans of the day evidently took a very special interest in everything connected with Britain. The leaders of Roman society, like Maecenas, drove about in British chariots,[122] smart ladies dyed their hair red in imitation of British warriors,[123] tapestry inwoven with British figures was all the fashion,[124] and constant hopes were expressed by the poets that, before long, so interesting a land might be finally incorporated in the Roman Empire.[125]

A. 8.—Augustus was too prudent to be stirred up by this "forward" policy; which, indeed, he had sanctioned once too often in the fatal invasion of Germany by Varus. But the diseased brain of Caligula *was* for a moment fired with the ambition of so vast an enterprise. He professed that the fugitive Adminius had ceded to him the kingship of the whole island,

and sent home high-flown dispatches to that effect. He had no fleet, but drew up his army in line of battle on the Gallic shore, while all wondered what mad freak he was purposing; then suddenly bade every man fill his helmet with shells as "spoils of the Ocean" to be dedicated in the Capitol. Finally he commemorated this glorious victory by the erection of a lofty lighthouse,[126] probably at the entrance of Boulogne harbour.

A. 9.—It was clear, however, that sooner or later Britain must be drawn into the great system so near her, and the next reign furnished the needful occasion. Yet another exiled British pretender appealed to the Emperor to see him righted—this time one Vericus. His name suggests that he may have been Verica son of Commius; but the theory of Professor Rhys and Sir John Evans seems more probable—that he was a Prince of the Iceni. The earliest name found on the coins of that clan is Addeomarus (Aedd Mawr, or Eth the Great, of British legend), who was contemporary with Tasciovan. After this the tribe probably became subject to Cymbeline, at whose death[127] the chieftainship seems to have been disputed between two pretenders, Vericus and Antedrigus; and on the success of the latter (presumably by Cateuchlanian favour) the former fled to Rome. Claudius, who now sat on the Imperial throne, eagerly seized the opportunity for the renown he was always coveting, and in A.D. 44 set in motion the forces of the Empire to subdue our island.

SECTION B.

Aulus Plautius—Reluctance to embark—Narcissus—Passage of Channel—Landing at Portchester—Strength of expedition—Vespasian's legion—British defeats—Line of Thames held—Arrival of Claudius—Camelodune taken—General submission of island.

B. 1.—The command of the expedition was entrusted to Aulus Plautius Laelianus, a distinguished Senator, of Consular rank. But the reluctance of the soldiery to advance "beyond the limits of this mortal world" (ἔξω τῆς οἰκουμένης) [exô tas oikoumenês], and entrust themselves to the mysterious tides of the ocean which was held to bound it, caused him weeks of delay on the shores of Gaul. Nor could anything move them, till they found this malingering likely to expose them to the degradation of a quasi-imperial scolding from Narcissus, the freed-man favourite of Claudius, who came down express from Rome as the Emperor's mouthpiece.[128] To bear reproof from one who had been born a slave was too much for Roman soldiers. When Narcissus mounted the tribune to address them in the Emperor's name, his very first words were at once drowned by a derisive shout from every mouth of *"Io Saturnalia!"* the well-known cry with which Roman slaves inaugurated their annual Yule-tide licence of aping for the day the characters of their masters. The parade tumultuously broke off, and the troops hurried down to the beach to carry out the commands of their General—who was at least free-born.

B, 2.—The passage of the Channel was effected in three separate fleets, possibly at three separate points, and the landing on our shores was unopposed. The Britons, doubtless, had been lulled to security by the tidings of the mutinous temper in the camp of the invaders, and were quite unprepared for the very unexpected result of the mission of Narcissus. It seems likely, moreover, that the disembarkation was made much further to the west than they would have looked for. The voyage is spoken of as long, and amid its discomforts the drooping spirits of the soldiery were signally cheered by a meteor of special brilliance which one night darted westwards as their harbinger. Moreover we find that when the Romans did land, their first success was a defeat of the Dobuni, subject allies of the House of Cymbeline, who, as we gather from Ptolemy, dwelt in what is now Southern Gloucestershire.[129] This objective rather points to their landing-place having been in Portsmouth harbour[130] (*the* Port, as its name still reminds us, of Roman Britain), where the undoubtedly Roman site of Portchester may well mark the exact spot where the expedition first set foot on shore.

B. 3.—Besides an unknown force of Gallic auxiliaries, its strength comprised four veteran legions, one (the Ninth *Hispanica*)[131] from the Danube frontier, the rest (Twentieth, Fourteenth, and Second) from the Rhine. This last, an "Augustan"[132] legion, was commanded by the future Emperor Vespasian—a connection destined to have an important influence on the *pronunciamento* which, twenty-five years later, placed him on the throne.[133] As yet he was only a man of low family, whom favouritism was held to have hurried up the ladder of promotion more rapidly than his birth warranted.[134] Serving under him as Military Tribunes were his brother Sabinus and his son Titus; and in this British campaign all three Flavii are said to have distinguished themselves,[135] especially at the passage of an unnamed river, where the Britons made an obstinate stand. The ford was not passed till after three days' continuous fighting, of which the issue was finally decided by the "Celtic" auxiliaries swimming the stream higher up, and stampeding the chariot-horses tethered behind the British lines.

B. 4.—What this stream may have been is a puzzle.[136] Dion Cassius brings it in after a victory over the sons of Cymbeline, Caradoc (or Caractacus, as historians commonly call him) and Togodumnus, wherein the latter was slain. And he adds that from its banks the Britons fell back upon their next line of defence, the *tide-way* on the Thames. He tells us that, though tidal, the river was, at this point, fordable at low water for those who knew the shallows; and incidentally mentions that at no great distance there was even a bridge over it. But it was bordered by almost impassable[137] swamps. It must be remembered that before the canalizing of the Thames the influence of the tide was perceptible at least as high as Staines, where was also a crossing-place of immemorial antiquity. And hereabouts may very probably have been the key of the British position, a position so strong that it brought Plautius altogether to a standstill. Not till overwhelming reinforcements, including even an elephant corps, were summoned from Rome, with Claudius in person at their head, was a passage forced. The defence then, however, collapsed utterly, and within a fortnight of his landing, Claudius was able to re-embark for Rome, after taking Camelodune, and securing for the moment, without the loss of a man,[138] as it would seem, the nominal submission of the whole island, including even the Orkneys.[139]

SECTION C.

Claudius triumphs—Gladiatorial shows—Last stand of Britons—Gallantry of Titus—Ovation of Plautius—Distinctions bestowed—Triumphal arch— Commemorative coinage—Conciliatory policy—British worship of Claudius— Cogidubnus—Attitude of clans—Britain made Imperial Province.

C. 1.—The success thus achieved was evidently felt to be something quite exceptionally brilliant and important. Not once, as was usual, but four several times was Claudius acclaimed "Imperator"[140] even before he left our shores; and in after years these acclamations were renewed at Rome as often as good news of the British war arrived there, till, ere Claudius died, he had received no fewer than twenty-one such distinctions, each signalized by an issue of commemorative coinage. His "Britannic triumph" was celebrated on a scale of exceptional magnificence. In addition to the usual display, he gave his people the unique spectacle of their Emperor climbing the ascent to the Capitol not in his triumphal car, nor even on foot, but on his knees (as pilgrims yet mount the steps of the Ara Coeli), in token of special gratitude to the gods for so signal an extension of the glory and the Empire of Rome. In the gladiatorial shows which followed, he presided in full uniform [*paludatus*],[141] with his son (whose name, like his own, a *Senatus consultum* had declared to be *Britannicus*)[142] on his knee.[143] One of the spectacles represented the storm of a British *oppidum* and the surrender of British kings. The kings were probably real British chieftains, and the storm was certainly real, with real Britons, real blood, real slaughter, for Claudius went to every length in this direction.

C. 2.—The narrative of Suetonius[144] connects these shows with the well-known tale of the unhappy gladiators who fondly hoped that a kind word from the Emperor meant a reprieve of their doom. He had determined to surpass all his predecessors in his exhibition of a sea-fight, and had provided a sheet of water large enough for the manoeuvres of real war-galleys, carrying some five hundred men apiece.[145] The crews, eleven thousand in all, made their usual preliminary march past his throne, with the usual mournful acclaim, "*Ave Caesar! Salutant te morituri!*" Claudius responded, "*Aut non:*" and these two words were enough to inspire the doomed ranks with hopes of mercy. With one accord they refused to play their part, and he had to come down in person and solemnly assure them that if his show was spoilt he would exterminate every man of them "with fire and sword," before they would embark. Once entered upon the combat, however, they fought desperately; so well, indeed, that at its close the survivors were declared exempt from any further performance. Such was the fate which awaited those who dared to defend their freedom against the Fortune of Rome, and such the death died by many a brave Briton for the glory of his subjugators. Dion Cassius[146] tells us that Aulus Plautius made a special boast of the numbers so butchered in connection with his own "Ovation."

C. 3.—This ceremony was celebrated A.D. 47, two years after that of Claudius. Plautius had remained behind in Britain to stamp out the last embers of resistance,—a task which all but proved fatal to Vespasian, who got hemmed in by the enemy. He was only saved by the personal heroism and devotion of Titus, who valiantly made in to his father's rescue, and succeeded in cutting him out. This seems to have been in the last desperate stand made by the Britons during this campaign. After this, with Togodumnus slain, Caradoc probably a fugitive in hiding, and the best and bravest of the land slaughtered either in the field or in the circus at Rome, British resistance was for the moment utterly crushed out. Claudius continued his demonstrations of delight; when Plautius neared Rome he went out in person to meet him,[147] raised him when he bent the knee in homage, and warmly shook hands with him[148] (καλῶς διαχείσας) [kalos diacheirisas]; afterwards himself walking on his left hand in the triumphal procession along the Via Sacra.[149]

C. 4.—Rewards were at the same time showered on the inferior officers. Cnaeus Ostorius Geta, the hero of the first riverside fight in Britain, was allowed to triumph in consular fashion, though not yet of consular rank; and an inscription found at Turin speaks of collars, gauntlets and phalera bestowed on one Caius Gavius, along with a golden wreath for Distinguished Service. Another, found in Switzerland,[150] records the like wreath assigned to Julius Camillus, a Military Tribune of the Fourth Legion, together with the decoration of the *Hasta Pura* (something, it would seem, in the nature of the Victoria Cross); which was also, according to Suetonius,[151] given to Posides, one of the Emperor's favourite freedmen.

C. 5.—To Claudius himself, besides his triumph, the Senate voted two triumphal arches,[152] one in Rome, the other in the Gallic port whence he had embarked for Britain. Part of the inscription on the former of these was found in 1650 on the site where it stood (near the Palazzo Sciarra), and is still to be seen in the gardens of the Barberini Palace. It runs as follows (the conjectural restoration of the lost portions which have been added being enclosed in brackets):

TI CLAVD [IO. CAES.]
AVG [VSTO]
PONTIFIC [I. MAX. TR. P. IX]
COS. VI. IM [P. XVI. PP]
SENATVS. PO [PVL. Q.R. QVOD]
REGES. BRIT [ANNIAE. ABSQ]
VLLA. JACTV [RA. DOMVERIT]

GENTES QVE [BARBARAS]
PRIMVS. INDI [CIO. SVBEGERIT]

"To Tiberius Claudius Caesar, Augustus, Pontifex Maximus, holding for the 9th time the authority of Tribune, Consul for the 6th time, acclaimed Imperator for the 16th, the Senate and People of Rome [have dedicated this arch]. Because that without the loss of a man he hath subdued the Kings of Britain, and hath been the first to bring under her barbarous clans under our sway."

Claudius also affixed to the walls of the imperial house on the Palatine (which was destined to give the name of "palace" to royal abodes for all time),[153] a "*corona navalis*"—a circlet in which the usual radiations were made to resemble the sails, etc. of ships—in support of his proud claim to have tamed the Ocean itself [*quasi domiti oceani*] and brought it under Roman sway:

"*Et jam Romano cingimur Oceano.*"[154]

C. 6.—As usual, coins were struck to commemorate the occasion, the earliest of the long series of Roman coins relating to Britain. They bear on the obverse the laureated head of Claudius to the right, with the superscription TI. CLAVD. CAESAR. AVG. P.M. TR. P. VIIII. IMP. XVI. On the reverse is an equestrian figure, between two trophies, surmounting a triumphal arch, over which is inscribed the legend DE. BRITAN. This coin, being of gold, was struck not by the Senate (who regulated the bronze issue), but by the Imperial mint, and dates from the year 46, when Claudius was clothed for the ninth time with the authority of Tribune. By that time the arch was doubtless completed, and the coin may well show what it was actually like. Another coin, also bearing the words DE. BRITAN., shows Claudius in his triumphal chariot with an eagle on his sceptre. Even poor little Britannicus, who never came to his

112

father's throne, being set aside through the intrigues of his stepmother Agrippina and finally poisoned (A.D. 55) by Nero, had a coin of his own on this occasion issued by the Senate and inscribed TI. CLAVD. CAESAR. AVG. F. [*Augusti Filius*] BRITANNICVS.

C.7.—Seneca, whose own connection with Britain was that of a grinding usurer,[155] speaks with intense disgust of the conciliatory attitude of Claudius towards the populations, or more probably the kinglets, who had submitted to his sway. He purposed, it seems, even to see some of them raised to Roman citizenship [*Britannos togatos videre*]. That the grateful provincials should have raised a temple to him at Camelodune, and rendered him worship as an incarnate deity, adds to the offence. And, writing on the Emperor's death, the philosopher points with evident satisfaction to the wretched fate of the man who triumphed over Britain and the Ocean, only to fall at last a victim to the machinations of his own wife.

C. 8.—An interesting confirmation of this information as to the relations between Claudius and his British subjects is to be found in a marble tablet[156] discovered at Chichester, which commemorates the erection of a temple (dedicated to Neptune and Minerva) for the welfare of the Divine [*i.e.* Imperial] Household by a Guild of Craftsmen [*collegium fabrorum*] on a site given by Pudens the son of Pudentinus;[157] all under the authority of Tiberius Claudius Cogidubnus, at once a native British kinglet and Imperial Legate in Britain. This office would imply Roman citizenship, as would also the form of his name. That (doubtless on his enfranchisement) he should have been allowed to take such a distinguished *nomen* and *praenomen* as Tiberius Claudius marks the special favour in which he was held by the Emperor.[158] To this witness is also borne by Tacitus, who says that certain states in Britain were placed under Cogidubnus not as a tributary Kingdom but as a Roman Province. Hence his title of Imperial Legate. These states were doubtless those of the Cantii and Regni in Kent, Surrey and Sussex.

C. 9.—The Iceni, on the other hand, were subject allies of Rome, with Vericus, in all probability, on the throne.[159] The Atrebates would seem also to have been "friendlies." But the great mass of the British clans were chafing under the humiliation and suffering which the invaders had wrought for them, and evidently needed a strong hand to keep them down. Under the Empire provinces requiring military occupation were committed not to Pro-consuls chosen by the Senate, but to Pro-praetors nominated by the Emperor, and were called "Imperial" as opposed to "Senatorial" governments.[160] Britain was now accordingly declared an Imperial Province, and Ostorius Scapula sent by Claudius to administer it as Pro-praetor.

SECTION D.

Ostorius Pro-praetor—Pacification of Midlands—Icenian revolt—Camb's dykes—Iceni crushed—Cangi—Brigantes—Silurian war—Storm of Caer Caradoc—Treachery of Cartismandua—Caradoc at Rome—Death of Ostorius— Uriconium and Caerleon—Britain quieted—Death of Claudius.

D. 1.—When Ostorius, in A.D. 50, reached Britain he found things in a very disturbed state. The clans which had submitted to the Romans were being raided by their independent neighbours, who calculated that this new governor would not venture on risking his untried levies in a winter campaign against them. Ostorius, however, was astute enough to realize that such a first impression of his rule would be fatal, and, by a sudden dash with a flying column (*citas cohortes*), cut the raiders to pieces. As usual the Britons hoisted the white flag in their familiar manner, making a surrender which they had no intention whatever of keeping to longer than suited their plans; and they were proportionately disgusted when Ostorius set to work at a real pacification of the Midlands, constructing forts at strategic points along the Trent and Severn, and requiring all natives whatsoever within this Roman Pale to give up their arms.

D. 2.—This demand the Britons looked upon as an intolerable dishonour, even as it seemed to the Highlanders two centuries ago. The first to resent it were the chieftain and clan whose alliance with Rome had been the *raison d'être* of the Conquest, Vericus and his Iceni.[161] Was this brand of shame to be their reward for bringing in the invaders? They received the mandate of Ostorius with a burst of defiance, and hastily organized a league of the neighbouring tribes to resist so intolerable a degradation. Before their allies could come in, however, Ostorius was upon them, and it became a matter of defending their own borders.

D. 3.—The spot they selected for resistance was a space shut in by earthworks *(agresti aggere)* accessible only by one narrow entrance. This description exactly applies to the locality where we should look for an Icenian Thermopylae. The clan dwelt, as we have said, in East Anglia, their borders to the south being the marshy course of the Stour, running from the primaeval forest that capped the "East Anglian Heights," and, to the west, the Cambridgeshire Fens. They thus lived within a ring fence almost unassailable. Only in one spot was there an entrance. Between the Fen and the Forest stretched a narrow strip of open turf, some three or four miles across, affording easy marching. And along it ran their own great war-path, the Icknield Street, extending from the heart of their realm right away to the Thames at Goring. It never became a Roman road, though a few miles are now metalled. Along most of its course it remains what it was in British days, a broad, green track seamed with scores of rut-marks. And even where it has been obliterated, its course may be traced by the names of Ickborough in Norfolk, Iclingham in Suffolk, Ickleton in Cambridgeshire, and Ickleford in Hertfordshire.[162]

D. 4.—The Iceni had long ago taken care to fortify this approach to their land. The whole space between fen and forest in the Cam valley was cut across by four (or five) great dykes which may still be traced, constructed for defence against invaders from the westward. Of these, the two innermost are far more formidable than the rest, the "Fleam Dyke" near Cambridge, and the "Devil's Ditch" by Newmarket. The outer fosse of each is from twenty to thirty feet deep; and the rampart, when topped by a stockade, must have constituted an obstacle to troops unprovided with artillery which the Iceni might justifiably think insuperable. The "one narrow entrance" along the whole length of the dykes (five miles and ten miles respectively) is where the Icknield Way cuts through them.

D. 5.—Here then, probably, the Icenian levies confidently awaited the onslaught of Ostorius—the more confidently inasmuch as he had not waited to call up his legionaries from their winter quarters, but attacked only with the irregulars whom he had been employing against the marauders in the midlands. The Iceni, doubtless, imagined that such troops would be unequal to assaulting their dyke at all. But Ostorius was no ordinary leader. Such was the enthusiasm which he inspired in his troops that they surprised the revolters by attacking along the whole line of the Fleam Dyke at once, and that with such impetuosity that in a moment they were over it. The hapless Iceni were now caught in a death-trap. Behind them the Devil's Ditch barred all retreat save through its one narrow entrance, and those who failed to force their way through the mad crush there could only fight and die with the courage of despair. "Many a deed of desperate valour did they," says Tacitus [*multa et clara facinora*], and the Romans displayed like courage; the son of Ostorius winning in the fray the "civic crown"[163] awarded for the rescue of a Roman citizen. But no quarter seems to have been given, and the flower of the Icenian tribe perished there to a man.

D. 6.—This slaughter effectually scotched the rising which the Icenians were hoping to organize. All Central Britain submitted, and, we may presume, was quietly disarmed; though the work cannot have been very effectually done, as these same tribes were able to rise under Boadicea twelve years later. The indefatigable Ostorius next led his men against the Cangi in North Wales[164] (who seem to have been stirred to revolt by the Icenian Prince Antedrigus), and gained much booty, for the

Britons dared not venture upon a battle, and had no luck in their various attempts at surprise. But before he quite reached the Irish Sea he was recalled by a disturbance amongst the Brigantes, which by a judicious mixture of firmness and clemency he speedily suppressed. And all this he did without employing a single legionary.

D. 7.—But neither firmness nor clemency availed to put an end to the desperate struggle for freedom maintained by the one clan in Britain which still held out against the Roman yoke. The Silurians of South Wales were not to be subdued without a regular campaign which was to tax the Legions themselves to the utmost. Naturally brave, stubborn, and with a passionate love of liberty, they had at this juncture a worthy leader, for Caradoc was at their head. We hear nothing of his doings between the first battle against Aulus Plautius, when his brother Togodumnus fell, leaving him the sole heir of Cymbeline, until we find him here. But we may be pretty sure that he was the animating spirit of the resistance which so long checked the conquerors on the banks of the Thames, and that he took no part in the general submission to Claudius. Probably he led an outlaw life in the forest, stirring up all possible resistance to the Roman arms, till finally he found himself left with this one clan of all his father's subjects still remaining faithful.

D. 8.—But he never thought of surrender. He was everywhere amongst his followers, says Tacitus, exhorting them to resist to the death, reminding them how Caswallon had "driven out" the great Julius, and binding one and all by a solemn national covenant [*gentili religione*] never to yield "either for wound or weapon." Ostorius had to bring against him the whole force he could muster, even calling out the veterans newly settled at the Colony[165] of Camelodune. Caradoc and his Silurians, on their part, did not wait at home for the attack, but moved northwards into the territory of the Ordovices, who at least sympathized if they did not actually aid. Here he entrenched himself upon a mountain, very probably that Caer Caradoc, near Shrewsbury, which still bears his name. Those who know the ground will not wonder that Ostorius hesitated at assaulting so impregnable a position. His men, however, were eager for the attack. "Nothing," they cried, "is impregnable to the brave." The legionaries stormed the hill on one side, the auxiliaries on the other; and once hand to hand, the mail-clad Romans had a fearful advantage against defenders who wore no defensive armour, nor even helmets. The Britons broke and fled, Caradoc himself seeking refuge amongst the Brigantes of the north.

D. 9.—At this time the chief power in this tribe was in the hands of a woman, Cartismandua, the heiress to the throne, with whose name and that of her Prince Consort scandal was already busy. The disturbances amongst the clan which Ostorius had lately suppressed were probably connected with her intrigues. Anyhow she posed as the favourite and friend of the Romans; and now showed her loyalty by arresting the national hero and handing him over to the enemy. With his family and fellow-captives he was [A.D. 52] deported to Rome, and publicly exhibited by the Emperor in his chains, as the last of the Britons, while the Praetorian Guards stood to their arms as he passed.

D. 10.—According to Roman precedent the scene should have closed with a massacre of the prisoners. But while the executioners awaited the order to strike, Caradoc stepped forward with a spirited appeal, the substance of which there is every reason to believe is truthfully recorded by Tacitus. Disdaining to make the usual pitiful petitions for mercy, he boldly justified his struggle for his land and crown, and reminded Claudius that he had now an exceptional opportunity for winning renown. "Kill me, as all expect, and this affair will soon be forgotten; spare me, and men will talk of your clemency from age to age." Claudius was touched; and even the fierce Agrippina, who, to the scandal of old Roman sentiment, was seated beside him at the saluting-point "as if she had been herself a General," and who must have reminded Caradoc of Cartismandua, was moved to mercy. Caradoc was spared, and assigned a residence in Italy; and the Senate, believing the war at an end with his capture, voted to

Ostorius "triumphal insignia"[166]—the highest honour attainable by any Roman below Imperial rank.[167]

D. 11.—But even without their King the stubborn clan still stood desperately at bay. Their pertinacious resistance in every pass and on every hill-top of their country at length fairly wore Ostorius out. The incessant fatigues of the campaign broke down his health, and he died [A.D. 54] on the march; to the ferocious joy of the Silurians, who boasted that their valour had made an end of the brave enemy who had vowed to "extinguish their very name,"[168] no less than if they had slain him upon the field of battle.

D. 12.—Before he died, however, he had curbed them both to north and south by the establishment of strong Roman towns at Uriconium on the Severn (named after the neighbouring Wrekin), and Isca Silurum at the mouth of the Usk. The British name of the latter place, Caerleon [Castra Legionum], still reminds us that it was one of the great legionary stations of the island, while the abundant inscriptions unearthed upon the site, tell us that here the Second Legion had its head-quarters till the last days of the Roman occupation.[169]

D. 13.—The unremitting pressure of these two garrisons crushed out at last the Silurian resistance. The fighting men of the clan must indeed have been almost wholly killed off during these four years of murderous warfare. Thus Avitus Didius Gallus, the successor of Ostorius, though himself too old to take the field, was able to announce to Claudius that he had completed the subjugation of Britain. The Silurians after one last effort, in which they signally defeated an entire Legion, lay in the quietude of utter exhaustion; and though Cartismandua caused some little trouble by putting away her husband Venusius and raising a favourite to the throne, the matter was compromised by Roman intervention; and Claudius lived to hear that the island was, at last, peacefully submissive to his sway. Then Agrippina showed herself once more the Cartismandua of Rome, and her son Nero sat upon the throne of her poisoned husband [A.D. 55].

SECTION E.

Neronian misgovernment—Seneca—Prasutagus—Boadicea's revolt—Sack of Camelodune—Suetonius in Mona—"Druidesses"—Sack of London and Verulam—Boadicea crushed at Battle Bridge—Peace of Petronius.

E. 1.—Under Nero the unhappy Britons first realized what it was to be Roman provincials. Though Julius Caesar and Augustus had checked the grossest abuses of the Republican proconsulates, yet enough of the evil tradition remained to make those abuses flourish with renewed vigour under such a ruler as Nero. The state of things which ensued can only be paralleled with that so vividly described by Macaulay in his lurid picture of the oppression of Bengal under Warren Hastings. The one object of every provincial governor was to exploit his province in his own pecuniary interest and that of his friends at Rome. Requisitions and taxes were heaped on the miserable inhabitants utterly beyond their means, with the express object of forcing them into the clutches of the Roman money-lenders, whose frightful terms were, in turn, enforced by military licence.

E. 2.—The most virtuous and enlightened citizens were not ashamed thus to wring exorbitant interest from their victims. Cicero tells us[170] how no less austere a patriot than Brutus thus exacted from the town of Salamis in Cyprus, 48 per cent. compound interest, and, after starving five members of the municipality to death in default of payment, was mortally offended because he, Cicero, as proconsul, would not exercise further military pressure for his ends.

E. 3.—The part thus played in Cyprus by Brutus was played in Britain by Seneca, another of the choice examples of the highest Roman virtue. By a series of blood-sucking transactions[171] he drove the Britons to absolute despair, his special victim being Prasutagus, now Chief of the Iceni, presumably set up by the Romans on the suppression of the

120

revolt under Vericus. As a last chance of saving any of his wealth for his children, Prasutagus, by will, made the Emperor his co-heir. This, however, only hastened the ruin of his family. His property was pounced upon by the harpies of Seneca and Nero, with the Procurator[172] of the Province, Catus Decimus, at their head, his kin sold into slavery, his daughters outraged, and his wife Boadicea, or, more correctly, *Boudicca*, brutally scourged. This was in A.D. 61.

E. 4.—A convulsive outburst of popular rage and despair followed. The wrongs of Boadicea kindled the Britons to madness, and she found herself at once at the head of a rising comprising all the clans of the east and the Midlands. Half-armed as they were, their desperate onset carried all before it. The first attack was made upon the hated Colony at Camelodune, where the great Temple of "the God" Claudius, rising high above the town, bore an ever-visible testimony to Rome's enslavement of Britain,[173] and whence the lately-established veterans were wont, by the connivance of the Procurator, to treat the neighbourhood with utterly illegal military licence, sacking houses, ravaging fields, and abusing their British fellow-subjects as "caitiff slaves."[174]

E. 5.—These marauders were, however, as great cowards as bullies, and were now trembling before the approach of vengeance. How completely they were cowed is shown by the gloomy auguries which passed from lip to lip as foreshadowing the coming woe. The statue of Victory had fallen on its face, women frantic with fear rushed about wildly shrieking "Ruin!", strange moans and wailings were heard in Courthouse and Theatre, on the Thames estuary the ruddy glow of sunset looked like blood and flame, the sand-ripples and sea-wrack left by the ebb suggested corpses; everything ministered to their craven fear.

E. 6.—So hopeless was the demoralization that the very commonest precautions were neglected. The town was unfortified, yet these old soldiers made no attempt at entrenchment; even the women and children were not sent away while the roads were yet open. And when the storm burst on the town the hapless non-combatants were simply abandoned to massacre, while the veterans, along with some two hundred badly-armed recruits (the only help furnished by their precious Procurator, who himself fled incontinently to Gaul), shut themselves up in the Temple, in hopes of thus saving their own skins till the Ninth Legion, which was hastening to their aid, should arrive.

E. 7.—It is a satisfaction to read that in this they were disappointed. Next day their refuge was stormed, and every soul within put to the sword. The Temple itself, and all else at Camelodune, was burnt to the ground, and the wicked Colony blotted off the face of the earth. The approaching Legion scarcely fared better. The victorious Britons swept down upon it on the march, cut to pieces the entire infantry, and sent the cavalry in headlong flight to London, where Suetonius Paulinus, the Governor of Britain, was now mustering such force as he could make to meet the overwhelming onslaught.

E. 8.—When the outbreak took place he had been far away, putting down the last relics of the now illicit Druidism in the island of Mona or Anglesey. The enterprise was one which demanded a considerable display of force, for the defenders of the island fought with fanatical frenzy, the priests and priestesses alike taking part in the fray, and perishing at last in their own sacrificial fires, when the passage over the Menai Straits was made good.

E. 9—It is noticeable that in Mona alone do we meet with "Druidesses." Female ministers of religion, whether priestesses or prophetesses, are always exceptional, and usually mark a survival from some very primitive cult. The Pythoness at Delphi, and the Vestals at Rome, obviously do so. And amongst the races of Gaul and Britain the same fact is testified to by such female ministrations being invariably confined to far western islands. Pytheas, as he passed Cape Finisterre (in Spain) by night, heard a choir of women worshipping "Mother Earth and her Daughter"[175] with shrill yells and music. A little further he tells of the barbarous rites observed by the *Samnitae* or *Amnitae*[176] in an island near the mouth of the Loire, on which no male person might ever set foot; and of another island at the extreme point of Gaul, already known as Uxisana (Ushant), where nine virgin sorceresses kept alight the undying fire on their sacred hearth and gave oracular responses. These cults clearly represented a much older worship than Druidism, though the latter may very probably have taken them under its shadow (as in India so many aboriginal rites are recognized and adopted by modern Brahmanism). And the priestesses in Mona were, in like manner, not "Druidesses" at all, but representatives of some more primitive cult, already driven from the mainland of Britain and finding a last foothold in this remote island.

E. 10.—The stamping out of the desperate fanaticism of Mona was barely accomplished, when tidings were brought to Suetonius of Boadicea's revolt. By forced marches he reached London before her, only to find himself too weak, after the loss of the Ninth Legion, to hold it. London, though no Colony, was already the largest and most thriving of the Roman settlements in Britain, and piteous was the dismay of the citizens when Suetonius bade the city be evacuated. But neither tears nor prayers could postpone his march, and such non-combatants as from age or infirmity could not retire with his column, were massacred by the furious Britons even as those at Camelodune. Next came the turn of Verulam, the Roman town on the site of Tasciovan's stronghold,[177] where like atrocities marked the British triumph. Every other consideration was lost in the mad lust of slaughter. No prisoners were taken, no spoil was made, no ransom was accepted; all was fire, sword, and hideous torturing. Tacitus declares that, to his own knowledge,[178] no fewer than seventy thousand Romans and pro-Romans thus perished in this fearful day of vengeance; the spirit of which has been caught by Tennyson, with such true poetic genius, in his 'Boadicea.'

E. 11.—Suetonius, however, now felt strong enough to risk a battle. The odds were enormous, for the British forces were estimated at two hundred and thirty thousand, while his own were barely ten thousand— only one legion (the Fourteenth) with the cavalry of the Twentieth. (Where its infantry was does not appear: it may have been left behind in the west.) The Ninth had ceased to exist, and the Second did not arrive

123

from far-off Caerleon till too late for the fight. The strength of legionary sentiment is shown by the fact that its commander actually slew himself for vexation that the Fourteenth had won without his men.

E. 12.—Where the armies met is quite uncertain, though tradition fixes on a not unlikely spot near London, whose name of "Battle Bridge" has but lately been overlaid by the modern designation of "King's Cross."[179] We only know that Suetonius drew up his line across a glade in the forest, which thus protected his flanks, and awaited the foe as they came pouring back from Verulam. In front of the British line Boadicea, arrayed in the Icenian tartan, her plaid fastened by a golden brooch, and a spear in her hand, was seen passing along "loftily-charioted" from clan to clan, as she exhorted each in turn to conquer or die. Suetonius is said to have given the like exhortation to the Romans; but every man in their ranks must already have been well aware that defeat would spell death for him. The one chance was in steadiness and disciplined valour; and the legionaries stood firm under a storm of missiles, withholding their own fire till the foe came within close range. Then, and not till then, they delivered a simultaneous discharge of their terrible *pila*[180] on the British centre. The front gave with the volley, and the Romans, at once wheeling into wedge-shape formation, charged sword in hand into the gap, and cut the British line clean in two. Behind it was a laager of wagons, containing their families and spoil, and there the Britons made a last attempt to rally. But the furious Romans entered the enclosure with them, and the fight became a simple massacre. No fewer than eighty thousand fell, and the very horses and oxen were slaughtered by the maddened soldiery to swell the heaps of slain. Boadicea, broken-hearted, died by poison; and (being reinforced by troops from Germany) Suetonius proceeded "to make a desert and call it Peace."[181]

E. 13.—The punishment he dealt out to the revolted districts was so remorseless that the new Procurator, Julius Classicianus, sent a formal complaint to Rome on the suicidal impolicy of his superior's measures. Nero, however, did not mend matters by sending (like Claudius) a freed-man favourite as Royal Commissioner to supersede Suetonius. Polycletus was received with derision both by Roman and Briton, and Suetonius remained acting Governor till the wreck of some warships afforded an excuse for a peremptory order to "hand over the command" to Petronius Turpilianus. Fighting now ceased by mutual consent; and this disgraceful slackness was called by the new Governor "Peace with Honour" [*honestum pacis nomen segni otio imposuit*].

SECTION F.

Civil war—Otho and Vitellius—Army of Britain—Priscus—Agricola— Vespasian Emperor—Cerealis—Brigantes put down—Frontinus—Silurians put down—Agricola Pro-praetor—Ordovices put down—Pacification of South Britain—Roman civilization introduced—Caledonian campaign—Galgacus— Agricola's rampart—Domitian—Resignation and death of Agricola.

F. 1.—Disgraceful as the policy of Petronius seemed to Tacitus (under the inspiration probably of his father-in-law Agricola), it did actually secure for Britain several years of much-needed peace. Not till the months of confusion which followed the death of Nero [June 10, A.D. 68] did any native rising take place, and then only in Wales and the north. The Roman Army of Britain was thus free to take sides in the contest for the throne between Otho and Vitellius, of which all that could be predicted was that the victor would be the worse of the two [*deteriorem fore quisquis vicisset*]. They were, however, so much ahead of their date that, before accepting this alternative, they actually thought of setting up an Emperor of their own, after the fashion so freely followed in later centuries. Fortunately the popular subaltern (ὑποστράτηγος) [hupostratêgos] on whom their choice fell, one Priscus, had the sense to see that the time was not yet come for such action, and sarcastically refused the crown. "I am no more fit," he said, "to be an Emperor (αὐτοκράτωρ) [autokrator] than you to be soldiers." The army now proceeded to "sit on the fence";

125

some legions, notably the famous Fourteenth, slightly inclined to Otho, others to Vitellius, till their hesitation was ended by their own special hero, Vespasian, fresh from his Judaean victories,[182] coming forward as Pretender. Agricola, now in command of the Twentieth, at once declared for him, and the other legions followed suit—the Fourteenth being gratified by the title *"Victores Britannici,"* officially conferred upon them by the Emperor's new Pro-praetor, Petilius Cerealis.

F. 2.—We now enter upon the last stage of the fifty years' struggle made by British patriots before they finally bowed to the Roman yoke. The glory of ending the long conflict is due to Agricola, whose praises are chronicled by his son-in-law Tacitus, and who does actually seem to have been a very choice example of Roman virtue and ability. The Army of Britain had been his training school in military life, and successive commanders had recognized his merits by promotion. Now his superiors gave him an almost independent command, in which he showed himself as modest as he was able. Thanks to him, Cerealis was able in A.D. 70 to end a Brigantian war (of which the inevitable Cartismandua was the *"teterrima causa"* now no less than twenty years earlier), and the next Pro-praetor, Frontinus, to put down, in 75, the very last effort of the indomitable Silurians. Yet another year, and he himself was made Military Governor of the island, and set about the task of permanently consolidating it as a Roman Province, with an insight all his own.

F. 3.—The only Britons yet in arms south of the Tyne were the Ordovices of North Wales, who had lately cut to pieces a troop of Roman cavalry. Agricola marched against them, and, by swimming his horsemen across the Menai Straits, surprised their stronghold, Anglesey, thus bringing about the same instant submission of the whole clan which through the same tactics he had seen won, seventeen years earlier, by Suetonius.

F. 4.—But Agricola was not, like Suetonius, a mere military conqueror. He saw that Britons would never unfeignedly submit so long as they were treated as slaves; and he set himself to remedy the grievances under which the provincials so long had suffered. Military licence, therefore, and civil corruption alike, he put down with a resolute hand, never acting through intermediaries, but himself investigating every complaint, rewarding merit, and punishing offences. The vexatious monopolies which previous governors had granted, he did away with; and, while he firmly dealt with every symptom of disloyalty, his aim was "not penalty but penitence" [*nom paena sed saepius paenitentia*]—penitence shown in a frank acceptance of Roman civilization. Under his influence Roman temples, Roman forums, Roman dwelling-houses, Roman baths and porticoes, rose all over the land, and, above all, Roman schools, where the youth of the upper classes learnt with pride to adopt the tongue[183] and dress of their conquerors. It is appropriate that the only inscription relating to him as yet found in Britain should be on two of the lead water-pipes (discovered in 1899 and 1902) which supplied his new Roman city (*Deva*) at Chester.[184]

F. 5.—This proved a far more effectual method of conquest than any yet adopted, and Southern Britain became so quiet and contented that Agricola could meditate an extension of the Roman sway over the wilder regions to the north, and even over Ireland.[185] He did not, indeed, actually accomplish either design, but he extended the Roman frontier to the Forth, and carried the Roman arms beyond the Tay. The game, however, proved not worth the candle. The regions penetrated were wild and barren, the inhabitants ferocious savages, who defended themselves with such fury that it was not worth while to subdue them.

F. 6.—The final battle [A.D. 84], somewhere near Inverness, is described in minute and picturesque detail by Tacitus, who was present. He shows us the slopes of the Grampians alive with the Highland host, some on foot, some in chariots, armed with claymore, dirk, and targe as in later ages. He puts into the mouth of the leader, Galgacus, an eloquent summary of the motives which did really actuate them, and he reports the exhortation to close the fifty years of British warfare with a glorious victory which Agricola, no doubt, actually addressed to his soldiers. He paints for us the wild charge of the clans, the varying fortunes of the conflict (which at one point was so doubtful that Agricola dismounted to fight on foot with his men), and the final hopeless rout of the Caledonian army, with the slaughter of ten thousand men; the Roman loss being under four hundred—including one unlucky colonel [*praefectus cohortis*] whose horse ran away with him into the enemy's ranks.

F. 7.—Agricola had now the prudence to draw his stakes while the game was still in his favour. He sent his fleet north-about (thus, for the first time, *proving* Britain to be an island),[186] and marched his army across to meet it on the Clyde, whence he had already drawn his famous rampart to the Forth, henceforward to be the extreme limit of Roman Britain.[187] His work was now done, and well done. He resigned his Province, and returned to Rome, in time to avoid dismissal by Domitian, to whom preeminent merit in any subject was matter for jealous hatred,[188] and who now made Agricola report himself by night, and received him without one word of commendation. Had his life been prolonged he would undoubtedly have perished, like so many of the best of the Roman aristocracy, by the despot's hands; but just before the unrestrained outbreak of tyranny, he suddenly died—"*felix opportunitate mortis*"—to be immortalized by the love and genius of his daughter's husband. And he left Britain, as it had never been before, truly within the comity of the Roman Empire.

* * * * *

CHAPTER IV

THE ROMAN OCCUPATION, A.D. 85-211

SECTION A.

Pacification of Britain—Roman roads—London their centre—Authority for names—Watling Street—Ermine Street—Icknield Way.

A. 1.—The work of Agricola inaugurated in Britain that wonderful *Pax Romana* which is so unique a phenomenon in the history of the world. That Peace was not indeed in our island so long continued or so unbroken as in the Mediterranean lands, where, for centuries on end, no weapon was used in anger. But even here swords were beaten into ploughshares and spears into pruning-hooks to an extent never known before or since in our annals. So profound was the quiet that for a whole generation Britain vanishes from history altogether. All through the Golden Age of Rome, the reigns of Nerva and Trajan, no writer even names her; and not till A.D. 120 do we find so much as a passing mention of our country. But we may be sure that under such rulers the good work of Agricola was developing itself upon the lines he had laid down, and that Roman civilization was getting an ever firmer hold. The population was recovering from the frightful drain of the Conquest, the waste cities were rebuilt, and new towns sprang up all over the land, for the most part probably on old British sites, connected by a network of roads, no longer the mere trackways of the Britons, but "streets" elaborately constructed and metalled.

A. 2.—All are familiar with the Roman roads of Britain as they figure on our maps. Like our present lines of railway, the main routes radiate in all directions from London, and for a like reason; London having been, in Roman days as now, the great commercial centre of the country. The reason for this, that it was the lowest place where the Thames could be bridged, we have already referred to.[189] We see the *Watling Street* roughly corresponding to the North-Western Railway on one side of the metropolis, and to the South-Eastern on the other; the *Ermine Street* corresponding to the Great Northern Railway; while the Great Western, the South-Western, the Great Eastern, and the Portsmouth branch of the South Coast system are all represented in like manner. We notice, perhaps, that, except the Watling Street and the Ermine Street, all these routes are nameless; though we find four minor roads with names crossing England from north-east to south-west, and one from north-west to south-east. The former are the *Fosse Way* (from Grimsby on the Humber to Seaton on the Axe), the *Ryknield Street* (from Newcastle-on-Tyne to Caerleon-upon-Usk), the *Akeman Street* (from Wells on the Wash to Aust on the Severn), and the *Icknield Way* (from Norfolk to Dorset). The latter is the *Via Devana* (from Chester to Colchester).

A. 3.—It comes as a surprise to most when we learn that all these names (except the Watling Street, the Fosse, and the Icknield Way only) are merely affixed to their respective roads by the conjectures of 17th-century antiquarianism, Gale being their special identifier. The names themselves (except in the case of the Via Devana) are old, and three of them, the Ermine Street, the Icknield Street, and the Fosse Way, figure in the inquisition of 1070 as being, together with the Watling Street, those of the Four Royal Roads (*quatuor chimini*) of England, the King's Highways, exempt from local jurisdiction and under the special guard of the King's Peace. Two are said to cross the length of the land, two its breadth. But their identification (except in the case of the main course of Watling Street) has been matter of antiquarian dispute from the 12th century downwards.[190] The very first chronicler who mentions them, Geoffrey of Monmouth, makes Ermine Street run from St. David's to Southampton, Icknield Street from St. David's to Newcastle, and the Fosse Way from Totnes in Devon to far Caithness; and his error has misled many succeeding authorities. That it *is* an error, at least with regard to the Icknield Way and the Fosse Way, is sufficiently proved by the various mediaeval charters which mention these roads in connection with localities along their course as assigned by our received geography.

As to the main Watling Street there is no dispute. Running right across the island from the Irish Sea[191] to the Straits of Dover, it suggested to the minds of our English ancestors the shining track of the Milky Way from end to end of the heavens. Even so Chaucer, in his 'House of Fame,' sings:

> "Lo there!" quod he, "cast up your eye,
> Se yonder, lo! the Galaxie,
> The whiche men clepe the Milky Way,
> For it is white, and some, parfay,
> Y-callen han it Watlinge-strete."

At Dover it still retains its name, and so it does in one part of its course through London (which it enters as the Edgware Road, and leaves as the Old Kent Road).[192]

A. 4.—This name, like that of the Ermine Street, is most probably derived from Teutonic mythology; the "Watlings" being the patrons of handicraft in the Anglo-Saxon Pantheon, and "Irmin" the War-god from whom "Germany" is called.[193] There is no reason to suppose that the roads of Britain had any Roman name, like those of Italy. The designations given them by our English forefathers show how deeply these mighty works impressed their imagination. The term "street" which they adopted for them shows, as Professor Freeman has pointed out, that such engineering ability was something quite new to their experience.[194] It is the Latin "Via *strata*" Anglicized, and describes no mere track, but the elaborately constructed Roman causeway, along which the soft alluvium was first dug away, and its place taken by layers of graduated road metal, with the surface frequently an actual pavement.[195]

A. 5.—For the assignment of the name Ermine Street to the Great North Road there is no ancient authority.[196] All we can say is that this theory is more probable than that set forth by Geoffrey of Monmouth. That the road existed in Roman times is certain, as London and York were the two chief towns in the island; and direct communication between them must have been of the first importance, both for military and economical reasons. Indeed it is probably older yet. (See p. 117.) But, with the exceptions already pointed out, the nomenclature of the Romano-British roads is almost wholly guess-work. Some archaeological maps show additional Watling Streets and Ermine Streets branching in all directions over the land,[197] presumably on the authority of local tradition. And these traditions may be not wholly unfounded; for the same motives which made the English immigrants of one district ascribe the handiwork of by-gone days to mythological powers might operate to the like end in another.

A. 6.—The origin of the names Ryknield Street and Akeman Street is beyond discovery;[198] but that of the Icknield Street is almost undoubtedly due to its connection with the great Icenian tribe, to whose territory it formed the only outlet.[199] By them, in the days of their greatness, it was probably driven to the Thames, the more southerly extension being perhaps later. It was never, as its present condition abundantly testifies, made into a regular Roman "Street." The final syllable may possibly, as Guest suggests, be the A.S. *hild* = war.

A. 7.—Besides these main routes, a whole network of minor roads must have connected the multitudinous villages and towns of Roman Britain, a fact which is borne witness to by the very roundabout route often given in the 'Itinerary' of Antoninus between places which we know were directly connected.[200] Moreover this network must have been at least as close as that of our present railways, and probably approximated to that of our present roads.

SECTION B.

Romano-British towns—Ancient lists—Methods of identification—Dense rural population—Remains in Cam valley—Coins—Thimbles—Horseshoes.

B. 1.—Of these many Romano-British towns we have five contemporary lists; those of Ptolemy in the 2nd century, of the Antonine 'Itinerary' in the 3rd, of the 'Notitia'[201] in the 5th, and those of Nennius and of the Ravenna Geographer, composed while the memory of the Roman occupation was still fresh. Ptolemy and Nennius profess to give complete catalogues; the 'Itinerary' and 'Notitia' contain only incidental references; while the Ravenna list, though far the most copious, is expressly stated to be composed only of selected names. Of these it has no fewer than 236, while the 'Notitia' gives 118, Ptolemy 60, and Nennius 28 (to which Marcus Anchoreta adds 5 more).

B. 2.—With this mass of material[202] it might seem to be an easy task to locate every Roman site in Britain; especially as Ptolemy gives the latitude (and sometimes the longitude[203] also) of every place he mentions, and the 'Itinerary' the distances between its stations. Unfortunately it is quite otherwise; and of the whole number barely fifty can be at all certainly identified, while more than half cannot even be guessed at with anything like reasonable probability. To begin with, the text of every one of these authorities is corrupt to a degree incredible; in Ptolemy we find *Nalkua*, for example, where the 'Itinerary' and Ravenna lists give *Calleva*; *Simeni* figures for *Iceni*, *Imensa* for *Tamesis*. The 'Itinerary' itself reads indiscriminately *Segeloco* and *Ageloco*, *Lagecio* and *Legeolio*; and examples might be multiplied indefinitely. In Nennius, particularly, the names are so disguised that, with two or three exceptions, their identification is the merest guess-work; *Lunden* is unmistakable, and *Ebroauc* is obviously York; but who shall say what places lie hid under *Meguaid, Urnath, Guasmoric,* and *Celemon*? And if this corruption is bad amongst the names, it absolutely runs riot amongst the numbers, both in Ptolemy and the 'Itinerary,' so that the degrees of the former and the distances of the latter are alike grievously untrustworthy guides. Ptolemy, for example, says that the longest day in London is 18 hours, an obvious mistake for 17, as the context clearly shows. There is further the actual equation of error in each authority: Ptolemy, for all his care, has confused Exeter (*Isca Damnoniorum*) with the more famous *Isca Silurum* (Caerleon-on-Usk); and there are blunders in his latitude and longitude which cannot wholly be ascribed to textual corruption. Still another difficulty is that then, as now, towns quite remote from each other bore the same name, or names very similar. Not only were two called *Isca*, but three were *Venta*, two *Calleva*, two *Segontium*, and no fewer than seven *Magna*; while *Durobrivae* is only too like to *Durocobrivae, Margiodunum* to *Moridunum, Durnovaria* to *Durovernum,* etc. The last name even gets confounded with *Dubris* by transcribers.

B. 3.—In all the lists we are struck by the extraordinary preponderance of northern names. Half the sites given by Ptolemy lie north of the Humber, and this is also the case with the Ravenna list, while in the 'Notitia' the proportion is far greater. In the last case this is due to the fact that the military garrisons, with which the catalogue is concerned, were mainly quartered in the north, and a like explanation probably holds good for the earlier and later lists also. Nennius, as is to be expected, draws most of his names from the districts which the Saxons had not yet reached; all being given with the Celtic prefix *Caer* (=city).

B. 4.—Amid all these snares the most certain identification of a Roman site is furnished by the discovery of inscriptions relating to the special troops with which the name is associated in historical documents. When, for example, we find in the Roman station at Birdoswald, on the Wall of Hadrian, an inscription recording the occupation of the spot by a

Dacian cohort, and read in the 'Notitia' that such a cohort was posted at *Amboglanna per lineam Valli*, we are sure that Amboglanna and Birdoswald are identical. This method, unfortunately, helps us very little except on the Wall, for the legionary inscriptions elsewhere are found in many places with which history does not particularly associate the individual legions thus commemorated.[204] However, the special number of such traces of the Second Legion at Caerleon, the Twentieth at Chester, and the Sixth at York, would alone justify us in certainly determining those places to be the Isca, Deva, and Eboracum given as their respective head-quarters in our documentary and historical evidence.

B. 5.—In the case of York another proof is available; for the name, different as it sounds, can be traced, by a continuous stream of linguistic development, through the Old English Eorfowic to the Roman *Eboracum*. In the same way the name of *Dubris* has unmistakably survived in Dover, *Lemannae* in Lympne, *Regulbium* in Reculver. *Colonia, Glevum, Venta, Corinium, Danum*, and *Mancunium*, with the suffix "chester,"[205] have become Colchester, Gloucester, Winchester, Cirencester, Doncaster, and Manchester. Lincoln is *Lindum Colonia*, Richborough, *Ritupis*; while the phonetic value of the word London has remained absolutely unaltered from the very first, and varies but slightly even in its historical orthography.

B. 6.—With names of this class, of which there are about thirty, for a starting-point, we can next, by the aid of our various lists (especially Ptolemy's, which gives the tribe in which each town lies, and the 'Itinerary'), assign, with a very high degree of probability, some thirty more—similarity of name being still more or less of a guide. For example, when midway between *Venta* (Winchester) and *Sorbiodunum* (Sarum) the 'Itinerary' places *Brige*, and the name *Broughton* now occupies this midway spot, *Brige* and *Broughton* may be safely assumed to be the same. This method shows Leicester to be the Roman *Ratae*, Carlisle to be *Luguvallum*, Newcastle *Pons Aelii*, etc., with so much probability that none of these identifications have been seriously disputed amongst antiquaries; while few are found to deny that Cambridge represents *Camboricum*,[206] Huntingdon (or Godmanchester) *Durolipons*, Silchester *Calleva*, etc. A list of all the sites which may be said to be fairly certified will be found at the end of this chapter.

B. 7.—Beyond them we come to about as many more names in our ancient catalogues of which all we can say is that we know the district to which they belong, and may safely apply them to one or other of the existing Roman sites in that district; the particular application being disputed with all the heat of the *odium archaeologicum*. Thus *Bremetonacum* was certainly in Lancashire; but whether it is now Lancaster, or Overborough, or Ribchester, we will not say; *Caesaromagum* was certainly in Essex; but was it Burghstead, Widford, or Chelmsford? And was the original *Camalodunum* at Colchester, Lexden, or Maldon?

B. 8.—And, yet further, we find, especially in the Ravenna list, multitudes of names with nothing whatever to tell us of their whereabouts; though nearly all have been seized upon by rival antiquaries, and ascribed to this, that, and the other of the endless Roman sites which meet us all over the country.[207]

B. 9.—For it must be remembered that there are very few old towns in England where Roman remains have not been found, often in profusion; and even amongst the villages such finds are exceedingly common wherever excavations on any large scale have been undertaken. Thus in the Cam valley, where the "coprolite" digging[208] resulted in the systematic turning over of a considerable area, their number is astounding, proving the existence of a teeming population. Many thousands of coins were turned up, scarcely ever in hordes, but scattered singly all over the land, testifying to the amount of petty traffic which must have gone on generation after generation. For these coins are very rarely of gold or silver, and amongst them are found the issues of every Roman Emperor from Augustus to Valentinian III. And, besides the coins, the soil was found to teem with fragments of Roman pottery; while the many "ashpits" discovered— as many as thirty in a single not very large field—have furnished other articles of domestic use, such as thimbles.[209] Even horseshoes have been found, though their use only came in with the 5th century of our era.[210]

B. 10.—Now there is no reason for supposing that the Cam valley was in any way an exceptionally prosperous or populous district in the Roman period. It contained but one Roman town of even third-class importance, Cambridge, and very few of the "villas" in which the great landed proprietors resided. The wealth of remains which it has furnished is merely a by-product of the "coprolite" digging, and it is probable that equally systematic digging would have like results in almost any alluvial district in the island. We may therefore regard it as fairly established that these districts were as thickly peopled under the Romans as at any other period of history, and that the agricultural population of our island has never been larger than in the 3rd and 4th centuries, till its great development in the 19th.

SECTION C.

Fortification of towns late—Chief Roman centres—London—York—Chester— Bath—Silchester—Remains there found—Romano-British handicrafts— Pottery—Basket work—Mining—Rural life—Villas—Forests—Hunting dogs—Husbandry—Britain under the Pax Romana.

C. 1.—The profound peace which reigned in these rural districts is shown by the fact that Roman weapons are the rarest of all finds, far less common than the earlier British or the ensuing Saxon.[211] At the same time it is worthy of note that every Roman town which has been excavated has been found to be fortified, often on a most formidable scale. Thus at London there still remains visible a sufficiently large fragment of the wall to show that it must have been at least thirty feet high, while that of Silchester was nine feet thick, with a fosse of no less than thirty yards in width. And at Cirencester the river Churn or Corin (from which the town took its name *Corinium*) was made to flow round the ramparts, which consisted first of an outer facing of stone, then of a core of concrete, and finally an earthen embankment within, the whole reaching a width of at least four yards. It is probable, however, that these defences, like those of so many of the Gallic cities, and like the Aurelian walls of Rome itself, belong to the decadent period of Roman power, and did not exist (except in the northern garrisons and the great legionary stations, York, Chester, and Caerleon) during the golden age of Roman Britain.[212]

C. 2.—Their circuit, where it has been traced, furnishes a rough gauge of the comparative importance of the Roman towns of Britain. Far at the head stands London, where the names of Ludgate, Newgate, Aldersgate, Moorgate, Bishopsgate, and Aldgate still mark the ancient boundary line, five miles in extent (including the river-front), nearly twice that of any other town.[213] And abundant traces of the existence of a flourishing suburb have been discovered on the southern bank of the river. To London ran nearly all the chief Roman roads, and the shapeless block now called London Stone was once the *Milliarium* from which the distances were reckoned along their course throughout the land.[214]

C. 3.—The many relics of the Roman occupation to be seen in the Museum at the Guildhall bear further testimony to the commercial importance of the City in those early days, an importance primarily due, as we have already seen, to the natural facilities for crossing the Thames at London Bridge.[215] The greatness of Roman London seems, however, to have been purely commercial. We do not even know that it was the seat of government for its own division of Britain. It was not a Colony, nor (in spite of the exceptional strength of the site, surrounded, as it was, by natural moats)[216] does it ever appear as of military importance till the campaign of Theodosius at the very end of the chapter.[217] In the 'Notitia' it figures as the head-quarters of the Imperial Treasury, and about the same date we learn that the name Augusta had been bestowed upon the town, as on Caerleon and on so many others throughout the Empire, though the older "London" still remained unforgotten.[218]

138

C. 4.—But, so far as Britain had a recognized capital at all, York and not London best deserved that name. For here was the chief military nerve-centre of the land, the head-quarters of the Army, where the Commander-in-Chief found himself in ready touch with the thick array of garrisons holding every strategic point along the various routes by which any invader who succeeded in forcing the Wall would penetrate into the land. At York, accordingly, the Emperors who visited Britain mostly held their court; beginning with Hadrian, who here established the Sixth Legion which he had brought over with him, possibly incorporating with it the remains of the Ninth, traces of which are here found. And here it remained permanently quartered to the very end of the Roman occupation, as abundant inscriptions, etc. testify. One of these, found in the excavations for the railway station, is a brass tablet with a dedication (in Greek) to *The Gods of the Head Praetorium* (θεοῖς τοῖς τοῦ ἡγεμονικοῦ πραιτωρίου) [theois tois tou haegemonikou praitoriou], bearing witness to the essential militarism of the city.

C. 5.—A Praetorium, moreover, was not merely a military centre. It was also, as at Jerusalem, a Judgment Hall; and here, probably, the *Juridicus Britanniae*[219] exercised his functions, which would seem to have been something resembling those of a Lord Chief Justice. Precedents laid down by his Court are quoted as still in force even by the Codex of Justinian (555). One of these incidentally lets us know that the Romans kept up not only a British Army, but a British Fleet in being.[220] The latter, probably, as well as the former, had its head-quarters at York, where the Ouse of old furnished a far more available waterway than now. Even so late as 1066 the great fleet of Harold Hardrada could anchor only a few miles off, at Riccall: and there is good evidence that in the Roman day the river formed an extensive "broad" under the walls of York itself. As at Portsmouth and Plymouth to-day, the presence of officers and seamen of the Imperial Navy must have added to the military bustle in the streets of Eboracum; while tesselated pavements, unknown in the ruder fortresses of the Wall, testify to the softer side of social life in a garrison town.

C. 6.—Chester [Deva] was also a garrison town, the head-quarters of the Twentieth Legion; so was Caerleon-upon-Usk [Isca], with the Second. A detachment was almost certainly detailed from one or other of these to hold Wroxeter [Uriconium], midway between them;[221] thus securing the line of the Marches between the wild districts of Wales and the more fertile and settled regions eastward. And the name of Leicester records the fact (not otherwise known to us) that here too was a military centre; probably sufficient to police the rest of the island.[222]

C. 7.—Gloucester, Colchester, and Lincoln, as being Colonies, may have been also, perhaps, always fortified, and possibly garrisoned. But in the ordinary Romano-British town, such as London, Silchester, or Bath,[223] the life was probably wholly civilian. The fortifications, if the place ever had any, were left to decay or removed, the soldiery were withdrawn or converted into a mere *gendarmerie*, and under the shield of the *Pax Romana*, the towns were as open as now. And as little as now did they look forward to a time when each would have to become a strongly-held place of arms girded in by massive ramparts, yet destined to prove all too weak against the sweep of barbarian invasion.

C. 8.—On most of these sites continuous occupation for many subsequent ages has blotted out the vestiges of their Roman day. Every town has a tendency literally to bury its past; and the larger the town the deeper the burial. Thus at London the Roman pavements, etc. found are some twenty feet below the present surface, at Lincoln some six or seven, and so forth. To learn how a Roman town was actually laid out we must have recourse to those places which for some reason have not been resettled since their destruction at the Anglo-Saxon conquest, such as Wroxeter and Silchester, where the remains accordingly lie only a foot or two below the ground. The former has been little explored, but the latter has for the last ten years been systematically excavated under the auspices of the Society of Antiquaries, the portions unearthed being reburied year by year, after careful examination and record.[224]

C. 9.—The greater part of the site has thus been already (1903) dealt with; proving the town to have been laid out on a regular plan, with straight streets dividing it, like an American city, into rectangular blocks. Twenty-eight of these have, so far, been excavated. They are from 100 to 150 yards in length and breadth, arranged, like the blocks in a modern town, with houses all round, and a central space for gardens, back-yards, etc. The remains found (including coins from Caligula to Arcadius) prove that the site was occupied during the whole of the Roman period. Originally it was, in all probability, one of the towns built for the Britons by Agricola[225] on the distinctive Roman pattern, with a central forum, town hall, baths, temples, and an amphitheatre outside the city limits.

C. 10.—The forum was flanked by a vast basilica, no less than 325 feet in length by 125 in breadth, with apses of 39 feet radius.[226] A smaller edifice of basilican type is generally supposed to have been a Christian church. It stands east and west, and consists of a nave 30 feet long by 10 broad, flanked by 5-feet aisles, with a narthex of 7 feet (extending right across the building) at the east end, and at the west an apse of 10 feet radius, having in the centre a tesselated pavement 6 feet square, presumably for the Altar.[227]

C. 11.—The main street of Silchester ran east and west, and *may* have been the main road from London to Bath; while that which crosses it at the forum was perhaps an extension of the Icknield Way from Wallingford to Winchester. A third road led straight to Old Sarum,[228] and there may have been others. Silchester lies about half-way between Reading and Basingstoke.

C. 12.—The relics of domestic life found indicate a high order of peaceful civilization. Abundance of domestic pottery (some of it the glazed ware manufactured at Caistor on the Nen), many bones of domestic animals (amongst them the cat),[229] finger-rings with engraved gems, and the like, have been discovered in the old wells[230] and ashpits.

More remarkable was the unearthing (in 1899) of the plant of a silver refinery,[231] showing that the method employed was analogous to that in vogue amongst the Japanese to-day, and that bone-ash was used in the construction of the hearths.[232] The houses were mainly built of red clay (on a foundation wall of flint and mortar) filled into a timber frame-work and supported by lath or wattle. The exterior was stamped with ornamental patterns, as in modern "parjetting" (which may thus very possibly be an actual survival from Roman days). This clay has in most cases soaked away into a mere layer of red mud overlying the pavements; but in 1901 there was unearthed a house in which a fortunate fire had calcined it into permanent brick, still retaining the parjetting and the impress of wattle and timber. But the whole site has not provided a single weapon of any sort or kind, and the construction of the defences clearly shows that they formed no part of the original plan on which the place was laid out.[233] They were probably, as we have said, added at the break up of the Pax Romana.

C. 13.—With the exception of the silver refinery above mentioned, nothing has appeared to tell us what handicrafts were practised at Silchester; but such industries formed a noteworthy feature of Romano-British life. Naturally the largest traces have been left in connection with that most imperishable of all commodities, pottery. The kilns where it was made are frequently met with in excavations; and individual vases, jugs,[234] cups, and amphorae (often of very large dimensions) constantly appear. Many of these are beautifully modelled and finished, and not unseldom glazed in various ways. But there is no evidence that the delicate "Samian" ware[235] was ever manufactured in Britain, though every house of any pretensions possessed a certain store of it. The indigenous art of basket-making[236] also continued as a speciality of Britain under the Romans, and the indigenous mining for tin, lead, iron, and copper was developed by them on the largest scale. In every district where these metals are found, in Cornwall, in Somerset, in Wales, in Derbyshire, and in Sussex, traces of Roman work are apparent, dating from the very beginning of the occupation to the very end. The earliest known Roman inscription found in Britain is one of A.D. 49 (the year before Ostorius subdued the Iceni) on a pig of lead from the Mendips,[237] and similar pigs bearing the Labarum, *i.e.* not earlier than Constantine presumably, have been dredged up in the Thames below London.[238] Inscriptions also survive to tell us of a few amongst the many other trades which must have figured in Romano-British life,—goldsmiths, silversmiths, iron-workers, stone-cutters, sculptors, architects, eye-doctors, are all thus commemorated.[239]

C. 14.—But then, as always, the life of Britain was mainly rural. The evidence for this unearthed in the Cam valley has already been spoken of, and in every part of England the "villas" of the great Roman landowners are constantly found. Hundreds have already been discovered, and year by year the list is added to. One of the most recent of the finds is that at Greenwich in 1901, and the best known, perhaps, that at Brading in the Isle of Wight. Here, as elsewhere, the tesselated pavements, the elaborate arrangements for warming (by hypocausts conveying hot air to every room), the careful laying out of the apartments, all testify to the luxury in which these old landlords lived. For the "villa" was the Squire's Hall of the period, and was provided, like the great country houses of to-day, with all the best that contemporary life could give.[240] And, like these also, it was the centre of a large circle of humbler dependencies wherein resided the peasantry of the estate and the domestics of the mansion.[241] The existence amongst these of huntsmen (as inscriptions tell) reminds us that not only was the chase, then as now, popular amongst the squirearchy, but that there was a far larger scope for its exercise. Great forests still covered a notable proportion of the soil (the largest being that which spread over the whole Weald of Sussex)[242], and were tenanted by numberless deer and wild swine, along with the wolves, and, perhaps, bears,[243] that fed upon them.

C. 15.—Hence it came about that during the Roman occupation the British products we find most spoken of by classical authors are the famous breeds of hunting-dogs produced by our island. Oppian[244] [A.D.

140] gives a long description of one sort, which he describes as small βαιον [baion], awkward γυϱον [guron], long-bodied, rough-haired, not much to look at, but excellent at scenting out their game and tackling it when found—like our present otter-hounds. The native name for this strain was Agasseus. Nemesianus[245] [A.D. 280] sings the swiftness of British hounds; and Claudian[246] refers to a more, formidable kind, used for larger game, equal indeed to pulling down a bull. He is commonly supposed to mean some species of mastiff; but, according to Mr. Elton[247] mastiffs are a comparatively recent importation from Central Asia, so that a boarhound of some sort is more probably intended, such as may be seen depicted (along with its smaller companion) on the fine tesselated pavement preserved in the Corinium Museum at Cirencester.[248] Whatever the creature was, it is probably the same as the Scotch "fighting dog," which figures in the 4th century polemics as a huge massive brute of savage temper[249] and evil odour,[250] to which accordingly controversialists rejoice in likening their ecclesiastical opponents.[251] Jerome incidentally tells us that "Alpine" dogs were of this Scotch breed, which thus may possibly be the original strain now developed into the St. Bernard.

C. 16.—But the existence of such tracts of forest, even when very extensive, is quite compatible (as the present state of France shows us) with a highly developed civilization, and a population thick upon the ground. And that a very large area of our soil came to be under the plough at least before the Roman occupation ended is proved by the fact that eight hundred wheat-ships were dispatched from this island by Julian the Apostate for the support of his garrisons in Gaul. The terms in which this transaction is recorded suggest that wheat was habitually exported (on a smaller scale, doubtless) from Britain to the Continent. At all events enough was produced for home consumption, and under the shadow of the Pax Romana the wild and warlike Briton became a quiet cultivator of the ground, a peaceful and not discontented dependent of the all-conquering Power which ruled the whole civilized world.

C. 17.—In the country the husbandman ploughed and sowed and reaped and garnered,[252] sometimes as a freeholder, oftener as a tenant; the miller was found upon every stream; the fisher baited his hook and cast his net in fen and mere; the Squire hunted and feasted amid his retainers (who were usually slaves); his wife and daughters occupied themselves in the management of the house. The language of Rome was everywhere spoken, the literature of Rome was read amongst the educated classes; while amongst the peasantry the old Celtic tongue, and with it, we may be sure, the old Celtic legends and songs, held its own. Intercourse was easy between the various districts; for along every great road a series of posting-stations, each with its stud of relays, was available for the service of travellers. In the towns were to be found schools, theatres, and courts of justice, with shops of every sort and kind, while travelling pedlars supplied the needs of the rural districts. No one, except actual soldiers, dreamt of bearing arms, or indeed was allowed to do so,[253] and the general aspect of the land was as wholly peaceful as now. But every one had to pay a substantial proportion of his income in taxes, in the collection of which there was not seldom a notable amount of corruption, as amongst the publicans of Judaea. In the bad days of the decadence this became almost intolerable;[254] but so long as the central administration retained its integrity the amount exacted was no more than left to every class a fair margin for the needs, and even the enjoyments, of life.

SECTION D.

The unconquered North—Hadrian's Wall—Upper and Lower Britain—Romano-British coinage—Wall of Antoninus—Britain Pro-consular.

D. 1.—The weak point of all this peaceful development was that the northern regions of the island remained unsubdued. It was all very well for the Roman Treasury, with true departmental shortsightedness, to declare (as Appian[255] reports) that North Britain was a worthless district, which could never be profitable ευπηορον [euphoron] to hold. The cost would have been cheap in the end. All through the Roman occupation it was from the north that trouble was liable to arise, and ultimately it was the ferocious independence of the Highland clans that brought Roman Britain to its doom. The Saxons, as tradition tells us, would never have been invited into the land but for the ravages of these Picts; and, in sober history, it may well be doubted whether they could ever have effected a permanent settlement here had not the Britons, in defending our shores, been constantly exposed to Pictish attacks from the rear.

D. 2.—Thus our earliest notice of Britain in this period tells us that Hadrian (A.D. 120), our first Imperial visitor since Claudius (A.D. 44), found it needful (after a revolt which cost many lives, and involved, as it seems, the final destruction of the unlucky Ninth Legion, which had already fared so badly in Boadicea's rebellion[256]) to supplement Agricola's rampart, between Forth and Clyde, with another from sea to sea, between Tynemouth and Solway, "dividing the Romans from the barbarians."[257] This does not mean that the district thus isolated was definitely abandoned,[258] but that its inhabitants were so imperfectly Romanized that the temptation to raid the more civilized lands to the south had better be obviated. The Wall of Hadrian marked the real limit of Roman Britain: beyond it was a "march," sometimes strongly, more often feebly, garrisoned, but never effectually occupied, much less civilized. The inhabitants, indeed, seem to have rapidly lost what civilization they had. Dion Cassius describes them, in the next generation, as far below the Caledonians who opposed Agricola, a mere horde of squalid and ferocious cannibals,[259] going into battle stark-naked (like their descendants the Galwegians a thousand years later),[260] having neither chief nor law, fields nor houses. The name Attacotti, by which they came finally to be known, probably means *Tributary*, and describes their nominal status towards Rome.

D. 3.—How hopeless the task of effectually incorporating these barbarians within the Empire appeared to Hadrian is shown by the extraordinary massiveness of the Wall which he built[261] to keep them out from the civilized Provinces[262] to the southwards. "Uniting the estuaries of Tyne and Solway it chose the strongest line of defence available. Availing itself of a series of bold heights, which slope steadily to the south, but are craggy precipices to the north, as if designed by Nature for this very purpose, it pursued its mighty course across the isthmus with a pertinacious, undeviating determination which makes its remains unique in Europe, and one of the most inspiriting scenes in Britain."[263] Its outer fosse (where the nature of the ground permits) is from 30 to 40 feet wide and some 20 deep, so sloped that the whole was exposed to direct fire from the Wall, from which it is separated by a small glacis [*linea*] 10 or 12 feet across. Beyond it the upcast earth is so disposed as to form the glacis proper, for about 50 feet before dipping to the general ground level. The Wall itself is usually 8 feet thick, the outer and inner faces formed of large blocks of freestone, with an interior core of carefully-filled-in rubble. The whole thus formed a defence of the most formidable character, testifying strongly to the respect in which the valour of the Borderers against whom it was constructed was held by Hadrian and his soldiers.[264]

D. 4.—This expedition of Hadrian is cited by his biographer, Aelius Spartianus, as the most noteworthy example of that invincible activity which led him to take personal cognizance of every region in his Empire: "*Ante omnes enitebatur ne quid otiosum vel emeret aliquando vel pasceret.*" His contempt for slothful self-indulgence finds vent in his reply to the doggerel verses of Florus, who had written:

Ego nolo Caesar esse,	["To be Caesar I'd not care,
Ambulare per Britannos,	Through the Britons far to fare,
Scythicas pati pruinas.	Scythian frost and cold to bear."]

Hadrian made answer:

Ego nolo Florus esse,   ["To be Florus I'd not care,
Ambulare per tabernas,   Through the tavern-bars to fare,
Cimices pati rotundas.   Noxious insect-bites to bear."]

To us its special interest (besides the Wall) is found in the bronze coins commemorating the occasion, the first struck with special reference to Britain since those of Claudius. These are of various types, but all of the year 120 (the third Consulate of Hadrian); and the reverse mostly represents the figure so familiar on our present bronze coinage, Britannia, spear in hand, on her island rock, with her shield beside her.[265] This type was constantly repeated with slight variations in the coinage of the next hundred years; and thus, when, after an interval of twelve centuries, the British mint began once more, in the reign of Charles the Second, to issue copper, this device was again adopted, and still abides with us. The very large number of types (approaching a hundred) of the Romano-British coinage, from this reign to that of Caracalla, shows that Hadrian inaugurated the system of minting coins not only with reference to Britain, but for special local use. They were doubtless struck within the island; but we can only conjecture where the earliest mints were situated.

D. 5.—Twenty years after Hadrian's visit we again find (A.D. 139) some little trouble in the north, owing to a feud between the Brigantes and Genuini, a clan of whom nothing is known but the name. The former seem to have been the aggressors, and were punished by the confiscation of a section of their territory by Lollius Urbicus, the Legate of Antoninus Pius; who further "shut off the excluded barbarians by a turf wall" (*muro cespitio submotis*[266] *barbaris ducto*). The context connects this operation with the Brigantian troubles; but it is certain that Lollius repaired and strengthened Agricola's rampart between Forth and Clyde. His name is found in inscriptions along that line,[267] and that of Antoninus is frequent. This work consisted of a *vallum* some 40 miles in length, from Carriden to

Dumbarton, with fortified posts at frequent intervals. It is locally known as "Graham's Dyke," and, since 1890, has been systematically explored by the Glasgow Archaeological Society. It is in the strictest sense "a turf wall"—no mere grass-grown earthwork, but regularly built of squared sods in place of stones (sometimes on a stone base). Roman engineers looked upon such a rampart as being the hardest of all to construct.

SECTION E.

Commodus Britannicus—Ulpius Marcellus—Murder of Perennis—Era of military turbulence—Pertinax—Albinus—British Army defeated at Lyons—Severus—Caledonian war—Severus overruns Highlands.

E. 1.—It may very probably be owing to the energy of Lollius that Britain, "Upper" and "Lower" together as it seems, as inscriptions tell us, was about this date ranked amongst the Senatorial Provinces of the Empire, the Pro-consul being C. Valerius Pansa. That it should have been made a Pro-consulate shows (as is pointed out on p. 142) that they were now considered amongst the more peaceful governorships. In fact, though some slight disturbances threatened at the death of Antoninus (A.D. 161), the country remained quiet till Commodus came to the throne (A.D. 180). Then, however, we hear of a serious inroad of the northern barbarians, who burst over the Roman Wall and were not repulsed without a hard campaign. The Roman commander was Ulpius Marcellus, a harsh but devoted officer, who fared like a common soldier, and insisted on the strictest vigilance, being himself "the most sleepless of generals."[268] The British Army, accordingly, swore by him, and were minded to proclaim him Emperor,[2] a matter which all but cost him his life at the hands of Commodus; who, however, contented himself with assuming, like Claudius, the title of Britannicus, in virtue of this success.[2] The further precaution was taken of cashiering not only Ulpius but all the superior officers of this dangerous army; men of lower rank and less influence being substituted. The soldiers, however, defeated the design by breaking out into open mutiny, and tearing to pieces the "enemy of the Army," Perennis, Praefect of the Praetorian Guards, who had been sent from Rome (A.D. 185) to carry out the reform.[269]

E. 2.—This episode shows us how great a solidarity the Army of Britain had by this time developed. It was always the policy of Imperial Rome to recruit the forces stationed throughout the Provinces not from the natives around them, but from those of distant regions. Inscriptions tell that the British Legions were chiefly composed of Spaniards, Aquitanians, Gauls, Frisians, Dalmatians, and Dacians; while from the 'Notitia' we know that, in the 5th century, such distant countries as Mauretania, Libya, and even Assyria,[270] furnished contingents. Britons, in turn, served in Gaul, Spain, Illyria, Egypt, and Armenia, as well as in Rome itself.

E. 3.—The outburst which led to the slaughter of Perennis was but the dawn of a long era of military turbulence in Britain. First came the suppression of the revolt A.D. 187 by the new Legate,[271] Pertinax, who, at the peril of his life, refused the purple offered him by the mutineers,[272] and drafted fifteen hundred of the ringleaders into the Italian service of Commodus;[273] then Commodus died (A.D. 192), and Pertinax became one of the various pretenders to the Imperial throne; then followed his murder by Julianus, while Albinus succeeded to his pretensions as well as to his British government; then that of Julianus by Severus; then the desperate struggle between Albinus and Severus for the Empire; the crushing defeat (A.D. 197) of the British Army at Lyons, the death of Albinus,[274] and the final recognition of Severus[275] as the acknowledged ruler of the whole Roman world.

E. 4.—Of all the Roman Emperors Severus is the most closely connected with Britain. The long-continued political and military confusion amongst the conquerors had naturally excited the independent tribes of the north. In A.D. 201 the Caledonians beyond Agricola's rampart threatened it so seriously that Vinius Lupus, the Praetor, was fain to buy off their attack; and, a few years later, they actually joined hands with the nominally subject Meatae within the Pale, who thereupon broke out into open rebellion, and, along with them, poured down upon the civilized districts to the south. So extreme was the danger that the Prefect of Britain sent urgent dispatches to Rome, invoking the Emperor's own presence with the whole force of the Empire.

E. 5.—Severus, in spite of age and infirmity,[276] responded to the call, and, in a marvellously short time, appeared in Britain, bringing with him his worthless sons, Caracalla[277] and Geta[278]—"my Antonines," as he fondly called them,[279] though his life was already embittered by their wickedness,—and Geta's yet more worthless mother, Julia Domna. Leaving her and her son in charge south of Hadrian's Wall, Severus and Caracalla undertook a punitive expedition[280] beyond it, characterized by ferocity so exceptional[281] that the names both of Caledonians and Meatae henceforward disappear from history. The Romans on this occasion penetrated further than even Agricola had gone, and reached Cape Wrath, where Severus made careful astronomical observations.[282]

E. 6.—But the cost was fearful. Fifty thousand Roman soldiers perished through the rigour of the climate and the wiles of the desperate barbarians; and Severus felt the north so untenable that he devoted all his energies to strengthening Hadrian's Wall,[283] so as to render it an impregnable barrier beyond which the savages might be allowed to range as they pleased.[284]

E. 7.—In what, exactly, his additions consisted we do not know, but they were so extensive that his name is no less indissolubly connected with the Wall than that of Hadrian. The inscriptions of the latter found in the "Mile Castles" show that the line was his work, and that he did not merely, as some have thought, build the series of "stations" to support the "Vallum." But it is highly probable that Severus so strengthened the Wall both in height and thickness as to make it[285] far more formidable than Hadrian had left it. For now it was intended to be the actual *limes* of the Empire.

SECTION F.

Severus completes Hadrian's Wall—Mile Castles—Stations—Garrison—
Vallum—Rival theories—Evidence—Remains—Coins—Altars—Mithraism—
Inscription to Julia Domna— "Written Rock" on Gelt—Cilurnum aqueduct.

F. 1.—It is to Severus, therefore, that we owe the final development
of this magnificent rampart, the mere remains of which are impressive
so far beyond all that description or drawing can tell. Only those who
have stood upon the heights by Peel Crag and seen the long line of
fortification crowning ridge after ridge in endless succession as far as
the eye can reach, can realize the sense of the vastness and majesty of
Roman Imperialism thus borne in upon the mind. And if this is so now
that the Wall is a ruin scarcely four feet high, and, but for its greater
breadth, indistinguishable from the ordinary local field-walls, what must
it have been when its solid masonry rose to a height of over twenty feet;
with its twenty-three strong fortresses[286] for the permanent quarters of
the garrison, its great gate-towers[287] at every mile for the accommodation
of the detachments on duty, and its series of watch-turrets which, at
every three or four hundred yards, placed sentinels within sight and call
of each other along the whole line from sea to sea?

F. 2.—Of all this swarming life no trace now remains. So entirely did
it cease to be that the very names of the stations have left no shadow
of memories on their sites. Luguvallum at the one end, and Pons Aelii
at the other, have revived into importance as Carlisle and Newcastle,[288]
but of the rest few indeed remain save as solitary ruins on the bare
Northumbrian fells tenanted only by the flock and the curlew. But this
very solitude in which their names have perished has preserved to us the
means of recovering them. Thanks to it there is no part of Britain so
rich in Roman remains and Roman inscriptions. At no fewer than twelve
of these "stations" such have been already found relating to troops

whom we know from the 'Notitia' to have been quartered at given spots *per lineam valli.* A Dacian cohort (for example) has thus left its mark at Birdoswald, and an Asturian at Chesters, thereby stamping these sites as respectively the *Amboglanna* and *Cilurnum,* whose Dacian and Asturian garrisons the 'Notitia' records. The old walls of Cilurnum, moreover, are still clothed with a pretty little Pyrenaean creeper, *Erinus Hispanicus,* which these Asturian exiles must have brought with them as a memorial of their far-off home.

F. 3.—Many such small but vivid touches of the past meet those who visit the Wall. At "King Arthur's Well," for example, near Thirlwall, the tiny chives growing in the crevices of the rock are presumably descendants of those acclimatized there by Roman gastronomy. At Borcovicus ("House-steads") the wheel-ruts still score the pavement; at Cilurnum the hypocaust of the bath is still blackened with smoke, and at various points the decay of Roman prestige is testified to by the walling up of one half or the other in the wide double gates which originally facilitated the sorties of the garrisons.

F. 4.—The same decay is probably the key to the problem of the "Vallum," that standing crux to all archaeological students of the Wall. Along the whole line this mysterious earthwork keeps company with the Wall on the south, sometimes in close contact, sometimes nearly a mile distant. It has been diversely explained as an earlier British work, as put up by the Romans to cover the fatigue-parties engaged in building the Wall, and as a later erection intended to defend the garrison against attacks from the rear. Each of these views has been keenly debated; the last having the support of the late Dr. Bruce, the highest of all authorities on the mural antiquities. And excavations, even the very latest, have produced results which are claimed by each of the rival theories.[289]

F. 5.—Quite possibly all are in measure true. The "Vallum" as we now see it is obviously meant for defence against a southern foe. But the spade has given abundant evidence that the rampart has been altered, and that, in many places at least, it at one time faced northwards. Though not an entirely satisfactory solution of the problem, the following sequence of events would seem, on the whole, best to explain the phenomena with which we are confronted. Originally a British earthwork[290] defending the Brigantes against the cattle-lifting raids of their restless northern neighbours, the "Vallum" was adapted[291] for like purposes by the Romans, and that more than once. After being thus utilized, first, perhaps, by Agricola, and afterwards by Hadrian (for the protection of his working-parties engaged in quarrying stone for the outer fortifications), it became useless when the Wall was finally completed,[292] and remained a mere unfortified mound so long as the Roman power in Southern Britain continued undisturbed.

But when the garrison of the Wall became liable to attacks from the rear, the "Vallum" was once more repaired, very probably by Theodosius,[293] and this time with a ditch to the south, to enable the soldiers to meet, if needful, a simultaneous assault of Picts in front and Scots[294] or Saxons behind. Weak though it was as compared to the Wall, it would still take a good deal of storming, if stoutly held, and would effectually guard against any mere raid both the small parties marching along the Military Way[295] from post to post, and the cattle grazing along the rich meadows which frequently lie between the two lines of fortification.

F.6.—As we have said, the line of country thus occupied teems with relics of the occupation. Coins by the thousand, ornaments, fragments of statuary, inscriptions to the Emperors, to the old Roman gods, to the strange Pantheistic syncretisms of the later Mithraism[296], to unknown (perhaps local) deities such as Coventina, records of this, that, and the other body of troops in the garrison, personal dedications and memorials—all have been found, and are still constantly being found, in rich abundance. Of the whole number of Romano-British inscriptions known, nearly half belong to the Wall.[297]

F.7.—As an example of these inscriptions we may give one discovered at Caervoran (the Roman *Magna*), and now in the Newcastle Antiquarian Museum,[298] the interpretation of which has been a matter of considerable

154

discussion amongst antiquaries. It is written in letters of the 3rd century and runs as follows:—

IMMINET ·LEONIVIRGO ·CAELES
TI ·SITV SPICIFERA ·IVSTI ·IN
VENTRIXVRBIVM ·CONDITRIX
EXQVISMVNERIBVS ·NOSSECON
TIGITDEOS ·ERGOEADEMMATERDIVVM
PAX ·VIRTVS ·CERES ·DEA ·SYRIA
LANCEVITAMETIVRAPENSITANS
IN ·CAELOVISVMSYRIASIDVSEDI
DIT ·LIBYAE ·COLENDVMINDE
CVNCTIDIDICIMVS
ITAINTELLEXITNVMINEINDVCTVS
TVO ·MARCVSCAECILIVSDO
NATIANVS ·MILITANS ·TRIBVNVS
INPRAEFECTODONO ·PRINCIPIS.

Here we have ten very rough trochaic lines:

Imminet Leoni Virgo caelesti situ
Spicifera, justi inventrix, urbium conditrix;
Ex quis muneribus nosse contigit Deos.
Ergo eadem Mater Divum, Pax, Virtus, Ceres,
Dea Syria, lance vitam et jura pensitans.
In caelo visum Syria sidus edidit
Libyae colendum: inde cuncti didicimus.
Ita intellexit, numine inductus tuo,
Marcus Caecilius Donatianus, militans
Tribunus in Praefecto, dono Principis.

This may be thus rendered:

O'er the Lion hangs the Virgin, in her place in heaven,
With her corn-ear;—justice-finder, city-foundress, she:
And in them that do such office Gods may still be known.
She, then, is the Gods' own Mother, Peace, Strength, Ceres, all;
Syria's Goddess, in her Balance weighing life and Law.
Syria sent this Constellation shining in her sky
Forth for Libya's worship:—thence we all have learnt the lore.
Thus hath come to understanding, by the Godhead led,
Marcus Caecilius Donatianus
Serving now as Tribune-Prefect, by the Prince's grace.

F. 8.—These obscure lines Dr. Hodgkin refers to Julia Domna, the wife of Severus, the one Emperor that Africa gave to the Roman world. He was an able astrologer, and from early youth considered himself destined by his horoscope for the throne. He was thus guided by astrological considerations to take for his second wife a Syrian virgin, whose nativity he found to forecast queenship. As his Empress she shared in the aureole of divinity which rested upon all members of the Imperial family. This theory explains the references in the inscription to the constellation Virgo, with its chief star Spica, having Leo on the one hand and Libra on the other, also to the Syrian origin of Julia and her connection with Libya, the home of Severus. It may be added that Dr. Hodgkin's view is confirmed by the fact that this Empress figures, on coins found in Britain, as the Mother of the Gods, and also as Ceres. The first line may possibly have special reference to her influence in Britain during the reign of Severus and her stepson[299] Caracalla (who was also her second husband), Leo being a noted astrological sign of Britain.[300] The inscription was evidently put up in recognition of promotion gained by her favour, though the exact interpretation of *Tribunus in praefecto* requires a greater knowledge of Roman military nomenclature than we possess. Dr. Hodgkin's "Tribune instead of Prefect" seems scarcely admissible grammatically.

F. 9.—Another inscription which may be mentioned is that referred to by Tennyson in 'Gareth and Lynette' (l. 172), which

> "the vexillary
> Hath left crag-carven over the streaming Gelt."[301]

This is one of the many such records in the quarries south of the Wall telling of the labours of the fatigue-parties sent out by Severus to hew stones for his mighty work, and cut on rocks overhanging the river. It sets forth how a *vexillatio*[302] of the Second Legion was here engaged, under a lieutenant [*optio*] named Agricola, in the consulship of Aper and Maximus (A.D. 207);[303] perhaps as a guard over the actual workers, who were probably a *corvée* of impressed natives.

F. 10.—Yet another inscription worth notice was unearthed in 1897, and tells how a water supply to Cilurnum was brought from a source in the neighbourhood through a subterranean conduit by Asturian engineers under Ulpius Marcellus (A.D. 160). That this should have been done brings home to us the magnificent thoroughness with which Rome did her work. Cilurnum stood on a pure and perennial stream, the North Tyne, with a massively-fortified bridge, and thus could never be cut off from water; it was only some six acres in total area; yet in addition to the river it received a water supply which would now be thought sufficient for a fair-sized town.[304] Well may Dr. Hodgkin say that "not even the Coliseum of Vespasian or the Pantheon of Agrippa impresses the mind with a sense of the majestic strength of Rome so forcibly" as works like this, merely to secure the passage of a "little British stream, unknown to the majority even of Englishmen."

SECTION G.

Death of Severus—Caracalla and Geta—Roman citizenship—Extended to veterans—Tabulae honestae, missionis—Bestowed on all British provincials.

G.I.—This mighty work kept Severus in Britain for the rest of his life. He incessantly watched over its progress, and not till it was completed turned his steps once more (A.D. 211) towards Rome. But he was not to reach the Imperial city alive. Scarcely had he completed the first stage of the journey than, at York, omens of fatal import foretold his speedy death. A negro soldier presented him with a cypress crown, exclaiming, "*Totum vicisti, totum fuisti. Nunc Deus esto victor.*"[305] When he would fain offer a sacrifice of thanksgiving, he found himself by mistake at the dark temple of Bellona; and her black victims were led in his train even to the very door of his palace, which he never left again. Dark rumours were circulated that Caracalla, who had already once attempted his father's life, and was already intriguing with his stepmother, was at the bottom of all this, and took good care that the auguries should be fulfilled. Anyhow, Severus never left York till his corpse was carried forth and sent off for burial at Rome. With his last breath he is said solemnly to have warned "my Antonines" that upon their own conduct depended the peace and well-being of the Empire which he had so ably won for them.[306]

G. 2.—The warning was, as usual, in vain. Caracalla and Julia were now free to work their will, and, having speedily got rid of her son Geta, entered upon an incestuous marriage. The very Caledonians, whose conjugal system was of the loosest,[307] cried shame;[308] but the garrison of the Wall which kept them off was, as we have seen, officered by Julia's creatures, and all beyond it was definitely abandoned,[309] not to be recovered for two centuries.[310] The guilty pair returned to Rome, and a hundred and thirty years elapsed before another Augustus visited Britain.[311]

G. 3.—They left behind them no longer a subject race of mere provincials, but a nation of full Roman citizens. For it was Caracalla, seemingly, who, by extending it to the whole Roman world, put the final stroke to the expansion, which had long been in progress, of this once priceless privilege; with its right of appeal to Caesar, of exemption from torture, of recognized marriage, and of eligibility to public office. Originally confined strictly to natives of Rome and of Roman Colonies, it was early bestowed *ipso facto* on enfranchised slaves, and sometimes given as a compliment to distinguished strangers. After the Social War (B.C. 90) it was extended to all Italians, and Claudius (A.D. 50) allowed Messalina to make it purchasable ("for a great sum," as both the Acts of the Apostles and Dion Cassius inform us) by provincials.

G. 4.—And they could also earn it by service in the Imperial armies. A bronze tablet, found at Cilurnum,[312] sets forth that Antoninus Pius confers upon the *emeriti*, or time-expired veterans, of the Gallic, Asturian, Celtiberian, Spanish, and Dacian cohorts in Britain, who have completed twenty-five years' service with the colours, the right of Roman citizenship, and legalizes their marriages, whether existing or future.[313] As there is no reason to suppose that such discharged soldiers commonly returned to their native land, this system must have leavened the population of Britain with a considerable proportion of Roman citizens, even before Caracalla's edict. Besides its privileges, this freedom brought with it certain liabilities, pecuniary and other; and it was to extend the area of these that Caracalla took this apparently liberal step, which had been at least contemplated by more worthy predecessors[314] on philanthropic grounds. Any way, Britain was, by now, in the fullest sense Roman.

ROMANO-BRITISH PLACE-NAMES.[315]

TOWNS, ETC.
Aballaba = Watch-cross
AESICA = GREAT CHESTERS

AMBOGLANNA = BIRDOSWALD
AQUAE (SULIS) = BATH
BORCOVICUS = HOUSE-STEADS
Branodunum = Brancaster
Braboniacum = Ribchester
Brige = Broughton
Caesaromagum = *Chelmsford*
Calcaria = Tadcaster
Calleva = Silchester
Camboricum = Cambridge
Cataractonis = Catterick
Clausentum = *Southampton*
CILURNUM = CHESTERS
Colonia = Colchester
Concangium = Kendal
CORINIUM = CIRENCESTER
DANUM = DONCASTER
DEVA = CHESTER
Devonis = *Devonport*
Dictis = Ambleside
DUBRIS = DOVER
DURNOVARIA = DORCHESTER
Durobrivis = Rochester
Durolipons = Godmanchester
Durnovernum = Canterbury
EBORACUM = YORK
Etocetum = *Uttoxeter*
GLEVUM = GLOUCESTER
Gobannium = Abergavenny
ISCA SILURUM = CAERLEON
Isca Damnoniorum = Exeter

Isurium = Aldborough (York)
LEMANNAE = LYMPNE
LINDUM COLONIA = LINCOLN
Longovicum = Lancaster
LONDINIUM = LONDON
Lugovallum = Carlisle
Magna = Caervoran
Mancunium = Manchester
Moridunum = Seaton
Muridunum = Caermarthen
Olikana = Ilkley
Pons Aelii = Newcastle
Pontes = Staines
PORTUS = PORTCHESTER
Procolitia = Carrawburgh
RATAE = LEICESTER
Regnum = Chichester
REGULBIUM = RECULVER
RITUPIS = RICHBOROUGH
Segedunum = Wall's End
SORBIODUNUM = SARUM
Spinae = Speen (Berks)
URICONUM = WROXETER
VENTA BELGARUM = WINCHESTER
VENTA ICENONUM = CAISTOR-BY-NORWICH
VENTA SILURUM = CAER GWENT
VERULAMIUM = VERULAM
Vindoballa = Rutchester
Vindomara = Ebchester
Vindolana = Little Chesters

RIVERS AND ESTUARIES.

Alaunus Fl. = Tweed
Belisama Est. = Mouth of Mersey
CLOTA EST. = FIRTH OF CLYDE
Cunio Fl. = Conway
TUNA EST. = SOLWAY
MORICAMBE EST. = MORCAMBE BAY
SABRINA FL. = SEVERN
Setantion Est. = Mouth of Ribble
Seteia Est. = Mouth of Dee
TAMARIS FL. = TAMAR
TAMESIS FL. = THAMES
Tava Est. = Firth of Tay
Tuerobis Fl. = Tavy VARAR EST. = MORAY FIRTH
Vedra Fl. = Wear

CAPES AND ISLANDS.

BOLERIUM PR. = LAND'S END
CANTIUM PR. = N. FORELAND
Epidium Pr. = Mull of Cantire
Herculis Pr. = Hartland Point
MANNA I. = MAN
MONA I. = ANGLESEY
Noranton Pr. = Mull of Galloway
OCRINUM PR. = THE LIZARD
OCTAPITARUM PR. = ST. DAVID'S HEAD
Orcas Pr. = Dunnet Head
Taexalum Pr. = Kinnaird Head
TANATOS I. = THANET
VECTIS I. = I. OF WIGHT

VIRVEDRUM PR. = CAPE WRATH

N.B.—Many of these names vary notably in our several authorities: e.g. Manna is also written Mona, Monaoida, Monapia, Mevania.

* * * * *

CHAPTER. V

THE END OF ROMAN BRITAIN, A.D. 211-455

SECTION A.

Era of Pretenders—Probus—Vandlebury—First notice of Saxons—Origin of name—Count of the Saxon Shore—Carausius—Allectus—Last Romano-British coinage—Britain Mistress of the Sea—Reforms of Diocletian—Constantius Chlorus—Re-conquest of Britain—Diocletian provinces—Diocletian persecution—The last "Divus"—General scramble for Empire—British Army wins for Constantine—Christianity established.

A. 1.—After the death of Severus in A.D. 211, Roman historians tell us nothing more concerning Britain till we come to the rise of the only other Emperor who died at York, Constantius Chlorus. During the miserable period which the wickedness of Caracalla brought upon the Roman world, when Pretender after Pretender flits across the scene, most to fail, some for a moment to succeed, but all alike to end their brief course in blood, our island remained fairly quiet. The Army of Britain made one or two futile pronunciamentos (the least unsuccessful being those for Postumus in A.D. 258, and Victorinus in A.D. 265), and in 277 the Emperor Probus, probably to keep it in check, leavened it with a large force recruited from amongst his Vandal prisoners,[316] whose name may, perhaps, still survive in Vandlebury Camp, on the Gog-Magog[317] Hills, near Cambridge. But not till the energy and genius of Diocletian began to bring back to order the chaos into which the Roman world had fallen does Britain play any real part in the higher politics.

A. 2.—Then, however, we suddenly find ourselves confronted with names destined to exert a supreme influence on the future of our land. The Saxons from the Elbe, and the Franks from the Rhine had already begun their pirate raids along the coasts to the westwards.[318] Each tribe derived its name from its peculiar national weapon (the Franks from their throwing-axe (*franca*),[319] the Saxons from the *saexes*, long murderous knives, snouted like a Norwegian knife of the present day, which they used with such deadly effect);[320] and their appearance constituted a new and fearful danger to the Roman Empire. Never, since the Mediterranean pirates were crushed by Pompey (B.C. 66) had it been exposed to attacks by sea. A special effort was needed to meet this new situation, and we find, accordingly, a new officer now added to the Imperial muster,—the Count of the Saxon Shore. His jurisdiction extended over the northern coast of Gaul and the southern and eastern shores of Britain, the headquarters of his fleet being at Boulogne.

A. 3.—The first man to be placed in this position was Carausius,[321] a Frisian adventurer of low birth, but great military reputation, to which unfortunately he proved unequal. When his command was not followed by the looked-for putting-down of the pirate raiders, he was suspected, probably with truth, of a secret understanding with them. The Government accordingly sent down orders for his execution, to which he replied (A.D. 286) by open rebellion, took the pirate fleets into his pay, and having thus got the undisputed command of the sea, succeeded in maintaining himself as Emperor in Britain for the rest of his life.

A. 4.—His reign and that of his successor (and murderer) Allectus are marked by the last and most extraordinary development of Romano-British coinage. Since the time of Caracalla no coins which can be definitely proved to deserve this name are found; but now, in less than ten years, our mints struck no fewer than five hundred several issues,

165

all of different types. Nearly all are of bronze, with the radiated head of the Emperor on the obverse, and on the reverse devices of every imaginable kind. The British Lion once more figures, as in the days of Cymbeline; and we have also the Roman Wolf, the Sea-horse, the Cow (as a symbol of Prosperity), Plenty, Peace, Victory, Prudence, Health, Safety, Might, Good Luck, Glory, all symbolized in various ways. But the favourite type of all is the British warship; for now Britannia, for the first time, ruled the waves, and was, indeed, so entirely Mistress of the Sea that her fleet appeared even in Mediterranean waters.[322] The vessels figured are invariably not Saxon "keels," but classical galleys, with their rams and outboard rowing galleries, and are always represented as cleared for action (when the great mainsail and its yard were left on shore).

A. 5.—The usurpation of Carausius, "the pirate," as the Imperial panegyrists called him,[323] brought Diocletian's great reform of the Roman administration within the scope of practical politics in Britain. The old system of Provinces, some Imperial, some Senatorial, with each Pro-praetor or Pro-consul responsible only and immediately to the central government at Rome, had obviously become outgrown. And the Provinces themselves were much too large. Diocletian accordingly began by dividing the Empire into four "Prefectures," two in the east and two in the west. Each pair was to be under one of the co-Augusti, who again was to entrust one of his Prefectures to the "Caesar"[324] or heir-apparent of his choice. Thus Diocletian held the East, while Galerius, his "Caesar," took the Prefecture of Illyricum. His colleague Maximian, as Augustus of the West, ruled in Italy; and the remaining Prefecture, that of "the Gauls," fell to the Western Caesar, Constantius Chlorus. Each Prefecture, again, was divided into "Dioceses" (that of Constantius containing those of Britain, Gaul, Spain, and Mauretania), each under a "Vicar," and comprising a certain number of "Provinces" (that of Britain having four). Thus a regular hierarchy with rank above rank of responsibility was established, and so firmly that Diocletian's system lasted (so far as provincial government was concerned) till the very latest days of the Roman dominion.

A. 6.—When Constantius thus became Caesar of the West, his first task was to restore Britain to the Imperial system. He was already, it seems, connected with the island, and had married a British lady named Helen.[325] Their son Constantine, a youth of special promise (according to the panegyrists), had been born at York, about A.D. 274, and now appeared on the scene to aid his father's operations with supernatural speed, "*quasi divino quodam curriculo.*"[326] Extraordinary celerity, indeed, marked all these operations. Allectus was on his guard, with one squadron at Boulogne to sweep the coast of Gaul, and another cruising in the Channel. By a sudden dash Constantius [in A.D. 296] seized the mouth of Boulogne harbour, threw a boom across it, "*defixis in aditu trabibus,*" and effectually barred the pirates from access to the sea.[327] Meanwhile the fleet which he had been building simultaneously in various Gallic ports was able to rendezvous undisturbed at Havre.

A. 7.—His men were no expert mariners like their adversaries; and, for this very reason, were ready, with their Caesar at their head, to put to sea in threatening weather, which made their better-skilled pilots hesitate. "What can we fear?" was the cry, "Caesar is with us." Dropping down the Seine with the tide on a wild and rainy morning, they set sail with a cross wind, probably from the north-east, a rare thing with ancient ships. As they neared the British coast the breeze sank to a dead calm, with a heavy mist lying on the waveless sea, in which the fleet found it impossible to keep together. One division, with Constantius himself on board, made their land-fall somewhere in the west, perhaps at Exeter, the other far to the east, possibly at Richborough.

A. 8.—But the wonderful luck which attended Constantius, and on which his panegyrists specially dwell, made all turn out for the best. The mist enabled both his divisions to escape the notice of the British fleet, which was lying off the Isle of Wight on the watch for him; and the unexpected landing at two such distant points utterly demoralized the usurper. Of the large force which had been mustered for land defence, only the Frankish auxiliaries could be got together in time to meet Constantius—who, having burnt his ships (for his only hope now lay in victory), was marching, with his wonted speed, straight on London. One battle,[328] in which scarcely a single Roman fell on the British side, was enough; the corpse of Allectus [*ipse vexillarius latrocinii*] was found, stripped of the Imperial insignia, amongst the heaps of slain barbarians, and the routed Franks fled to London. Here, while they were engaged in sacking the city before evacuating it, they were set upon by the eastern division of the Roman army (under Asclepiodotus the Praetorian Prefect)[329] and slaughtered almost to a man. The rescued metropolis eagerly welcomed its deliverers, and the example was followed by the rest of Britain; the more readily that the few surviving Franks were distributed throughout the land to perish in the provincial amphitheatres.

A. 9.—The Diocletian system was now introduced; and, instead of Hadrian's old divisions of Upper and Lower Britain, the island south of his Wall was distributed into four Provinces, "Britannia Prima," "Britannia Secunda," "Maxima Caesariensis," and "Flavia Caesariensis." That the Thames, the Severn, and the Humber formed the frontier lines between these new divisions is probable. But their identification, in the current maps of Roman Britain, with the later Wessex, Wales, Northumbria, and Mercia (with East Anglia), respectively, is purely conjectural.[330] All that we know is that when the district between Hadrian's Wall and Agricola's Rampart was reconquered in 369, it was made a fifth British Province under the name Valentia. The Governor of each Province exercised his functions under the "Vicar" of the "Diocese," an official of "Respectable" rank—the second in precedence of the Diocletian hierarchy (exclusive of the Imperial Family).

A. 10.—With the Diocletian administration necessarily came the Diocletian Persecution—an essential feature of the situation. There is no reason to imagine that the great reforming Emperor had, like his colleague Maximian, any personal hatred for Christianity. But Christianity was not among the *religiones licitae* of the Empire. Over and over again it had been pronounced by Imperial Rescript unlawful. This being so, Diocletian saw in its toleration merely one of those corruptions of lax government which it was his special mission to sweep away, and proceeded to deal with it as with any other abuse,—to be put down with whole-hearted vigour and rigour.

A. 11.—The Faith had by this time everywhere become so widespread that the good-will of its professors was a political power to be reckoned with. Few of the passing Pretenders of the Era of Confusion had dared to despise it, some had even courted it; and thus throughout the Empire the Christian hierarchy had been established, and Christian churches been built everywhere; while Christians swarmed in every department of the Imperial service,—their neglect of the official worship winked at, while they, in turn, were not vigorous in rebuking the idolatry of their heathen fellow-servants. Now all was changed. The sacred edifices were thrown down, or (as in the famous case of St. Clement's at Rome) made over for heathen worship, the sacred books and vessels destroyed, and every citizen, however humble, had to produce a *libellus*,331 or magisterial certificate, testifying that he had formally done homage to the Gods of the State, by burning incense at their shrines, by pouring libations in their name, and by partaking of the victims sacrificed upon their altars. Torture and death were the lot of all recusants; and to the noble army of martyrs who now sealed their testimony with their blood Britain is said (by Gildas) to have contributed a contingent of no fewer than seventeen thousand, headed by St. Alban at Verulam.

A. 12.—So thorough-going a persecution the Church had never known. But it came too late for Diocletian's purpose; and it was probably the latent consciousness of his failure that impelled him, in 305, to resign the purple and retire to his cabbage-garden at Dyrrhachium. Maximian found himself unwillingly obliged to retire likewise; and the two Caesars, Galerius and Constantius, became, by the operation of the new constitution, *ipso facto* Augusti.

A. 13.—But already the mutual jealousy and distrust in which that constitution was so soon to perish began to manifest themselves. Galerius, though properly only Emperor of the East, seized on Rome, and with it on the person of the young Constantine, whom he hoped to keep as hostage for his father's submission. The youth, however, contrived to flee, and post down to join Constantius in Gaul, slaughtering every stud of relays along the entire road to delay his pursuers. Both father and son at once sailed for Britain, where the former shortly died, like Severus, at York. With their arrival the persecution promptly ceased;[332] for Helena, at least, was an ardent Christian, and her husband well-affected to the Faith. Yet, on his death, he was, like his predecessors, proclaimed *Divus*; the last formal bestowal of that title being thus, like the first,[333] specially connected with Britain. Constantius was buried, according to Nennius,[334] at Segontium, wherever that may have been; and Constantine, though not yet even a Caesar, was at once proclaimed by the soldiers (at his native York) Augustus in his father's room.

A. 14.—This was the signal for a whole outburst of similar proclamations all over the Roman world, Licinius, Constantine's brother-in-law, declared himself Emperor at Carnutum, Maxentius, son of Maximian and son-in-law of Galerius, in Rome, Severus in the Illyrian provinces, and Maximin (who had been a Caesar) in Syria. Galerius still reigned, and even Maximian revoked his resignation and appeared once more as Augustus. But one by one this medley of Pretenders swept each other away, and the survival of the fittest was exemplified by the final victory of Constantine over them all. For a few years he bided his time, and then, at the head of the British army, marched on Rome. Clear-sighted enough to perceive that events were irresistibly tending to the triumph of Christianity, he declared himself the champion of the Faith; and it was not under the Roman Eagle, but the Banner of Christ,[335] that his soldiers fought and won. Coins of his found in Britain, bearing the Sacred Monogram which led his men to the crowning victory of 312 at the Milvian Bridge (the intertwined letters X [Chi] and P [Rho] between A [Alpha] and Ω [Omega], the whole forming the word ΧΡΑΩ [ARChÔ], "I reign"), with the motto *Hoc Signo Victor Eris*, testify to the special part taken by our country in the establishment of our Faith as the officially recognized religion of Rome,—that is to say, of the whole civilized world. And henceforward, as long as Britain remained Roman at all, it was a monarch of British connection who occupied the Imperial throne. The dynasties of Constantius, Valentinian, and Theodosius, who between them (with the brief interlude of the reign of Julian) fill the next 150 years (300-450), were all markedly associated with our island. So, indeed, was Julian also.

SECTION B.

Spread of Gospel—Arianism—Britain orthodox—Last Imperial visit—Heathen temples stripped—British Emperors—Magnentius—Gratian—Julian—British corn-trade—First inroad of Picts and Scots—Valentinian—Saxon raids— Campaign of Theodosius—Re-conquest of Valentia.

B. 1.—For a whole generation after the triumph of Constantine tranquillity reigned in Britain. The ruined Christian churches were everywhere restored, and new ones built; and in Britain, as elsewhere, the Gospel spread rapidly and widely—the more so that the Church here was but little troubled[336] by the desperate struggle with Arianism which was convulsing the East. Britain, as Athanasius tells us, gave an assenting vote to the decisions of Nicaea (σύμψηφος ἐτύγχανε) [sumpsêphos etunchane], and British Bishops actually sat in the Councils of Arles (314) and of Ariminum (360).

B. 2.—The old heathen worship still continued side by side with the new Faith; but signs soon appeared that the Church would tolerate no such rivalry when once her power was equal to its suppression. Julius Firmicus (who wrote against "Profane Religions" in 343) implores the sons of Constantine to continue their good work of stripping the temples and melting down the images;—in special connection with a visit paid by them that year to Britain[337] (our last Imperial visit), when they had actually been permitted to cross the Channel in winter-time; an irrefragable proof of Heaven's approval of their iconoclasm. It is highly probable that they pursued here also a course at once so pious and so profitable, and that the fanes of the ancient deities but lingered on in poverty and neglect till finally suppressed by Theodosius (A.D. 390).

B. 3.—And now Britain resumed her *rôle* of Emperor-maker.[338] After the death of Constans, (A.D. 350), Magnentius, an officer in the Gallic army of British birth, set up as Augustus, and was supported by Gratian, the leader of the Army of Britain, and by his son Valentinian. Magnentius himself had his capital at Treves, and for three years reigned over the whole Prefecture of the Gauls. He professed a special zeal for orthodoxy, and was the first to introduce burning, as the appropriate punishment for heresy, into the penal code of Christendom. Meanwhile his colleague Decentius advanced against Constantius, and was defeated, at Nursa on the Drave, with such awful slaughter that the old Roman Legions never recovered from the shock. Henceforward the name signifies a more or less numerous body, more or less promiscuously armed, such as we find so many of in the 'Notitia.' Magnentius, in turn, was slain (A.D. 353), and the supreme command in Britain passed to the new Caesar of the West, Julian "the Apostate."

B. 4.—Under him we first find our island mentioned as one of the great corn-growing districts of the Empire, on which Gaul was able to draw to a very large extent for the supply of her garrisons. No fewer than eight hundred wheat-ships sailed from our shores on this errand; a number which shows how large an area of the island must have been brought under cultivation, and how much the country had prospered during the sixty years of unbroken internal peace which had followed on the suppression of Allectus.

B. 5.—That peace was now to be broken up. The northern tribes had by this recovered from the awful chastisement inflicted upon them by Severus,[339] and, after an interval of 150 years, once more (A.D. 362) appeared south of Hadrian's Wall. Whether as yet they *burst through* it is uncertain; for now we find a new confederacy of barbarians. It is no longer that of Caledonians and Meatae, but of Picts and Scots. And these last were seafarers. Their home was not in Britain at all, but in the north of Ireland. In their "skiffs"[340] they were able to turn the flank of the Roman defences, and may well have thus introduced their allies from beyond Solway also. Anyhow, penetrate the united hordes did into the quiet cornfields of Roman Britain, repeating their raids ever more frequently and extending them ever more widely, till their spearmen were cut [Errata: to] pieces in 450 at Stamford by the swords of the newly-arrived English.[341]

B. 6.—For the moment they were driven back without much difficulty, by Lupicinus, Julian's Legate (the first Legate we hear of in Britain since Lollius Urbicus), who, when the death of Constantius II. (in 361) had extinguished that royal line, aided his master to become "*Dominus totius orbis*"—as he is called in an inscription[342] describing his triumphant campaigns "*ex oceano Britannico.*" And after "the victory of the Galilaean" (363) had ended Julian's brief and futile attempt to restore the Higher Paganism (to which several British inscriptions testify),[343] it was again to an Emperor from Britain that there fell the Lordship of the World—Valentinian, son of Gratian, whose dynasty lasted out the remaining century of Romano-British history.

B. 7.—His reign was marked in our land by a life-and-death struggle with the inrushing barbarians. The Picts and Scots were now joined by yet another tribe, the cannibal[344] Attacotti[345] of Valentia, and their invasions were facilitated by the simultaneous raids of the Saxon pirates (with whom they may perhaps have been actually in concert) along the coast. The whole land had been wasted, and more than one Roman general defeated, when Theodosius, father of the Great Emperor, was sent, in 368, to the rescue. Crossing from Boulogne to Richborough in a lucky calm,[346] and fixing his head-quarters at London, or Augusta, as it was now called [*Londinium vetus oppidum, quod Augustam posteritas apellavit*], he first, by a skilful combination of flying columns, cut to pieces the scattered hordes of the savages as they were making off with their booty, and finally not only drove them back beyond the Wall, which he repaired and re-garrisoned,[347] but actually recovered the district right up to Agricola's rampart, which had been barbarian soil ever since the days of Severus.[348] It was now (369) formed into a fifth British province, and named Valentia in honour of Valens, the brother and colleague of the Emperor.

B. 8.—The Twentieth Legion, whose head-quarters had so long been at Chester, seems to have been moved to guard this new province. Forty years later Claudian speaks of it as holding the furthest outposts in Britain, in his well-known description of the dying Pict:

> "Venit et extremis legio praetenta Britannis,
> Quae Scoto dat frena truci, ferroque notatas
> Perlegit exsangues Picto moriente figuras."

> ["From Britain's bound the outpost legion came,
> Which curbs the savage Scot, and fading sees
> The steel-wrought figures on the dying Pict."]

The same poet makes Theodosius fight and conquer even in the Orkneys and in Ireland;

> "—maduerunt Saxone fuso
> Orcades; incaluit Pictorum sanguine Thule;
> Scotorum cumulos flevit glacialis Ierne."[349]

["With Saxon slaughter flowed the Orkney strand,
With Pictish blood cold Thule warmer grew;
And icy Erin wept her Scotchmen slain."]

The relief, however, was but momentary. Five years later (374) another great Saxon raid is recorded; yet eight years more and the Picts and Scots have again to be driven from the land; and in the next decade their attacks became incessant.

SECTION C.

Roman evacuation of Britain begun—Maximus—Settlement of Brittany—Stilicho restores the Wall—Radagaisus invades Italy—Twentieth Legion leaves Britain— Britain in the 'Notitia'—Final effort of British Army—The last Constantine— Last Imperial Rescript to Britain—Sack of Rome by Alaric—Collapse of Roman rule in Britain.

C. 1.—By this time the evacuation of Britain by the Roman soldiery had fairly begun. Maximus, the last victor over the Scots, the "Pirate of Richborough," as Ausonius calls him, set up as Emperor (A.D. 383); and the Army of Britain again marched on Rome, and again, as under Constantine, brought its leader in triumph to the Capitol (A.D. 387). But this time it did not return. When Maximus was defeated and slain (A.D. 388) at Aquileia by the Imperial brothers-in-law Valentinian II. and Theodosius the Great[350] (sons of the so-named leaders connected with Britain), his soldiers, as they retreated homewards, straggled on the march; settling, amid the general confusion, here and there, mostly in Armorica, which now first began to be called Brittany.[351] This tale rests only on the authority of Nennius, but it is far from improbable, especially as his sequel—that a fresh legion dispatched to Britain by Stilicho (in 396) once more repelled the Picts and Scots, and re-secured the Wall—is confirmed by Claudian, who makes Britain (in a sea-coloured cloak and bearskin head-gear) hail Stilicho as her deliverer:

Inde Caledonio velata Britannia monstro, Ferro picta genas, cujus vestigia verrit Coerulus, Oceanique aestum mentitur, amictus: "Me quoque vicinis percuntem gentibus," inquit, "Munivit Stilichon, totam quum Scotus Iernen Movit, et infesto spumavit remige Tethys. Illius effectum curis, ne tela timerem Scotica, ne Pictum tremerem, ne litore toto Prospicerem dubiis venturum Saxona ventis."[352]

[Then next, with Caledonian bearskin cowled, Her cheek steel-tinctured, and her trailing robe Of green-shot blue, like her own Ocean's tide, Britannia spake: "Me too," she cried, "in act To perish 'mid the shock of neighbouring hordes, Did Stilicho defend, when the wild Scot All Erin raised against me, and the wave Foamed 'neath the stroke of many a foeman's oar. So wrought his pains that now I fear no more Those Scottish darts, nor tremble at the Pict, Nor mark, where'er to sea mine eyes I turn, The Saxon coming on each shifting wind."]

C. 2.—Which legion it was which Stilicho sent to Britain is much more questionable. The Roman legions were seldom moved from province to province, and it is perhaps more probable that he filled up the three quartered in the island to something like their proper strength. But a crisis was now at hand which broke down all ordinary rules. Rome was threatened with such a danger as she had not known since Marius, five hundred years before, had destroyed the Cimbri and Teutones (B.C. 101). A like horde of Teutonic invaders, nearly half a million strong, came pouring over the Alps, under "Radagaisus the Goth," as contemporary historians call him, though his claim, to Gothic lineage is not undisputed. And these were not, like Alaric and his Visigoths, who were to reap the fruits of this effort, semi-civilized Christians, but heathen savages of the most ferocious type. Every nerve had to be strained to crush them; and Stilicho did crush them. But it was at a fearful cost. Every Roman soldier within reach had to be swept to the rescue, and thus the Rhine frontier was left defenceless against the barbarian hordes pressing upon it. Vandals, Sueves, Alans, Franks, Burgundians, rushed tumultuously over the peaceful and fertile fields of Gaul, never to be driven forth again.

C. 3.—Of the three British legions one only seems to have been thus withdrawn,—the Twentieth, whose head-quarters had been so long at Chester, and whose more recent duty had been to garrison the outlying province of Valentia, which may now perhaps have been again abandoned. It seems to have been actually on the march towards Italy[353] when there was drawn up that wonderful document which gives us our last and completest glimpse of Roman Britain—the *Notitia Dignitatum Utriusque Imperii.*

C. 4.—This invaluable work sets forth in detail the whole machinery of the Imperial Government, its official hierarchy, both civil and military, in every land, and a summary of the forces under the authority of each commander. A reference in Claudian would seem to show that it was compiled by the industry of Celerinus, the *Primicerius Notariorum* or Head Clerk of the Treasury. The poet tells us how this indefatigable statistician—

> "Cunctorum tabulas assignat honorum,
> Regnorum tractat numeros, constringit in unum
> Sparsas Imperii vires, cuneosque recenset
> Dispositos; quae Sarmaticis custodia ripis,
> Quae saevis objecta Getis, quae Saxona frenat
> Vel Scotum legio; quantae cinxere cohortes
> Oceanum, quanto pacatur milite Rhenus."[354]

> ["Each rank, each office in his lists he shows,
> Tells every subject realm, together draws
> The Empire's scattered force, recounts the hosts
> In order meet;—which Legion is on guard

By Danube's banks, which fronts the savage Goth,
Which curbs the Saxon, which the Scot; what bands
Begird the Ocean, what keep watch on Rhine."]

To us the 'Notitia' is only known by the 16th-century copies of a 10th-century MS. which has now disappeared.[355] But these were made with exceptional care, and are as nearly as may be facsimiles of the original, even preserving its illuminated illustrations, including the distinctive insignia of every corps in the Roman Army.

C. 5.—The number of these corps had, we find, grown erormously since the days of Hadrian, when, as Dion Cassius tells us, there were 19 "Civic Legions" (of which three were quartered in Britain). No fewer than 132 are now enumerated, together with 108 auxiliary bodies. But we may be sure that each of these "legions" was not the complete Army Corps of old,[356] though possibly the 25 of the First Class, the *Legiones Palatinae*, may have kept something of their ancient effectiveness. Indeed it is not wholly improbable that these alone represent the old "civil" army; the Second and Third Class "legions," with their extraordinary names ("Comitatenses" and "Pseudo-Comitatenses"), being indeed merely so called by "courtesy," or even "sham courtesy."

C. 6.—In Britain we find the two remaining legions of the old garrison, the Second, now quartered not at Caerleon but at Richborough, under the Count of the Saxon Shore, and the Sixth under the "Duke of the Britains," holding the north (with its head-quarters doubtless, as of yore, at York, though this is not mentioned). Along with each legion are named ten "squads" [*numeri*], which may perhaps represent the ten cohorts into which legions were of old divided. The word cohort seems to have changed its meaning, and now to signify an independent military unit under a "Tribune." Eighteen of these, together with six squadrons [*alae*] of cavalry, each commanded by a "Praefect," form the garrison of the Wall;—a separate organization, though, like the rest of the northern forces, under the Duke of the Britains. The ten squads belonging to the Sixth Legion (each under a Prefect) are distributed in

178

garrison throughout Yorkshire, Lancashire, and Westmoreland. Those of the Second (each commanded by a "Praepositus") are partly under the Count of the Saxon Shore, holding the coast from the Wash to Arundel,[357] partly under the "Count of Britain," who was probably the senior officer in the island[358] and responsible for its defence in general. Besides these bodies of infantry the British Army comprised eighteen cavalry units; three, besides the six on the Wall, being in the north, three on the Saxon Shore, and the remaining six under the immediate command of the Count of Britain, to whose troops no special quarters are assigned. Not a single station is mentioned beyond the Wall, which supports the theory that the withdrawal of the Twentieth Legion had involved the practical abandonment of Valentia.[359]

C. 7.—The two Counts and the Duke were the military leaders of Britain. The chief civil officer was the "respectable" Vicar of the Diocese of Britain, one of the six Vicars under the "illustrious" Proconsul of Africa. Under him were the Governors of the five Provinces, two of these being "Consulars" of "Right Renowned" rank [*clarissimi,*] the other three "Right Perfect" [*perfectissimi*] "Presidents." The Vicar was assisted by a staff of Civil Servants, nine heads of departments being enumerated. Their names, however, have become so wholly obsolete as to tell us nothing of their respective functions.

C. 8.—Whatever these may have been they did not include the financial administration of the Diocese, the general management of which was in the hands of two officers, the "Accountant of Britain" [*Rationalis Summarum Britanniarum*] and the "Provost of the London Treasury" [*Praepositus thesaurorum Augustensium*].[360] Both these were subordinates of the "Count of the Sacred Largesses" [*Comes Sacrarum Largitionum*], one of the greatest officers of State, corresponding to our First Lord of the Treasury, whose name reminds us that all public expenditure was supposed to be the personal benevolence of His Sacred Majesty the Emperor, and all sources of public revenue his personal property. The Emperor, however, had actually in every province domains of his own, managed by the Count of the Privy Purse [*Comes Rei Privatae*], whose subordinate in Britain was entitled the "Accountant of the Privy Purse for Britain" [*Rationalis Rei Privatae per Britanniam*]. Both these Counts were "Illustrious" [*illustres*]; that is, of the highest order of the Imperial peerage below the "Right Noble" [*nobilissimi*] members of the Imperial Family.

C. 9.—Such and so complete was the system of civil and military government in Roman Britain up to the very point of its sudden and utter collapse. When the 'Notitia' was compiled, neither Celerinus, as he wrote, nor the officials whose functions and ranks he noted, could have dreamt that within ten short years the whole elaborate fabric would, so far as Britain was concerned, be swept away utterly and for ever. Yet so it was.

C. 10.—For what was left of the British Army now made a last effort to save the West for Rome, and once more set up Imperial Pretenders of its own.[361] The first two of these, Marcus and Gratian, were speedily found unequal to the post, and paid the usual penalty of such incompetence; but the third, a private soldier named Constantine, all but succeeded in emulating the triumph of his great namesake. For four years (407-411) he was able to hold not only Britain, but Gaul and Spain also under his sceptre; and the wretched Honorius, the unworthy son and successor of Theodosius, who was cowering amid the marshes of Ravenna, and had murdered his champion Stilicho, was fain to recognize the usurper as a legitimate Augustus. Only by treachery was he put down at last, the traitor being the commander of his British forces, Gerontius. Both names continued for many an age favourites in British nomenclature, and both have been swept into the cycle of Arturian romance, the latter as "Geraint."

C. 11.—Neither Gerontius nor his soldiers ever got back to their old homes in Britain. What became of them we do not know. But Zosimus[362] tells us that Honorius now sent a formal rescript to the British cities abrogating the Lex Julia, which forbade civilians to carry arms, and bidding them look to their own safety. For now the end had really come, and the Eternal City itself had been sacked by barbarian hands. Never before and never since does history record a sacked city so mildly treated by the conquerors. Heretics as the Visi-goths were, they never forgot that the vanquished Catholics were their fellow-Christians, and, barbarians

180

as they were, they left an example of mercy in victory which puts to the blush much more recent Christian and civilized warfare.

C. 12.—But, for all that, the moral effect of Alaric's capture of Rome was portentous, and shook the very foundations of civilization throughout the world. To Jerome, in his cell at Bethlehem, the tidings came like the shock of an earthquake. Augustine, as he penned his 'De Civitate Dei,' felt the old world ended indeed, and the Kingdom of Heaven indeed at hand. And in Britain the whole elaborate system of Imperial civil and military government seems to have crumbled to the ground almost at once. It is noticeable that the rescript of Honorius is addressed simply to "the cities" of Britain, the local municipal officers of each several place. No higher authority remained. The Vicar of Britain, with his staff, the Count and Duke of the Britains with their soldiery, the Count of the Saxon Shore with his coastguard,—all were gone. It is possible that, as the deserted provincials learnt to combine for defence, the Dictators they chose from time to time to lead the national forces may have derived some of their authority from the remembrance of these old dignities. "The dragon of the great Pendragonship,"[363] the tufa of Caswallon (633), and the purple of Cunedda[364] may well have been derived (as Professor Rhys suggests) from this source. But practically the history of Roman Britain ends with a crash at the Fall of Rome.

SECTION D.

Beginning of English Conquest—Vortigern—Jutes in Thanet—Battle of Stamford—Massacre of Britons—Valentinian III.—Latest Roman coin found in Britain—Progress of Conquest—The Cymry—Survival of Romano-British titles—Arturian Romances—Procopius—Belisarius—Roman claims revived by Charlemagne—The British Empire.

D. 1.—Little remains to be told, and that little rests upon no contemporary authority known to us. In Gildas, the nearest, writing in the next century, we find little more than a monotonous threnody over the awful visitation of the English Conquest, the wholesale and utter destruction of cities, the desecration of churches, the massacre of clergy and people. Nennius (as, for the sake of convenience, modern writers mostly agree to call the unknown author of the 'Historia Britonum') gives us legends of British incompetence and Saxon treachery which doubtless represent the substantial features of the break-up, and preserve, quite possibly, even some of the details. Bede and the 'Anglo-Saxon Chronicle' assign actual dates to the various events, but we have no means of testing their accuracy.

D. 2.—Broadly we know that the unhappy civilians, who were not only without military experience, but had up to this moment been actually forbidden to carry arms, naturally proved unable to face the ferocious enemies who swarmed in upon them. They could neither hold the Wall against the Picts nor the coast against the Saxons. It may well be true that they chose a *Dux Britannorum*,[365] and that his name may have been something like Vortigern, and that he (when a final appeal for Roman aid proved vain)[366] may have taken into his pay (as Carausius did) the crews of certain pirate "keels" [*chiulae*],[367] and settled them in Thanet. The very names of their English captains, "Hengist and Horsa," may not be so mythical as critics commonly assume.[368] And the tale of the victory at Stamford, when the spears of the Scottish invaders were cut to pieces by the swords of the English mercenaries,[369] has a very true ring about it. So has also the sequel, which tells how, when the inevitable quarrel arose between employers and employed, the Saxon leader gave the signal for the fray by suddenly shouting to his men, *Nimed eure saxes*[370] (*i.e.* "Draw your knives!"), and massacred the hapless Britons of Kent almost without resistance.

D. 3.—The date of this first English settlement is doubtful. Bede fixes it as 449, which agrees with the order of events in Gildas, and with the notice in Nennius that it was forty years after the end of Roman rule in Britain [*transacto Romanorum in Britannia imperio*]. But Nennius also declares that this was in the fourth year of Vortigern, and that his accession coincided with that of the nephew and successor of Honorius, Valentinian III., son of Galla Placidia, which would bring in the Saxons 428. It may perhaps be some very slight confirmation of the later date, that Valentinian is the last Emperor whose coins have been found in Britain.[371]

D. 4.—Anyhow, the arrival of the successive swarms of Anglo-Saxons from the mouth of the Elbe, and their hard-won conquest of Eastern Britain during the 5th century, is certain. The western half of the island, from Clydesdale southwards, resisted much longer, and, in spite of its long and straggling frontier, held together for more than a century. Not till the decisive victory of the Northumbrians at Chester (A.D. 607), and that of the West Saxons at Beandune (A.D. 614) was this Cymrian federation finally broken into three fragments, each destined shortly to disintegrate into an ever-shifting medley of petty principalities. Yet in each the ideal of national and racial unity embodied in the word Cymry[372] long survived; and titles borne to this day by our Royal House, "Duke of Cornwall," "Prince of Wales," "Duke of Albany," are the far-off echoes, lingering in each, of the Roman "Comes Britanniae" and "Dux Britanniarum." The three feathers of the Principality may in like manner be traced to the *tufa*, or plume, borne before the supreme authority amongst the Romans of old, as the like are borne before the Supreme Head of the Roman Church to this day. And age after age the Cymric harpers sang of the days when British armies had marched in triumph to Rome, and the Empire had been won by British princes, till the exploits of their mystical "Arthur"[373] became the nucleus of a whole cycle of mediaeval romance, and, even, for a while, a real force in practical politics.[374]

D. 5.—And as the Britons never quite forgot their claims on the Empire, so the Empire never quite forgot its claims on Britain. How entirely the island was cut off from Rome we can best appreciate by the references to it in Procopius. This learned author, writing under Justinian, scarcely 150 years since the day when the land was fully Roman, conceives of Britannia and Brittia as two widely distant islands—the one off the coast of Spain, the other off the mouth of the Rhine.[375] The latter is shared between the Angili, Phrissones,[376] and Britons, and is divided *from North to South*[377] by a mighty Wall, beyond which no mortal man can breathe. Hither are ferried over from Gaul by night the souls of the departed;[378] the fishermen, whom a mysterious voice summons to the work, seeing no one, but perceiving their barks to be heavily sunk in the water, yet accomplishing the voyage with supernatural celerity.

D. 6.—About the same date Belisarius offered to the Goths,[379] in exchange for their claim to Sicily, which his victories had already rendered practically nugatory, the Roman claims to Britain, "a much larger island," which were equally outside the scope of practical politics for the moment, but might at any favourable opportunity be once more brought forward. And, when the Western Empire was revived under Charlemagne, they were in fact brought forward, and actually submitted to by half the island. The Celtic princes of Scotland, the Anglians of Northumbria, and the Jutes of Kent alike owned the new Caesar as their Suzerain. And the claim was only abrogated by the triumph of the counter-claim first made by Egbert, emphasized by Edward the Elder, and repeated again and again by our monarchs their descendants, that the British Crown owes no allegiance to any potentate on earth, being itself not only Royal, but in the fullest sense Imperial.[380]

SECTION E.

Survivals of Romano-British civilization—Romano-British Church—Legends of its origin—St. Paul—St. Peter—Joseph of Arimathaea—Glastonbury—Historical notices—Claudia and Pudens—Pomponia—Church of St. Pudentiana—Patristic references to Britain—Tertullian—Origen—Legend of Lucius—Native Christianity—British Bishops at Councils—Testimony of Chrysostom and Jerome.

E. 1.—Few questions have been more keenly debated than the extent to which Roman civilization in Britain survived the English Conquest.

184

On the one hand we have such high authorities as Professor Freeman assuring us that our forefathers swept it away as ruthlessly and as thoroughly as the Saracens in Africa; on the other, those who consider that little more disturbance was wrought than by the Danish invasions. The truth probably lies between the two, but much nearer to the former than the latter. The substitution of an English for the Roman name of almost every Roman site in the country[381] could scarcely have taken place had there been anything like continuity in their inhabitants. Even the Roman roads, as we have seen,[382] received English designations. We may well believe that most Romano-British towns shared the fate of Anderida (the one recorded instance of destruction),[383] and that the word "chester" was only applied to the Roman *ruins* by their destroyers.[384] But such places as London, York, and Lincoln may well have lived on through the first generation of mere savage onslaught, after which the English gradually began to tolerate even for themselves a town life.

E. 2.—And though in the country districts the agricultural population were swept away pitilessly to make room for the invaders,[385] till the fens of Ely[386] and the caves of Ribblesdale[387] became the only refuge of the vanquished, yet, undoubtedly, many must have been retained as slaves, especially amongst the women, to leaven the language of the conquerors with many a Latin word, and their ferocity with many a recollection of the gentler Roman past.

E. 3.—And there was one link with that past which not all the massacres and fire-raisings of the Conquest availed to break. The Romano-British populations might be slaughtered, the Romano-British towns destroyed, but the Romano-British Church lived on; the most precious and most abiding legacy bestowed by Rome upon our island.

E. 4.—The origin of that Church has been assigned by tradition to directly Apostolic sources. The often-quoted passage from Theodoret,[388] of St. Paul having "brought help" to "the isles of the sea" (ταῖς ἐν τῷ πελάγει διακειμέναις νήσοις) [tais en to pelagei diakeimenais nêsois], can scarcely, however, refer to this island. No classical author ever uses the word πέλαγος [pelagos] of the Oceanic waters; and the epithet diakeime/nais [diakeimenais], coming, as it does, in connection with the Apostle's preaching in Italy and Spain, seems rather to point to the islands between these peninsulas—Sardinia, Corsica, and the Balearic Islands. But the well-known words of St. Clement of Rome,[389] that St. Paul's missionary journeys extended to "the End of the West" τό τέρμα τῆς δύσεως [to terma tês duseôs], were, as early as the 6th century, held to imply a visit to Britain (for our island was popularly supposed by the ancients to lie west of Spain).[390] The lines of Venantius (A.D. 580) even seem to contain a reference to the tradition that he landed at Portsmouth:

"Transit et Oceanum, vel qua facit insula portum,
Quasque Britannus habet terras atque ultima Thule."
    ["Yea, through the ocean he passed, where the Port is made by an island, And through each British realm, and where the world endeth at Thule."]

E. 5.—The Menology of the Greek Church (6th century) ascribes the organization of the British Church to the visitation, not of St. Paul, but of St. Peter in person.

Ο Πέτρος . . . εἰς Βρεταννίαν παραγίνεται. Ενθα δὴ χειροτριβήσας [*sic*] καὶ πολλὰ τῶν ἀκατανομάτων ἐθνῶν εἰς τὴν τοῦ Χριστοῦ πίστιν ἐπισπασάμενος . . . καί πολούς τῷ λόγῳ φωτίσας τῆς χάριτος, ἐκκλησιάς τε συστησάμενος, ἐπισκοπούς τε καὶ πρεσβυτέρους καὶ διακόνους χειροτονησας, δωδεκάτῳ ἔτει τοῦ Καίσαρος αὖθις Πώμην παραγίνεται.

[O Petros . . . ehis Bretannian paraginetai. Entha dô cheirotribôsas [*sic*] kai polla tôn hakatanomatôn hethnôn eis

186

tôn tou Christou pistin cpispasamenos ... kai pollous toi logoi photisas tôs charitos, ekklaesias te sustêsamenos, episkopous te kai presbuterous kai diakonous cheipotonhêsas, dôdekatôi etei tou Kaisaros authis eis Rômên paraginetai.][391]

["Peter ... cometh even unto Britain. Yea, there abode he long, and many of the lawless folk did he draw to the Faith of Christ ... and many did he enlighten with the Word of Grace. Churches, too, did he set up, and ordained bishops and priests and deacons. And in the twelfth year of Caesar[392] came he again unto Rome."]

The 'Acta Sanctorum' also mentions this tradition (filtered through Simeon Metaphrastes), and adds that St. Peter was in Britain during Boadicea's rebellion, when he incurred great danger.

E. 6—The 'Synopsis Apostolorum,' ascribed to Dorotheus (A.D. 180), but really a 6th-century compilation, gives us yet another Apostolic preacher, St. Simon Zelotes. This is probably due to a mere confusion between Μαβριτανία [Mabritania] [Mauretania] and Βρεταννία [Bretannia]. But it is impossible to deny that the Princes of the Apostles *may* both have visited Britain, nor indeed is there anything essentially improbable in their doing so. We know that Britain was an object of special interest at Rome during the period of the Conquest, and it would be quite likely that the idea of simultaneously conquering this new Roman dominion for Christ should suggest itself to the two Apostles so specially connected with the Roman Church.[393]

E. 7.—But while we may *possibly* accept this legend, it is otherwise with the famous and beautiful story which ascribes the foundation of our earliest church at Glastonbury to the pilgrimage of St. Joseph of Arimathaea, whose staff, while he rested on Weary-all Hill, took root, and became the famous winter thorn, which

"Blossoms at Christmas, mindful of our Lord,"[394]

and who, accordingly, set up, hard by, a little church of wattle to be the centre of local Christianity.

E. 8.—Such was the tale which accounted for the fact that this humble edifice developed into the stateliest sanctuary of all Britain. We first find it, in its final shape, in Geoffrey of Monmouth (1150); but already in the 10th century the special sanctity of the shrine was ascribed to a supernatural origin,[395] as a contemporary Life of St. Dunstan assures us; and it is declared, in an undisputed Charter of Edgar, to be "the first church in the Kingdom built by the disciples of Christ." But no earlier reference is known; for the passages cited from Gildas and Melkinus are quite untrustworthy. So striking a phenomenon as the winter thorn would be certain to become an object of heathen devotion;[396] and, as usual, the early preachers would Christianize the local cult, as they Christianized the Druidical figment of a Holy Cup (perhaps also local in its origin), into the sublime mysticism of the Sangreal legend, connected likewise with Joseph of Arimathaea.[397]

E. 9.—That the original church of Glaston was really of wattle is more than probable, for the remains of British buildings thus constructed have been found abundantly in the neighbouring peat. The Arimathaean theory of its consecration became so generally accepted that at the Council of Constance (1419) precedence was actually accorded to our Bishops as representing the senior Church of Christendom. But the oldest variant of the legend says nothing about Arimathaea, but speaks only of an undetermined "Joseph" as the leader [decurio][398] of twelve missionary comrades who with him settled down at Glastonbury. And this may well be true. Such bands (as we see in the Life of Columba) were the regular system in Celtic mission work, and survived in that of the Preaching Friars:

"For thirteen is a Covent, as I guess."[399]

E. 10.—And though such high authorities as Mr. Haddan have come to the conclusion that Christianity in Britain was confined to a small minority even amongst the Roman inhabitants of the island, and almost vanished with them, yet the catena of references to British converts can scarcely be thus set aside. They begin in Apostolic times and in special connection with St. Paul. Martial tells us of a British princess named Claudia Rufina[400] (very probably the daughter of that Claudius Cogidubnus whom we meet in Tacitus as at once a British King and an Imperial Legate),[2] whose beauty and wit made no little sensation in Rome; whither she had doubtless been sent at once for education and as a hostage for her father's fidelity. And one of the most beautiful of his Epigrams speaks of the marriage of this foreigner to a Roman of high family named Pudens, belonging to the Gens Aemilia (of which the Pauline family formed a part):

> "Claudia, Rufe, meo nubet peregrina Pudenti,
> Macte esto taedis, O Hymenaee, suis.
> Diligat illa senem quondam; sed et ipsa marito,
> Tunc quoque cum fuerit, non videatur anus."[401]

> [To RUFUS.
> Claudia, from far-off climes, my Pudens weds:
> With choicest bliss, O Hymen, crown their heads!
> May she still love her spouse when gray and old,
> He in her age unfaded charms behold.]

It may have been in consequence of this marriage that Pudens joined with Claudius Cogidubnus in setting up the Imperial Temple at Chichester.[402] And the fact that Claudia was an adopted member of the

Rufine family shows that she was connected with the Gens Pomponia to which this family belonged.

E. 11.—Now Aulus Plautius, the conqueror of Britain, had married a Pomponia, who in A.D. 57 was accused of practising an illicit religion, and, though pronounced guiltless by her husband (to whose domestic tribunal she was left, as Roman Law permitted), passed the rest of her life in retirement.[403] When we read of an illicit religion in connection with Britain, our first thought is, naturally, that Druidism is intended.[404] But there are strong reasons for supposing that Pomponia was actually a Christian. The names of her family are found in one of the earliest Christian catacombs in Rome, that of Calixtus; and that Christianity had its converts in very high quarters we know from the case of Clemens and Domitilla, closely related to the Imperial throne.

E. 12.—Turning next to St. Paul's Second Epistle to Timothy, we find, in close connection, the names of Pudens and Claudia (along with that of the future Pope Linus) amongst the salutations from Roman Christians. And recent excavations have established the fact that the house of Pudens was used for Christian worship at this date, and is now represented by the church known as St. Pudentiana.[405] That this should have been so proves that this Pudens was no slave going under his master's name (as was sometimes done), but a man of good position in Rome. Short of actual proof it would be hard to imagine a series of evidences more morally convincing that the Pudens and Claudia of Martial are the Pudens and Claudia of St. Paul, and that they, as well as Pomponia, were Christians. Whether, then, St. Paul did or did not actually visit Britain, the earliest British Christianity is, at least, closely connected with his name.

E. 13.—Neither legendary nor historical sources tell us of any further development of British Christianity till the latter days of the 2nd century. Then, however, it had become sufficiently widespread to furnish a common-place for ecclesiastical declamation on the all-conquering influence of the Gospel. Both Tertullian and Origen[406] thus use it. The former numbers in his catalogue of believing countries even the districts of Britain beyond the Roman pale, *Britannorum inaccessa Romanis loca, Christo vero subdita*[407]. And in this lies the interest of his reference, as pointing to the native rather than the Roman element being the predominant factor in the British Church. For just at this period comes in the legend preserved by Bede,[408] that a mission was sent to Britain by Pope Eleutherius[409] in response to an appeal from "Lucius Britanniae Rex." The story, which Bede probably got from the 'Catalogus Pontificum,'[410] may be apocryphal; but it would never have been invented had British Christianity been found merely or mainly in the Roman veneer of the population. Modern criticism finds in it this kernel of truth, that the persecution which gave the Gallican Church the martyrs of Lyons, also sent her scattered refugees as missionaries into the less dangerous regions of Britain;—those remoter parts, in especial, where even the long arm of the Imperial Government could not reach them.

E. 14.—The Picts, however, as a nation, remained savage heathens even to the 7th century, and the bulk of our Christian population must have been within the Roman pale; but little vexed, it would seem, by persecution, till it came into conflict with the thorough-going Imperialism of Diocletian.[411] Its martyrs were then numbered, according to Gildas, by thousands, according to Bede by hundreds; and their chief, St. Alban, at least, is a fairly established historical entity.[412] Nor is there any reason to doubt that after Constantine South Britain was as fully Christian as any country in Europe. In the earliest days of his reign (A.D. 314) we find three bishops,[413] together with a priest and a deacon, representing[414] the British Church at the Council of Arles (which, amongst other things, condemned the marriage of the "innocent divorcee"[415]). And the same number figure in the Council of Ariminum (360), as the only prelates (out of the 400) who deigned to accept from the Emperor the expenses of their journey and attendance.

E. 15.—This Council was called by Constantius II. in the semi-Arian interest, and not allowed to break up till after repudiating the Nicene formula. But the lapse was only for a moment. Before the decade was out Athanasius could write of Britain as notoriously orthodox,[416] and before the century closes we have frequent references to our island as a fully Christian and Catholic land. Chrysostom speaks of its churches and its altars and "the power of the Word" in its pulpits,[417] of its diligent study of Scripture and Catholic doctrine,[418] of its acceptance of Catholic discipline,[419] of its use of Catholic formulae: "Whithersoever thou goest," he says, "throughout the whole world, be it to India, to Africa, or to Britain, thou wilt find *In the beginning was the Word*."[420] Jerome, in turn, tells of British pilgrimages to Jerusalem[421] and to Rome;[422] and, in his famous passage on the world-wide Communion of the Roman See, mentions Britain by name: "Nec altera Romanae Urbis Ecclesia, altera totius orbis existimanda est. Et Galliae, et Britanniae, et Africa, et Persis, et Oriens, et Indio, et omnes barbarae nationes, unum Christum adorant, unam observant regulam veritatis."[423]

["Neither is the Church of the City of Rome to be held one, and that of the whole world another. Both Gaul and Britain and Africa and Persia and the East and India, and all the barbarian nations, adore one Christ, observe one Rule of Truth."]

SECTION F.

British Missionaries—Ninias—Patrick—Beatus—Heresiarchs—Pelagius Fastidius—Pelagianism stamped out by Germanus—The Alleluia Battle— Romano-British churches—Why so seldom found—Conclusion.

F. 1.—The fruits of all this vigorous Christian life soon showed themselves in the Church of Britain by the evolution of noteworthy individual Christians. First in order comes Ninias, the Apostle of the Southern Picts, commissioned to the work, after years of training at Rome, by Pope Siricius (A.D. 394), and fired by the example of St. Martin, the great prelate of Gaul. To this saint (or, to speak more exactly, under his invocation) Ninias, on hearing of his death in A.D. 400, dedicated his newly-built church at Whithern[424] in Galloway, the earliest recorded example of this kind of dedication in Britain.[425] Galloway may have been the native home of Ninias, and was certainly the head-quarters of his ministry.

F. 2.—The work of Ninias amongst the Picts was followed in the next generation by the more abiding work of St. Patrick amongst the Scots of Ireland. Nay, even the Continent was indebted to British piety; though few British visitors to the Swiss Oberland remember that the Christianity they see around them is due to the zeal of a British Mission. Yet there seems no solid reason for doubting that so it is. Somewhere about the time of St. Patrick, two British priests, Beatus and Justus, entered the district by the Brunig Pass, and set up their first church at Einigen, near Thun. There Justus abode as the settled Missioner of the neighbourhood, while Beatus made his home in the ivy-clad cave above the lake which still bears his name,[426] sailing up and down with the Gospel message, and evangelizing the valleys and uplands now so familiar to his fellow-countrymen—Grindelwald, Lauterbrunnen, Mürren, Kandersteg.

F. 3.—And while the light of the Gospel was thus spreading on every side from our land, Britain was also becoming all too famous as the nurse of error. The British Pelagius,[427] who erred concerning the doctrine of free-will, grew to be a heresiarch of the first order;[428] and his follower Fastidius, or Faustus, the saintly Abbot of Lerins in the Hyères, the friend of Sidonius Apollinaris,[429] was, in his day, only less renowned. He asserted the materiality of the soul. Both were able writers; and Pelagius was the first to adopt the plan of promulgating his heresies not as his own, but as the tenets of supposititious individuals of his acquaintance.

F. 4.—Pelagianism spread so widely in Britain that the Catholics implored for aid from over-sea. St. Germanus of Auxerre, and St. Lupus, Bishop of Troyes (whose sanctity had disarmed the ferocity even of Attila), came[430] accordingly (in 429) and vindicated the faith in a synod held at Verulam so successfully that the neighbouring shrine of St. Alban was the scene of a special service of thanksgiving. In a second Mission, fifteen years later, Germanus set the seal to his work, stamping out throughout all the land both this new heresy and such remains of heathenism as were still to be found in Southern Britain. While thus engaged on the Border he found his work endangered by a raiding host of Picts or Saxons, or both. The Saint, who had been a military chieftain in his youth, promptly took the field at the head of his flock, many of whom were but newly baptized. It was Easter Eve, and he took advantage of the sacred ceremonies of that holy season, which were then actually performed by night. From the New Fire, the "Lumen Christi," was kindled a line of beacons along the Christian lines, and when Germanus intoned the threefold Easter Alleluia, the familiar strain was echoed from lip to lip throughout the host. Stricken with panic at the sudden outburst of light and song, the enemy, without a blow, broke and fled.[431]

F. 5.—This story, as told by Constantius, and confirmed by both Nennius and Bede, incidentally furnishes us with something of a key to the main difficulty in accepting the widely-spread Romano-British Christianity to which the foregoing citations testify. What, it is asked, has become of all the Romano-British churches? Why are no traces of them found amongst the abundant Roman remains all over the land? That they were the special objects of destruction at the Saxon invasion we learn from Gildas. But this does not account for their very foundations having disappeared; yet at Silchester[432] alone have modern excavations unearthed any even approximately certain example of them. Where are all the rest?

F. 6.—The question is partly answered when we read that the soldiers of Germanus had erected in their camp a church of wattle, and that such was the usual material of which, even as late as 446, British churches were built (as at Glastonbury). Seldom indeed would such leave any trace behind them; and thus the country churches of Roman Britain would be sought in vain by excavators. In the towns, however, stone or brick would assuredly be used, and to account for the paucity of ecclesiastical ruins three answers may be suggested.

F. 7.—First, the number of continuously unoccupied Romano-British cities is very small indeed. Except at Silchester, Anderida, and Uriconium, almost every one has become an English town. But when this took place early in the English settlement of the land, the ruins of the Romano-British churches would still be clearly traceable at the conversion of the English, and would be rebuilt (as St. Martin's at Canterbury was in all probability rebuilt)[433] for the use of English Christianity, the old material[434] being worked up into the new edifices. It is probable that many of our churches thus stand on the very spot where the Romano-British churches stood of old. But this very fact would obliterate the remains of these churches.

F. 8.—Secondly, it is very possible that many of the heathen temples may, after the edict of Theodosius (A.D. 392), have been turned into churches (like the Pantheon at Rome), so that *their* remains may mark ecclesiastical sites. There are reasons for believing that in various places, such as St. Paul's, London, St. Peter's, Cambridge, and St. Mary's, Ribchester, Christian worship did actually thus succeed Pagan on the same site.

F. 9.—Thirdly, as Lanciani points out, the earliest Christian churches were simply the ordinary dwelling-houses of such wealthier converts as were willing to permit meetings for worship beneath their roof, which in time became formally consecrated to that purpose. Such a dwelling-house usually consisted of an oblong central hall, with a pillared colonnade, opening into a roofed cloister or peristyle on either side, at one end into a smaller guest-room [*tablinum*], at the other into the porch of entry. The whole was arranged thus:

```
          Small
          Guest
          Room.
P                           P
e                           e
r                           r
i         Central Hall,     i
s          with pillars     s
t         on each side      t
y        (often roofless).  y
l              l
e                           e
          Porch
           of
          Entry.
```

It will be readily seen that we have here a building on the lines of an ordinary church. The small original congregation would meet, like other guests, in the reception-room. As numbers increased, the hall and adjoining cloisters would have to be used (the former being roofed in); the reception-room being reserved for the most honoured members, and ultimately becoming the chancel of a fully-developed church, with nave and aisles complete.[435] It *may* be, therefore, that some of the Roman villas found in Britain were really churches.[436]

F. 10.—This, however, is a less probable explanation of the absence of ecclesiastical remains; and the large majority of Romano-British church sites are, as I believe, still in actual use amongst us for their original purpose. And it may be considered as fairly proved, that before Britain was cut off from the Empire the Romano-British Church had a rite[437] and a vigorous corporate life of its own, which the wave of heathen invasion could not wholly submerge. It lived on, shattered, perhaps, and disorganized, but not utterly crushed, to be strengthened in due time by a closer union with its parent stem, through the Mission of Augustine, to feel the reflex glow of its own missionary efforts in the fervour of Columba and his followers,[438] and, finally, to form an integral part of that Ecclesia Anglicana whose influence knit our country into one, and inspired the Great Charter of our constitutional liberties.[439] Her faith and her freedom are the abiding debt which Britain owes to her connection with Rome.

* * * * *

FOOTNOTES

1. Published by the Record Office, 1848.
2. Published by the Royal Academy of Berlin. Vol. VII. contains the Romano-British Inscriptions.
3. His later books only survive in the epitome of Xiphilinus, a Byzantine writer of the 13th century.
4. See p. 171.
5. See p. 256.
6. In the British (?) village near Glastonbury the bases of shed antlers are found hafted for mallets.
7. This name is simply given for archaeological convenience, to indicate that these aborigines were non-Aryan, and perhaps of Turanian affinity.
8. Skeat, however, traces "ogre" (the Spanish "ogro") to the Latin *Orcus*.
9. The latest excavations (1902) prove Stonehenge to be a Neolithic erection. No metal was found, but quantities of flint implements, broken in the arduous task of dressing the great Sarsen monoliths. The process seems to have been that still used for granite, viz. to cut parallel channels on the rough surface, and then break and rub down the ridges between. This was done by the use of conical lumps of Sarsen stone, weighing from 20 to 60 lbs., several of which were discovered bearing traces of usage, both in pounding and rubbing. The monoliths examined were found to be thus tooled accurately down to the very bottom, 8 or 9 feet below ground. At Avebury the stones are not dressed.

10. *Sarsen* is the same word as *Saracen*, which in mediaeval English simply means *foreign* (though originally derived from the Arabic *sharq* = Eastern). Whence the stones came is still disputed. They *may* have been boulders deposited in the district by the ice-drift of the Glacial Epoch.

11. Professor Rhys assigns 600 B.C. as the approximate date of the first Gadhelic arrivals, and 200 B.C. as that of the first Brythonic.

12. Whether or no this word is (as some authorities hold) derived from the Welsh *Prutinach* (=Picts) rather than from the Brythons, it must have reached Aristotle through Brythonic channels, for the Gadhelic form is *Cruitanach*.

13. A certain amount of British folk-lore was brought back to Greece, according to Plutarch ('De defect. orac.' 2), by the geographer Demetrias of Tarsus about this time. He refers to the cavern of sleeping heroes, so familiar in our mediaeval legends.

14. The word is said to be derived from the root *kâsh*, "shine." Some authorities, however, maintain that it came into Sanscrit from the Greek.

15. 'Hist.' III. 112.

16. See p. 48.

17. For a full notice of Pytheas see Elton, 'Origins of English History,' pp. 13-75. See also Tozer's 'Ancient Geography,' chap. viii.

18. Posidonius of Rhodes, the tutor of Cicero, visited Britain about 100 B.C., and wrote a History of his travels in fifty volumes, only known to us by extracts in Strabo (iii. 217, iv. 287, vii. 293), Diodorus Siculus (v. 28, 30), Athenaeus, and others. See Bake's 'Posidonius' (Leyden, 1810).

19. The ingots of bronze found in the recent [1900] excavations at Gnossus, in Crete, which date approximately from 2000 B.C., are of this shape. Presumably the Britons learnt it from Phoenician sources.

20. *Saxon* coracles are spoken of even in the 5th century A.D. See p. 245.

21. 'Coins of the Ancient Britons,' p. 24.

22. This familiar feature of our climate is often touched on by classical authors. Minucius Felix (A.D. 210) is observant enough to connect it with our warm seas, "its compensation," due to the Gulf Stream.

23. 'Nat. Hist.' xviii. 18.

24. *Ibid.* xvii. 4.

25. Solinus (A.D. 80) adds that bees, like snakes, were unknown in Ireland, and states that bees will even desert a hive if Irish earth be brought near it!

26. Matthew Martin, 'Western Isles,' published 1673. Quoted by Elton ('Origins of English Hist.,' p. 16), who gives Martin's date as 1703.

27. Strabo, iv. 277. The word *basket* is itself of Celtic origin, and passed into Latin as it has passed into English. Martial ('Epig.' xiv. 299) says: "Barbara de pictis veni *bascauda* Britannis." Strabo wrote shortly before, Martial shortly after, the Roman Conquest of Britain.

28. One of these primitive mortars, a rudely-hollowed block of oolite, with a flint pestle weighing about 6 lbs., was found near Cambridge in 1885.

29. Diod. Siculus, 'Hist.' v. 21.

30. 'British Barrows,' p. 750.

31. 'Geog.' IV.

32. 'Legend of Montrose,' ch. xxii.

33. Diod. Sic. v. 30: "Saga crebris tessellis florum instar distincta." This *sagum* was obviously a tartan plaid such as are now in use. The kilt, however, was not worn. It is indeed a comparatively quite modern adaptation of the belted plaid. Ancient Britons wore trousers, drawn tight above the ankles, after the fashion still current amongst agricultural labourers. They were already called "breeches." Martial (Ep. x. 22) satirizes a life "as loose as the old breeches of a British pauper."

34. Pliny, 'Nat. Hist.' viii. 48.
35. *Id.* xxviii. 2. Fashions about hair seem to have changed as rapidly amongst Britons (throughout the whole period of this work) as in later times. The hair was sometimes worn short, sometimes long, sometimes strained back from the forehead; sometimes moustaches were in vogue, sometimes a clean shave, more rarely a full beard; but whiskers were quite unknown.
36. Tozer ('Ancient Geog.' p. 164) states that amber is also exported from the islands fringing the west coast of Schleswig, and considers that these rather than the Baltic shores were the "Amber Islands" of Pytheas.
37. 'Nat. Hist.' xxxvii. 1.
38. See p. 128.
39. A lump weighing nearly 12 lbs. was dredged up off Lowestoft in 1902.
40. A.D. 50.
41. Seneca speaks of the blue shields of the Yorkshire Brigantes.
42. See Elton, 'Origins of English History,' p. 116.
43. Thurnam, 'British Barrows' (Archaeol. xliii. 474).
44. Propertius, iv. 3, 7.
45. 'Celtic Britain,' p. 40.
46. This seems the least difficult explanation of this strange name. An alternative theory is that it = *Cenomanni* (a Gallic tribe-name also found in Lombardy). But with this name (which must have been well known to Caesar) we never again meet in Britain. And it is hard to believe that he would not mention a clan so important and so near the sphere of his campaign as the Iceni.
47. See p. 109.
48. These tribes are described by Vitruvius, at the Christian era, as of huge stature, fair, and red-haired. Skeletons of this race, over six feet in height, have been discovered in Yorkshire buried in "monoxylic"

coffins; i.e. each formed of the hollowed trunk of an oak tree. See Elton's 'Origins,' p. 168.

49. This correspondence, however, is wholly an antiquarian guess, and rests on no evidence. It is first found in the forged chronicle of "Richard of Cirencester." The *names* are genuine, being found in the 'Notitia,' though dating only from the time of Diocletian (A.D. 296). But, on our theory, the same administrative divisions must have existed all along. See p. 225.

50. General Pitt Rivers, however, in his 'Excavations in Cranborne Chase' (vol. ii. p. 237), proves that the ancient water level in the chalk was fifty feet higher than at present, presumably owing to the greater forest area. "Dew ponds" may also have existed in these camps. But these can scarcely have provided any large supply of water.

51. The word is commonly supposed to represent a Celtic form *Mai-dun*. But this is not unquestionable.

52. 'De Bello Gall.' vi. 13.

53. 'De Bell. Gall.' vi. 14.

54. Jerome ('Quaest. in Gen.' ii.) says that Varro, Phlegon, and all learned authors testify to the spread of Greek [at the Christian era] "from Taurus to Britain." And Solinus (A.D. 80) tells of a Greek inscription in Caledonia, "ara Graecis literis scripta"—as a proof that Ulysses (!) had wandered thither (Solinus, 'Polyhistoria,' c. 22). See p. 248.

55. 'De Bell, Gall.' vi. 16.

56. 'Hist.' v. 31.

57. 'Celtic Britain,' p. 69.

58. 'Nat. Hist.' xvi. 95.

59. So Caesar, 'De Bell. Gall.' vi. 17.

60. Pliny, 'Nat. Hist.' xxiv. 62. Linnaeus has taken *selago* as his name for club-moss, but Pliny here compares the herb to *savin*, which grows to the height of several feet. *Samolum* is water-pimpernel in

the Linnaean classification. Others identify it with the *pasch-flower*, which, however, is far from being a marsh plant.

61. Suetonius (A.D. 110), 'De xii. Caes.' v. 25.

62. Pliny, 'Nat. Hist.' xxx. 3.

63. Tacitus, 'Annals,' xiv. 30. See p. 154.

64. Pliny, 'Nat. Hist.' xxix. 12.

65. See Brand, 'Popular Antiquities,' under *Ovum Anguinum*. He adds that *Glune* is the Irish for glass.

66. Lampridius, in his life of Alexander Severus, tells us of a "Druid" sorceress who warned the Emperor of his approaching doom. Another such "Druidess" is said to have foretold Diocletian's rise. See Coulanges, '*Comme le Druidisme a disparu,*' in the *Revue Celtique*, iv. 37.

67. See Professor Rhys, 'Celtic Britain,' p. 70. The Professor's view that the "schismatical" tonsure of the Celtic clergy, which caused such a stir during the evangelization of England, was a Druidical survival, does not, however, seem probable in face of the very pronounced antagonism between those clergy and the Druids. That tonsure was indeed ascribed by its Roman denouncers to Simon Magus [see above], but this is scarcely a sufficient foundation for the theory.

68. They may very possibly have been connected with the Veneti of Venice at the other extremity of "the Gauls."

69. See p. 37.

70. Caesar, 'Bell. Gall.' iii. 9, 13.

71. Elton, 'Origins of English Hist.,' p. 237. Though less massive, these vessels are built much as the Venetian. But it is just as probable they may really be "picts." See p. 232.

72. This opening of Britain to continental influences may perhaps account for Posidonius having been able to make so thorough a survey of the islands. See p. 36.

73. Elton ('Origins of English Hist.') conjectures that these tribes did not migrate to Britain till after Caesar's day. But there is no evidence for this, and my view seems better to explain the situation.

74. Solinus (A.D. 80) says of Britain, "*alterius orbis nomen mereretur.*" This passage is probably the origin of the Pope's well-known reference to St. Anselm, when Archbishop of Canterbury, as "*quasi alterius orbis antistes.*"

75. A Roman legion at this date comprised ten "cohorts," *i.e.* some six thousand heavy-armed infantry, besides a small light-armed contingent, and an attached squadron of three hundred cavalry. Each of Caesar's transports must thus have carried from one hundred and fifty to two hundred men, and at this rate the eighteen cavalry vessels (reckoning a horse as equivalent to five men, the usual proportion for purposes of military transport) would suffice for his two squadrons.

76. An ancient ship could not sail within eight points of the wind (see Smith, 'Voyage of St. Paul'). Thus a S.W. breeze, while permitting Caesar to leave Boulogne, would effectually prevent these vessels from working out of Ambleteuse.

77. Hence the name Dubris = "the rivers."

78. The claims of Richborough [Ritupis] to be Caesar's actual landing-place have been advocated by Archdeacon Baddeley, Mr. G. Bowker, and others. But it is almost impossible to make this place square with Caesar's narrative.

79. This was four days before the full moon, so that the tide would be high at Dover about 6 p.m.

80. The "lofty promontory" rounded is specially noticed by Dio Cassius.

81. The principle of the balista that of the sling, of the catapult that of the bow. Ammianus Marcellinus (xv. 12) speaks of "the snowy arms" of the Celtic women dealing blows "like the stroke of a catapult."

82. Valerius Maximus (A.D. 30) has recorded one such act of daring on the part of a soldier named Scaeva, who with four comrades held an isolated rock against all comers till he alone was left, when he plunged into the sea and swam off, with the loss of his shield. In spite of this disgrace Caesar that evening promoted him on the field. The story has a suspicious number of variants, but off Deal there *is* such a patch of rocks, locally called the Malms; so that it may possibly be true ('Memorabilia,' III. 2, 23).

83. Valerius Maximus (A.D. 30) states that the Romans landed on a *falling* tide, which cannot be reconciled with Caesar's own narrative (see p. 88). The idea may have originated in the fact that it was probably the approaching turn of the tide which forced him to land at Deal. He could not have reached Richborough before the ebb began.

84. Every soldier was four feet from his nearest neighbour to give scope for effective sword-play. No other troops in history have ever had the morale thus to fight at close quarters.

85. See Plutarch, 'De placitis philosophorum.'

86. Each chariot may have carried six or seven men, like those of the Indian King Porus. See Dodge, 'Alexander,' p. 554.

87. Pomponius Mela ('De Situ Orbis,' I) tells us that by his date (50 A.D.) it had come in: "Covinos vocant, quorum falcatis axîbus utuntur."

88. It is thus represented by Giraldus Cambrensis, who gives us the story of Caesar's campaigns from the British point of view, as it survived (of course with gross exaggerations) in the Cymric legends of his day.

89. Lucan, the last champion of anti-Caesarism, sung, two generations after its overthrow, the praises and the dirge of the Oligarchy.

90. See my 'Alfred in the Chroniclers,' p. 44.

91. 'Ad Treb.' Ep. VI.

92. 'Ad Treb.' Ep. VII.

93. Ep. 10.

94. Ep. 16.
95. Ep. 17.
96. IV. 15.
97. III. 1.
98. II. 16.
99. II. 15.
100. III. 10.
101. Wace ('Roman de Ron,' 11,567) gives 696 as the exact total.
102. 'Strategemata,' viii. 23.
103. This was probably not Deal, which had not proved a satisfactory station, but Richborough, where the Wantsum, then a broad arm of the sea between Kent and Thanet, provided an excellent harbour for a large fleet. It was, moreover, the regular emporium of the tin trade (see p. 36), and a British trackway thus led to it.
104. Otherwise *Cadwallon*, which, according to Professor Rhys, signifies War King, and may possibly have been a title rather than a personal name. But it remained in use as the latter for many centuries of British history.
105. Vine, 'Caesar in Kent,' p. 171. The spot is "in Bourne Park, not far from the road leading up to Bridge Hill."
106. See p. 244.
107. See II. G. 8. The tradition of this sentiment long survived. Hegesippus (A.D. 150) says: "Britanni . . . quidesse servitus ignorabant; soli sibi nati, semper sibi liberi" ('De Bello Judiaco,' II. 9).
108. Polyaenus (A.D. 180) in his 'Strategemata' (viii. 23) ascribes their panic to Caesar's elephant. See p. 107.
109. At Ilerda. See Dodge, 'Caesar,' xxviii.
110. Frontinus (A.D. 90), 'Strategemata II.' xiii. II.
111. Coins of all three bear the words COMMI. F. (*Commii Filius*), but Verica alone calls himself REX. Those of Eppillus were struck at Calleva (Silchester?).
112. See p. 54.

113. This is the spelling adopted by Suetonius.

114. The lion was already a specially British emblem. Ptolemy ('de Judiciis II.' 3) ascribes the special courage of Britons to the fact that they are astrologically influenced by Leo and Mars. It is interesting to remember that our success in the Crimean War was prognosticated from Mars being in Leo at its commencement (March 1854). Tennyson, in 'Maud,' has referred to this—"And pointed to Mars, As he hung like a ruddy shield on the Lion's breast."

115. See p. 38.

116. The site of this town is quite unknown. Caesar mentions the Segontiaci amongst the clans of S.E. Britain.

117. In S.E. Essex, near Colchester. See p. 176.

118. See pp. 109, 122.

119. Aelian (A.D. 220), 'De Nat. Animal.' xv. 8.

120. Ελεφάντινα ψάλια καὶ, περιαυχένια, καὶ νιγγούρια καὶ ὑαλᾶ σκεύη ὑαλᾶ σκεύη, καὶ ῥῶπος τοίουτος [Elephantina psalia, kai periauchenia, kai lingouria kai huala skeuê, kai rhôpos toioutos]. Strabo is commonly supposed to mean that these were the *imports* from Gaul. But his words are quite ambiguous, and such of the articles he mentions as are found in Britain are clearly of native manufacture. British graves are fertile (see p. 48) in the "amber and glass ornaments" (the former being small roughly-shaped fragments pierced for threading, the latter coarse blue or green beads), and produce occasional armlets of narwhal ivory. Glass beads have been found (1898) in the British village near Glastonbury, and elsewhere.

121. Strabo, v. 278.

122. Propertius, II. 1. 73: Esseda caelatis siste Britanna jugis.

123. *Ibid.* II. 18. 23. See p. 47.

124. Virgil, 'Georg.' III. 24.

125. Virgil, 'Eccl.' I. 65; Horace, 'Od.' I. 21. 13, 35. 30, III. 5. 3; Tibullus, IV. 1. 147; Propertius, IV. 3. 7.

126. Suetonius, 'De XII. Caes.' IV. 19.

127. The lofty spur of the Chiltern Hills which overhangs the church of Ellsborough is traditionally the site of his tomb.

128. This whole episode is from 'Dio Cassius' (lib. xxxix. Section 50).

129. He places Cirencester in their territory, while both Bath and Winchester belonged to the Belgae. To secure Winchester, where they would be on the line of the tin-trade road (see p. 36), would be the first object of the Romans if they did land at Portsmouth. Their further steps would depend upon the disposition of the British armies advancing to meet them,—the final objective of the campaign being Camelodune, the capital of the sons of Cymbeline.

130. This is stated by both Geoffrey of Monmouth and Matthew of Westminster.

131. For three centuries this legion was quartered at Caerleon-upon-Usk, and the Twentieth at Chester. See Mommsen, 'Roman Provinces,' p. 174.

132. This was the honorary title of several legions; as there are several "Royal" regiments.

133. Tac, 'Hist.' III. 44.

134. The Flavian family was of very humble origin.

135. Bede, from Suetonius, tells us that Vespasian with his legion fought in Britain thirty-two battles and took twenty towns, besides subduing the Isle of Wight ('Sex. Aet.' A.D. 80).

136. If the Romans were advancing eastward from the Dobunian territory it may have been the Loddon. Mommsen cuts the knot in true German fashion by refusing to identify the Dobuni of Ptolemy with those of Dion, and placing the latter in Kent on his own sole authority. ('Roman Provinces,' p. 175.)

137. δυσδιέξοδα [dusdiexoda [138.See p. 139.]

139. 'Orosius,' VII. 5.

140. A victorious Roman general was commonly thus hailed by his troops after any signal victory. But by custom this could only be done once in the same campaign.
141. Suet. v. 21.
142. Dio Cassius, lx. 23. The boy, who was the child of Messalina, had previously been named *Germanicus*.
143. Suet. v. 28.
144. Suet. v. 21.
145. Tac., 'Ann.' xii. 56.
146. Dio Cassius, lx. 30.
147. Suet. v. 24.
148. Dio Cassius, lx. 30.
149. Eutropius, vii. 13.
150. Muratori, Thes. mcii. 6.
151. 'De XII. Caesaribus,' v. 28.
152. Dio Cassius, lx. 23.
153. See Haverfield in 'Authority and Archaeology,' p. 319
154. 'Laus Claudii' (Burmann, 'Anthol.' ii. 8).
155. See p. 152.
156. The inscription runs thus:
    NEPTVNO. ET. MINERVAE
        TEMPLVM
    pro SALVTE. DO *mus* DIVINAE
    ex AVCTORITATE. *Ti.* CLAVD
    Co GIDVBNI. R. LEGATI. AVG. IN. BRIT.
    Colle GIVM. FABRO. ET. QVI. IN. E.
    . . . . D.S.D. DONANTE. AREAM.
    Pud ENTE. PVDENTINI. FIL*iae*
    (The italics are almost certain restoration of illegible letters.)
157. See p. 256.
158. Claudia, the British Princess mentioned by Martial as making a distinguished Roman marriage, may very probably be his daughter.

159. See p. 130.
160. Thus in St. Luke ii. we find Cyrenius *Pro-praetor* (ἡγεμων [hêgemôn]) of Syria, but in Acts xviii. Gallio *Pro-consul* (ἀνθύπατος [hanthupatos]) of Achaia.
161. See p. 131.
162. See p. 170.
163. His reputation for strength, skill, and daring cost him his life a few years later, under Nero (Tac, 'Ann.' xvi. 15).
164. Pigs of lead have been found in Denbighshire stamped CANGI or DECANGI. Mr. Elton, however, locates the tribe in Somerset. Coins testify to Antedrigus, the Icenian, being somehow connected with this tribe.
165. A Roman "Colony" was a town peopled by citizens of Rome (old soldiers being preferred) sent out in the first instance to dominate the subject population amid whom they were settled. Such was Philippi.
166. Tacitus, 'Annals,' xii. 38.
167. The distinction of an actual triumph was reserved for Emperors alone.
168. Tacitus, 'Annals,' xii. 39.
169. See p. 239. Uriconium alone has as yet furnished inscriptions of the famous Fourteenth Legion, *"Victores Britannici."* (See p. 160.)
170. 'Ep. ad Atticum,' vi. 1.
171. See Dio Cassius, xii. 2.
172. The Procurator of a Province was the Imperial Finance Administrator. (See Haverfield, 'Authority and Archaeology,' p. 310.)
173. An inscription calls the place *Colonia Victricensis*.
174. Tacitus, 'Ann.' xiv. 32.
175. Demeter and Kore. M. Martin ('Hist. France,' i. 63) thinks there is here a confusion between the Greek Kore (Proserpine) and Koridwen, the White Fairy, the Celtic Goddess of the Moon and also (as amongst the Greeks) of maidenhood. But this is not proven.

176. The former is Strabo's variant of the name (which may possibly be connected with σεμνός [semnos]), the latter that of Dionysius Periegetes ('De Orbe,' 57). In Caesar we find a third form *Namnitae*, which Professor Rhys connects with the modern Nantes.

177. See p. 127.

178. As Agricola, his father-in-law, was actually with Suetonius, Tacitus had exceptional opportunities for knowing the truth.

179. Suetonius probably retreated southward when he left London, and reoccupied its ruins when the Britons, instead of following him, turned northwards to Verulam.

180. The Roman *pilum* was a casting spear with a heavy steel head, nine inches long.

181. Tac., 'Agricola,' c. 12.

182. That the well-known coins commemorating these victories and bearing the legend IVDAEA CAPTA are not infrequently found in Britain, indicates the special connection between Vespasian and our island. The great argument used by Titus and Agrippa to convince the Jews that even the walls of Jerusalem would fail to resist the onset of Romans was that no earthly rampart could compare with the ocean wall of Britain (Josephus, D.B.J., II. 16, vi, 6).

183. The spread of Latin oratory and literature in Britain is spoken of at this date by Juvenal (Sat. xv. 112), and Martial (Epig. xi. 3), who mentions that his own works were current here: "Dicitur et nostros cantare Britannia versus."

184. Mr. Haverfield suggests that Silchester may also be an Agricolan city (see p. 184).

185. Juvenal mentions these designs (II. 159):

"—Arma quidem ultra
Litora Juvernae promovimus, et modo captas
Orcadas, et minima contentos nocte Britannos" (i.e. those furthest north).

186. According to Dio Cassius this voyage of discovery was first made by some deserters ('Hist. Rom.' lxix. 20).

187. The little that is known of this rampart will be found in the next chapter (see p. 198).

188. Sallustius Lucullus, who succeeded Agricola as Pro-praetor, was slain by Domitian only for the invention of an improved lance, known by his name (as rifles now are called Mausers, etc.).

189. See p. 117.

190. All highways were made Royal Roads before the end of the 12th century, so that the course of the original four became matter of purely antiquarian interest.

191. Where it struck that sea is disputed, but Henry of Huntingdon's assertion that it ran straight from London to Chester seems the most probable.

192. The lines of these roads, if produced, strike the Thames not at London Bridge, but at the old "Horse Ferry" to Lambeth. This *may* point to an alternative (perhaps the very earliest) route.

193. Guest ('Origines Celticae') derives "Ermine" from A.S. *eorm*=fen, and "Watling" from the Welsh Gwyddel=Goidhel=Irish. The Ermine Street, however, nowhere touches the fenland; nor did any Gaelic population, so far as is known, abut upon the Watling Street, at any rate after the English Conquest. Verulam was sometimes called Watling-chester, probably as the first town on the road.

194. The distinction between "Street" and "Way" must not, however, be pressed, as is done by some writers. The Fosse Way is never called a Street, though its name [*fossa*] shows it to have been constructed as such; and the Icknield Way is frequently so called, though it was certainly a mere track—often a series of parallel tracks (*e.g.* at Kemble-in-the-Street in Oxfordshire)—as it mostly remains to this day.

195. This may still be seen in places; *e.g.* on the "Hardway" in Somerset and the "Maiden Way" in Cumberland. See Codrington, 'Roman Roads in Britain.'

196. Camden, however, speaks of a Saxon charter so designating it near Stilton ('Britannia,' II. 249).

197. The whole evidence on this confused subject is well set out by Mr. Codrington ('Roman Roads in Britain').

198. It is, however, possible that the latter is named from Ake-manchester, which is found as A.S. for Bath, to which it must have formed the chief route from the N. East.

199. See p. 144. Bradley, however, controverts this, pointing out that the pre-Norman authorities for the name only refer to Berkshire.

200. Thus Iter V. takes the traveller from London to Lincoln *viâ* Colchester, Cambridge, and Huntingdon, though the Ermine Street runs direct between the two. The 'Itinerary' is a Roadbook of the Empire, giving the stages on each route set forth, assigned by commentators to widely differing dates, from the 2nd century to the 5th. In my own view Caracalla is probably the Antoninus from whom it is called. But after Antoninus Pius (138 A.D.) the name was borne (or assumed) by almost every Emperor for a century and more.

201. See p. 237.

202. Ptolemy also marks, in his map of Britain, some fifty capes, rivers, etc., and the Ravenna list names over forty.

203. The longitude is reckoned from the "Fortunate Isles," the most western land known to Ptolemy, now the Canary Islands. Ferro, the westernmost of these, is still sometimes found as the Prime Meridian in German maps.

204. Thus the north supplies not only inscriptions relating to its own legion (the Sixth), but no fewer than 32 of the Second, and 22 of the Twentieth; while at London and Bath indications of all three are found.

205. The Latin word *castra*, originally meaning "camp," came (in Britain) to signify a fortified town, and was adopted into the various dialects of English as *caster, Chester,* or *cester;* the first being the distinctively N. Eastern, the last the S. Western form.

206. Amongst these, however, must be named the high authority of Professor Skeat. See 'Cambs. Place-Names.'

207. Pearson's 'Historical Maps of England' gives a complete list of these.

208. This industry flourished throughout the last half of the 19th century. The "coprolites" were phosphatic nodules found in the greensand and dug for use as manure.

209. These are of bronze, with closed ends, pitted for the needle as now, but of size for wearing upon the *thumb*.

210. There seems no valid reason for doubting that the horseshoes found associated with Roman pottery, etc., in the ashpits of the Cam valley, Dorchester, etc., are actually of Romano-British date. Gesner maintains that our method of shoeing horses was introduced by Vegetius under Valentinian II. The earlier shoes seem to have been rather such slippers as are now used by horses drawing mowing-machines on college lawns. They were sometimes of rope: *Solea sparta pes bovis induitur* (Columella), sometimes of iron: *Et supinam animam gravido derelinquere caeno Ferream ut solam tenaci in voragine mula* (Catullus, xvii. 25). Even gold was used: *Poppaea jumentis suis soleas ex auro induebat* (Suet., 'Nero,' xxx.). The Romano-British horseshoes are thin broad bands of iron, fastened on by three nails, and without heels. See also Beckmann's 'History of Inventions' (ed. Bohn).

211. This is true of the whole of Britain, even along the Wall, as a glance at the cases in the British Museum will show. There may be seen the most interesting relic of this class yet discovered, a bronze shield-boss, dredged out of the Tyne in 1893 [see 'Lapid. Sept.' p. 58], bearing the name of the owner, Junius Dubitatus, and his Centurion, Julius Magnus, of the Ninth Legion.

212. The wall of London is demonstrably later than the town, old material being found built into it. So is that of Silchester.
213. York was not three miles in circumference, Uriconium the same, Cirencester and Lincoln about two, Silchester and Bath somewhat smaller.
214. Roman milestones have been found in various places, amongst the latest and most interesting being one of Carausius discovered in 1895, at Carlisle. It had been reversed to substitute the name of Constantius (see p. 222.). It may be noted that the earliest of post-Roman date are those still existing on the road between Cambridge and London, set up in 1729.
215. See p. 117. When the existing bridge was built, Roman remains were found in the river-bed.
216. The Thames to the south, the Fleet to the west, and the Wall Brook to the east and north.
217. See p. 233. The city wall may well be due to him.
218. See p. 233.
219. On this functionary, see article by Domaszewski in the 'Rheinisches Review,' 1891. His appointment was part of the pacificatory system promoted by Agricola.
220. An *archigubernus* (master pilot) of this fleet left his property to one of his subordinates in trust for his infant son. The son died before coming of age, whereupon the estate was claimed by the next of kin, while the trustee contended that it had now passed to him absolutely. He was upheld by the Court. Another York decision established the principle that any money made by a slave belonged to his *bonâ fide* owner. And another settled that a *Decurio* (a functionary answering to a village Mayor in France) was responsible only for his own *Curia*.
221. Inscriptions of the Twentieth have been found here.
222. *Legra-ceaster*, the earliest known form of the name, signifies Camp-chester *(Legra = Laager)*. In Anglo-Saxon writings the name is often

216

applied to Chester. This, however, was *the* Chester, *par excellence*, as having remained so long unoccupied. In the days of Alfred it is still a "waste Chester" in the A.S. Chronicle. The word *Chester* is only associated with Roman fortifications in Southern Britain. But north of the wall, as Mr. Haverfield points out, we find it applied to earthworks which cannot possibly have ever been Roman. (See 'Antiquary' for 1895, p. 37.)

223. Bath was frequented by Romano-British society for its medicinal waters, as it has been since. The name *Aquae* (like the various *Aix* in Western Europe) records this fact. Bath was differentiated as *Aquae Solis*; the last word having less reference to Apollo the Healer, than to a local deity *Sul* or *Sulis*. Traces of an elaborate pump-room system, including baths and cisterns still retaining their leaden lining, have here been discovered; and even the stock-in-trade of one of the small shops, where, as now at such resorts, trinkets were sold to the visitors.(See 'Antiquary,' 1895, p. 201.)

224. Similar excavations are in progress at Caergwent, but, as yet, with less interesting results. Amongst the objects found is a money-box of pottery, with a slit for the coins. A theatre [?] is now (1903) being uncovered.

225. See II. F. 4; also Mr. Haverfield's articles in the 'Athenaeum' (115, Dec. 1894), and in the 'Antiquary' (1899, p. 71).

226. Mr. Haverfield notes ('Antiquary,' 1898, p. 235) that British basilicas are larger than those on the Continent, probably because more protection from weather was here necessary. Almost as large as this basilica must have been that at Lincoln, where sections of the curious multiple pillars (which perhaps suggested to St. Hugh the development from Norman to Gothic in English architecture) may be seen studding the concrete pavement of Ball Gate.

227. A plan of this "church" is given by Mr. Haverfield in the 'English Hist. Review,' July 1896.

228. An inspection of the Ordnance Map (1 in.) shows this clearly. It is the road called (near Andover) the *Port Way*.

229. See p. 46.

230. The water supply of Silchester seems to have been wholly derived from these wells, which are from 25 to 30 feet in depth, and were usually lined with wood. In one of them there were found (in 1900) stones of various fruit trees (cherry, plum, etc.), the introduction of which into Britain has long been attributed to the Romans, (See Earle, 'English Plant Names.') But this find is not beyond suspicion of being merely a mouse's hoard of recent date.

231. Roman refineries for extracting silver existed in the lead-mining districts both of the Mendips and of Derbyshire, which were worked continuously throughout the occupation. But the Silchester plant was adapted for dealing with far more refractory ores; for what purpose we cannot tell.

232. See paper by W. Gowland in Silchester Report (Society of Antiquaries) for 1899.

233. A glance at the maps issued by the Society of Antiquaries will show this. The massive rampart, forming an irregular hexagon, cuts off the corners of various blocks in the ground plan.

234. The well-known Cambridge jug of Messrs. Hattersley is a typical example.

235. "Samian" factories existed in Gaul.

236. See p. 43.

237. TI. CLAVDIVS CAESAR AVG. P.M. TRIB. P. VIIII. IMP, XVI. DE BRITAN. This was found at Wokey Hole, near Wells.

238. Haverfield, 'Ant.' p. 147.

239. See 'Corpus Inscript. Lat.' Vol. VII.

240. A specially interesting touch of this old country house life is to be seen in the Corinium Museum at Cirencester—a mural painting whereon has been scratched a squared word (the only known classical example of this amusement):

ROTAS
OPERA
TENET
AREPO
SATOR

241. The word *mansio*, however, at this period signified merely a posting-station on one or other of the great roads.

242. Selwood, Sherwood, Needwood, Charnwood, and Epping Forest are all shrunken relics of these wide-stretching woodlands, with which most of the hill ranges seem to have been clothed. See Pearson's 'Historical Maps of England.'

243. Classical authorities only speak of bears in Scotland. See P. 236.

244. Cyneget., I. 468.

245. *Ibid.* 69.

246. In II. Cons. Stilicho, III. 299: *Magnaque taurorum fracturae colla Britannae.*

247. 'Origins of English History,' p. 294.

248. A brooch found at Silchester also represents this dog.

249. Symmachus (A.D. 390) represents them as so fierce as to require iron kennels (Ep. II. 77).

250. Prudentius (contra Sab. 39): *Semifer, et Scoto sentit cane milite pejor.*

251. Proleg. to Jeremiah, lib. III.

252. Flavius Vopiscus (A.D. 300) tells us that vine-growing was also attempted, by special permission of the Emperor Probus.

253. The Lex Julia forbade the carrying of arms by civilians.

254. See Elton's 'Origins,' p. 347.

255. Proem, v.

256. See Fronto,'De Bello Parthico', I. 217. The latest known inscription relating to this Legion is of A.D. 109 [C.I.L. vii. 241].

257. Spartianus (A.D. 300), 'Hist. Rom.'

258. About a fifth of the known legionary inscriptions of Britain have been found in Scotland.

259. See p. 233.

260. At the Battle of the Standard, 1138.

261. That Hadrian and not Severus (by whose name it is often called) was the builder of the Wall as well as of the adjoining fortresses is proved by his inscriptions being found not only in them, but in the "mile-castles" [see C.I.L. vii. 660-663]. Out of the 14 known British inscriptions of this Emperor, 8 are on the Wall; out of the 57 of Severus, 3 only.

262. Hadrian divided the Province of Britain [see p. 142] into "Upper" and "Lower"; but by what boundary is wholly conjectural. All we know is that Dion Cassius [Xiph. lv.] places Chester and Caerleon in the former and York in the latter. The boundary *may* thus have been the line from Mersey to Humber; "Upper" meaning "nearer to Rome."

263. Neilson, 'Per Lineam Valli,' p.I.

264. See further pp. 203-212.

265. The figure has been supposed to represent Rome seated on Britain. But the shield is not the oblong buckler of the Romans, but a round barbaric target.

266. So Tacitus speaks of *"Submotis velut in aliam insulam hostibus"* by Agricola's rampart. And Pliny says, *"Alpes Germaniam ab Italia submovent."*

267. Corpus Inscript. Lat, vii. 1125.

268. Dio Cassius, lxxii. 8.

269. Aelius Lampridius, 'De Commodo,' c. 8.

270. Inscriptions in the Newcastle Museum show that bargemen from the Tigris were quartered on the Tyne.

271. Dio Cassius, lxxii. 9.

272. Julius Capitolinus, 'Pertinax,' c. 3.

273. Orosius, 'Hist' 17.

274. Herodian, 'Hist.' iii. 20.

275. Lucius Septimus Severus.

276. Herodian, 'Hist. III.' 46. He is a contemporary authority.

277. Also called Bassianus. His throne name was Marcus Aurelius Antoninus Pius.

278. Publius Septimus Geta Antoninus Pius.

279. Aelius Spartianus, 'Severus,' c. 23.

280. Dion Cassius, lxxvi. 12.

281. Severus gave as a *mot d'ordre* to his soldiers the "No quarter" proclamation of Agamemnon. ('Iliad,' vi. 57): τῶν μήτις κφύγοι αἰπὺν ὄλεθρον [ton mêtis hupekphugoi aipun olethron].

282. Dion Cassius, lxxvi. 12.

283. See p. 195.

284. Aurelius Victor (20) makes him (as Mommsen and others think) restore *Antonine's* rampart: "*vallum per* xxxii. *passuum millia a mari ad mare.*" But more probably xxxii. is a misreading for lxxii.

285. The very latest spade-work on the Wall (undertaken by Messrs. Haverfield and Bosanquet in 1901) shows that the original wall and ditch ran through the midst of the great fortresses of Chesters and Birdoswald, which are now astride, so to speak, of the Wall; pointing to the conclusion that Severus rebuilt and enlarged them. In various places along the Wall itself the stones bear traces of mortar on their exterior face, showing that they have been used in some earlier work.

286. This is the number *per lineam valli* given in the 'Notitia.' Only twelve have been certainly identified. They are commonly known as "stations."

287. Antiquaries have given these structures the name of "mile-castles." They are usually some fifty feet square.

288. The familiar name of "Wallsend" coals reminds us of this connection between the Tynemouth colliery district and the Wall's end.

289. So puzzling is the situation that high authorities on the subject are found to contend that the work was perfunctorily thrown up, in obedience to mistaken orders issued by the departmental stupidity

of the Roman War Office, that in reality it was never either needed or used, and was obsolete from the very outset. But this suggestion can scarcely be taken as more than an elaborate confession of inability to solve the *nodus*.

290. It should be noted that the "Vallum" is no regular Roman *muris caespitius* like the Rampart of Antoninus, though traces have been found here and there along the line of some intention to construct such a work (see 'Antiquary,' 1899, p. 71).

291. In more than one place the line of fortification swerves from its course to sweep round a station.

292. Near Cilurnum the fosse was used as a receptacle for shooting the rubbish of the station, and contains Roman pottery of quite early date.

293. See p. 233.

294. See p. 232.

295. The existing military road along the line of the Wall does not follow the track of its Roman predecessor. It was constructed after the rebellion of 1745, when the Scots were able to invade England by Carlisle before our very superior forces at Newcastle could get across the pathless waste between to intercept them.

296. Mithraism is first heard of in the 2nd century A.D., as an eccentric cult having many of the features of Christianity, especially the sense of Sin and the doctrine that the vicarious blood-shedding essential to remission must be connected with a New Baptismal Birth unto Righteousness. The Mithraists carried out this idea by the highly realistic ceremonies of the *Taurobolium*; the penitent neophyte standing beneath a grating on which the victim was slain, and thus being literally bathed in the atoning blood, afterwards being considered as born again [*renatus*]. It thus evolved a real and heartfelt devotion to the Supreme Being, whom, however (unlike Christianity), it was willing to worship under the names of the old Pagan Deities; frequently combining their various attributes in joint

Personalities of unlimited complexity. One figure has the head of Jupiter, the rays of Phoebus, and the trident of Neptune; another is furnished with the wings of Cupid, the wand of Mercury, the club of Hercules, and the spear of Mars; and so forth. Mithraism thus escaped the persecution which the essential exclusiveness of their Faith drew down upon Christians; gradually transforming by its deeper spirituality the more frigid cults of earlier Paganism, and making them its own. The little band of truly noble men and women who in the latter half of the 4th century made the last stand against the triumph of Christianity over the Roman world were almost all Mithraists. For a good sketch of this interesting development see Dill, 'Roman Society in the Last Century of the Western Empire.'

297. Of the 1200 in the 'Corpus Inscript. Lat.' (vol. vii.), 500 are in the section *Per Lineam Valli*.

298. 'Corpus Inscript. Lat.' vol. vii., No. 759.

299. Some authorities consider him to have been her own son.

300. See p. 126.

301. The Gelt is a small tributary joining the Irthing shortly before the latter falls into the Eden.

302. Polybius (vi. 24) tells us that in the Roman army of his day a *vexillum* or *manipulum* consisted of 200 men under two centurions, each of whom had his *optio*. Vegetius (II. 1) confines the word *vexillatio* to the cavalry, but gives no clue as to its strength.

303. On this inscription see Huebner, C.I.L. vii. 1. A drawing will be found in Bruce's 'Handbook to the Wall' (ed. 1895), p. 23.

304. The name *Cilurnum* may be connected with this wealth of water. In modern Welsh *celurn* = caldron.

305. "All hast thou won, all hast thou been. Now be God the winner." (These final words are equivocal, in both Latin and English. They might signify, "Now let God be your conqueror," and "Now, thou conqueror, be God," *i. e.* "die"; for a Roman Emperor was deified at his decease.) Spartianus, 'De Severo,' 22.

306. Aelius Spartianus, 'Severus,' c. 22.
307. See p. 46.
308. Dio Cassius, lxxvi. 16.
309. *Ibid.* lxxvii. I.
310. In 369. See p. 230.
311. Constans in 343. See p. 230.
312. See Bruce, 'Handbook to Wall' (ed. 1895), p. 267.
313. Such tablets, called *tabulae honestae missionis* ("certificates of honourable discharge"), were given to every enfranchised veteran, and were small enough to be carried easily on the person. Four others, besides that at Cilurnum, have been found in Britain.
314. None of the above-mentioned *tabulae* found are later than A.D. 146, which, so far as it goes, supports the contention that Marcus Aurelius was the real extender of the citizenship; Caracalla merely insisting on the liabilities which every Roman subject had incurred by his rise to this status.
315. See pp. 175, 176. Only those fairly identifiable are given; the certain in capitals, the highly probable in ordinary type, and the reasonably probable in italics. For a full list of Romano-British place-names, see Pearson, 'Historical Maps of England.'
316. Probus was fond of thus dealing with his captives. He settled certain Franks on the Black Sea, where they seized shipping and sailed triumphantly back to the Rhine, raiding on their way the shores of Asia Minor, Greece, and Africa, and even storming Syracuse. They ultimately took service under Carausius. [See Eumenius, Panegyric on Constantius.] The Vandals he had captured on the Rhine, after their great defeat by Aurelius on the Danube.
317. This name may also echo some tradition of barbarians from afar having camped there.
318. Eutropius (A.D. 360), 'Breviarium,' x. 21.
319. By the analogy of Saxon and of Lombard (*Lango-bardi* = "Long-spears"), this seems the most probable original derivation of the

name. In later ages it was, doubtless, supposed to have to do with *frank* = free. The franca is described by Procopius ('De Bell. Goth.' ii. 25.), and figures in the Song of Maldon.

320. See Florence of Worcester (A.D. 1138); also the Song of Beowulf.
321. Eutropius, ix. 21.
322. The Franks of Carausius had already swept that sea (see p. 219).
323. Mamertinus, 'Paneg. in Maximian.'
324. Caesar, originally a mere family name, was adapted first as an Imperial title by the Flavian Emperors.
325. Henry of Huntingdon makes her the daughter of Coel, King of Colchester; the "old King Cole" of our nursery rhyme, and as mythical as other eponymous heroes. Bede calls her a concubine, a slur derived from Eutropius (A.D. 360), who calls the connection *obscurius matrimonium* (Brev. x. 1).
326. Eumenius, 'Panegyric on Constantine,' c. 8.
327. Eumenius, 'Panegyric on Constantius,' c. 6.
328. Salisbury Plain has been suggested as the field.
329. The historian Victor, writing about 360 A.D., ascribes the recovery of Britain to this officer rather than to the personal efforts of Constantius. The suggestion in the text is an endeavour to reconcile his statement with the earlier panegyrics of Eumenius.
330. See p. 59. An inscription found near Cirencester proves that place to have been in Britannia Prima. It is figured by Haverfield ('Eng. Hist. Rev.' July 1896), and runs as follows: *Septimius renovat Primae Provinciae Rector Signum et erectam prisca religione columnam.* This is meant for two hexameter lines, and refers to Julian's revival of Paganism (see p. 233).
331. Specimens of these are given by Harnack in the 'Theologische Literaturzeitung' of January 20 and March 17, 1894.
332. See Sozomen, 'Hist. Eccl.' I, 6.
333. See p. 123.

334. The name commonly given to the really unknown author of the 'History of the Britons.' He states that the tombstone of Constantius was still to be seen in his day, and gives Mirmantum or Miniamantum as an alternative name for Segontium. Bangor and Silchester are rival claimants for the name, and one 13th-century MS. declares York to be signified.

335. The Sacred Monogram known as *Labarum*. Both name and emblem were very possibly adapted from the primitive cult of the Labrys, or Double Axe, filtered through Mithraism. The figure is never found as a Christian emblem before Constantine, though it appears as a Heathen symbol upon the coinage of Decius (A.D. 250). See Parsons, 'Non-Christian Cross,' p. 148.

336. Hilary (A.D. 358), 'De Synodis,' § 2.

337. Ammianus Marcellinus, 'Hist.' XX. I.

338. Jerome calls her "fertilis tyrannorum provincia." ['Ad Ctesiph.' xliii.] It is noteworthy that in all ecclesiastical notices of this period Britain is always spoken of as a single province, in spite of Diocletian's reforms.

339. See p. 202.

340. These Scotch pirate craft (as it would seem) are described by Vegetius (A.D. 380) as skiffs (*scaphae*), which, the better to escape observation, were painted a neutral tint all over, ropes and all, and were thus known as *Picts*. The crews were dressed in the same colour—like our present khaki. These vessels were large open boats rowing twenty oars a side, and also used sails. The very scientifically constructed vessels which have been found in the silt of the Clyde estuary may have been *Picts*. See p. 80.

341. Henry of Huntingdon, 'History of the English,' ii. I.

342. Murat, CCLXIII. 4.

343. See p. 225.

344. Jerome, in his treatise against Jovian, declares that he could bear personal testimony to this.

345. See p. 194.

346. Marcellinus dwells upon the chopping seas which usually prevailed in the Straits; and of the rapid tide, which is also referred to by Ausonius (380), "Quum virides algas et rubra corallia nudat Aestus," etc.

347. To him is probably due the reconstruction of the "Vallum" as a defence against attacks from the south, such as the Scots were now able to deliver. See p. 207.

348. Marcellinus, 'Hist.' XXVIII. 3. See p. 202.

349. 'De Quarto Consulatu Honorii,' I. 31.

350. Theodosius married Galla, daughter of Valentinian I.

351. For the later migrations to Brittany see Elton's 'Origins,' p. 350. Samson, Archbishop of York, is said to have fled thither in 500, and settled at Dol. Sidonius Apollinaris speaks of Britons settled by the Loire.

352. 'In Primum Consulatum Stilichonis,' II. 247.

353. Alone amongst the legions it is not mentioned in the 'Notitia' as attached to any province.

354. 'Epithalamium Paladii,' 85.

355. The first printed edition was published 1552.

356. See p. 90.

357. *Portus Adurni*. Some authorities, however, hold this to be Shoreham, others Portsmouth, others Aldrington. The remaining posts are less disputed. They were Branodunum (Brancaster), Garianonum (Yarmouth), Othona (Althorne[?] in Essex), Regulbium (Reculver), Rutupiae (Richborough), Lemanni (Lyminge), Dubris (Dover), and Anderida.

358. There were six "Counts" altogether in the Western Empire, and twelve "Dukes." Both Counts and Dukes were of "Respectable" rank, the second in the Diocletian hierarchy.

359. See p. 237.

360. This word, however, may perhaps signify *Imperial* rather than *London*.
361. Olympiodorus (A.D. 425).
362. 'Hist. Nov.' vi. 10. He is a contemporary authority.
363. Tennyson, 'Guinevere,' 594. The dragon standard first came into use amongst the Imperial insignia under Augustus, and the red dragon is mentioned by Nennius as already the emblem of Briton as opposed to Saxon. The mediaeval Welsh poems speak of the legendary Uther, father of Arthur, as "Pendragon," equivalent to Head-Prince, of Britain.
364. See Rhys, 'Celtic Britain,' pp. 116, 136.
365. Gildas (xxiii.) so calls him.
366. "The groans of the Britons" are said by Bede to have been forwarded to Aetius "thrice Consul," *i.e.* in 446, on the eve of the great struggle with Attila.
367. Nennius (xxviii.) so calls them, and they are commonly supposed to have been clinker-built like the later Viking ships. But Sidonius Apollinaris (455) speaks of them as a kind of coracle. See p. 37.

> "Quin et Armorici piratam Saxona tractus
> Sperabant, cui *pelle* salum sulcare Britannum
> Ludus, et *assuto* glaucum mare findere lembo."
> ('Carm.' vii. 86.)

368. See Elton, 'Origins,' ch. xii.
369. Henry of Huntingdon, 'Hist. of the English,' ii. 1.
370. Nennius, xlix. This is the reading of the oldest MSS.; others are *Nimader sexa* and *Enimith saxas*. The regular form would be *Nimap eowre seaxas*.
371. A coin of Valentinian was discovered in the Cam valley in 1890. On the reverse is a Latin Cross surrounded by a laurel wreath.
372. *Cymry* signifies *confederate*, and was the name (quite probably an older racial appellation revived) adopted by the Western Britons in their resistance to the Saxon advance.

373. Arthur is first mentioned (in Nennius and the 'Life of Gildas') as a Damnonian "tyrant" (i.e. a popular leader with no constitutional status), fighting against "the kings of Kent." This notice must be very early—before the West Saxons came in between Devon and the Kentish Jutes. His early date is confirmed by his mythical exploits being located in every Cymric region—Cornwall, Wales, Strathclyde, and even Brittany.

374. The ambition of Henry V. for Continental dominion was undoubtedly thus quickened.

375. Procopius, 'De Bello Gothico,' iv. 20.

376. These presumably represent the Saxons, who were next-door neighbours to the Frisians of Holland. But Mr. Haverfield's latest (1902) map makes Frisians by name occupy Lothian.

377. Ptolemy's map shows how this error arose; Scotland, by some extraordinary blunder, being therein represented as an *eastward* extension at right angles to England, with the Mull of Galloway as its northernmost point.

378. This fable probably arose from the mythical visit of Ulysses (see p. 64 *n.*), who, as Claudian ('In Rut.' i. 123) tells, here found the Mouth of Hades.

379. Procopius, 'De Bello Gothico,' ii. 6.

380. See my 'Alfred in the Chroniclers,' p. 6.

381. See p. 175.

382. See p. 168.

383. 'Anglo-Saxon Chronicle,' A. 491: "This year Ella and Cissa stormed Anderida and slew all that dwelt therein, so that not one Briton was there left."

384. Chester itself, one of the last cities to fall, is called "a waste chester" as late as the days of Alfred ('A.-S. Chron.,' A. 894).

385. In the districts conquered after the Conversion of the English there was no such extermination, the vanquished Britons being fellow-Christians.

386. For the British survival in the Fenland see my 'History of Cambs.,' III., § 11.

387. Romano-British relics have been found in the Victoria Cave, Settle.

388. 'Comm. on Ps. CXVI.' written about 420 A.D.

389. 'Epist. ad. Corinth.' 5.

390. Catullus, in the Augustan Age, refers to Britain as the "extremam Occidentis," and Aristides (A.D. 160) speaks of it as "that great island opposite Iberia."

391. 'Menol. Graec.,' June 29. A suspiciously similar passage (on March 15) speaks of British ordinations by Aristobulus, the disciple of St. Paul.

392. Nero. This would be A.D. 66.

393. It is less generally known than it should be that the head of St. Paul as well as of St. Peter has always figured on the leaden seal attached to a Papal Bull.

394. Tennyson, 'Holy Grail,' 53. This thorn, a patriarchal tree of vast dimensions, was destroyed during the Reformation. But many of its descendants exist about England (propagated from cuttings brought by pilgrims), and still retain its unique season for flowering. In all other respects they are indistinguishable from common thorns.

395. See also William of Malmesbury, 'Hist. Regum,' § 20.

396. See p. 62.

397. See Introduction to Tennyson's 'Holy Grail' (G.C. Macaulay), p. xxix.

398. See Bp. Browne, 'Church before Augustine,' p. 46.

399. Chaucer, 'Sumpnour's Tale.'

400. Epig. xi. 54: "Claudia coeruleis . . . Rufina Britannis Edita."

401. See p. 141.

402. Epig. v. 13.

403. Tacitus, 'Ann.' xiii. 32.

404. See p. 69.

405. Lanciani, 'Pagan and Christian Rome,' p. 110. The house was bought by Pudens from Aquila and Priscilla, and made a titular church by Pius I.

406. Homily 4 on Ezechiel, 6 on St. Luke.

407. 'Adversus Judaeos,' c. 7.

408. 'Eccl. Hist.' iv.

409. Pope from 177-191.

410. Haddan and Stubbs, i. 25. The 'Catalogus' was composed early in the 4th century, but the incident is a later insertion.

411. See p. 225.

412. He is mentioned by Gildas, along with Julius and Aaron of Caerleon. These last were already locally canonized in the 9th century, as the 'Liber Landavensis' testifies; and the sites of their respective churches could still be traced, according to Bishop Godwin, in the 17th century.

413. Eborius of York, Restitutus of London, and Adelfius of "Colonia Londinensium." The last word is an obvious misreading. Haddan and Stubbs ('Concilia,' p. 7) suggest *Legionensium*, i.e. Caerleon.

414. It is more reasonable to assume this than to imagine, with Mr. French, that these three formed the entire British episcopate. And there is reason to suppose that York, London, and Caerleon were metropolitan sees.

415. Canon x.: De his qui conjuges suas in adulterio deprehendunt, et iidem sunt fideles, et prohibentur nubere; Placuit . . . ne viventibus uxoribus suis, licet adulteris, alias accipiant. [Haddan, 'Concilia,' p. 7. [416.   'Ad Jovian' (A.D. 363).

417. 'Contra Judaeos' (A.D. 387).

418. 'Serm. de Util. Lect. Script.'

419. Hom. xxviii., in II. Corinth.

420. This text seems from very early days to have been a sort of Christian watchword (being, as it were, an epitome of the Faith). The Coronation Oath of our English Kings is still, by ancient

precedent, administered on this passage, *i.e.* the Book is opened for the King's kiss at this point. In mediaeval romance we find the words considered a charm against ghostly foes; and to this day the text is in use as a phylactery amongst the peasantry of Ireland.

421. Ep. xlix. ad Paulinum. These pilgrimages are also mentioned by Palladius (420) and Theodoret (423).

422. Ep. lxxxiv. ad Oceanum.

423. Ep. ci. ad Evang.

424. Whithern (in Latin *Casa Candida*) probably derived its name from the white rough-casting with which the dark stone walls of this church were covered, a strange sight to Pictish eyes, accustomed only to wooden buildings.

425. The practice, now so general, of dedicating a church to a saint unconnected with the locality, was already current at Rome. But hitherto Britain had retained the more primitive habit, by which (if a church was associated with any particular name) it was called after the saint who first built or used it, or, like St. Alban's, the martyr who suffered on the spot. Besides Whithern, the church of Canterbury was dedicated about this time to St. Martin, showing the close ecclesiastical sympathy between Gaul and Britain.

426. The cave is on the northern shore of the Thuner-See, near Sundlauenen. Beatus is said to have introduced sailing into the Oberland by spreading his mantle to the steady breeze which blows down the lake by night and up it during the day. The name of Justus is preserved in the Justis-thal near Merlingen.

427. This name is merely the familiar Welsh *Morgan*, which signifies *sea-born*, done into Greek.

428. See Orosius, 'De Arbit. Lib.,' and other authorities in Haddan and Stubbs.

429. Sidonius, Ep. ix. 3.

430. Constantius, the biographer of Germanus, says they were sent by a Council of Gallican Bishops; but Prosper of Aquitaine (who was

in Rome at the time) declares they were commissioned by Pope Celestine. Both statements are probably true.

431. The lives of Germanus, Patrick, and Ninias will be found in a trustworthy and well-told form in Miss Arnold-Foster's 'Studies in Church Dedication.'

432. See p. 185.

433. Bede, 'Eccl. Hist.' I. xxvi.

434. Many existing churches are more or less built of Roman material. The tower of St. Albans is a notable example, and that of Stoke-by-Nayland, near Colchester. At Lyminge, near Folkestone, so much of the church is thus constructed that many antiquaries have believed it to be a veritable Roman edifice.

435. See Lanciani, 'Pagan and Christian Rome,' p. 115.

436. At Frampton, near Dorchester, and Chedworth, near Cirencester, stones bearing the Sacred Monogram have been found amongst the ruins of Roman "villas."

437. The British rite was founded chiefly on the Gallican, and differed from the Roman in the mode of administering baptism, in certain minutiae of the Mass, in making Wednesday as well as Friday a weekly fast, in the shape of the sacerdotal tonsure, in the Kalendar (especially with regard to the calculation of Easter), and in the recitation of the Psalter. From Canon XVI. of the Council of Cloveshoo (749) it appears that the observance of the Rogation Days constituted another difference.

438. The Mission of St. Columba the Irishman to Britain was a direct result of the Mission of St. Patrick the Briton to Ireland.

439. Magna Charta opens with the words *Ecclesia Anglicana libera sit;* and the Barons who won it called themselves "The Army of the Church."

BIBLIOBAZAAR

The essential book market!

Did you know that you can get any of our titles in large print?

Did you know that we have an ever-growing collection of books in many languages?

Order online:
www.bibliobazaar.com

Find all of your favorite classic books!

Stay up to date with the latest government reports!

At BiblioBazaar, we aim to make knowledge more accessible by making thousands of titles available to you- *quickly and affordably*.

Contact us:
BiblioBazaar
PO Box 21206
Charleston, SC 29413

Lightning Source UK Ltd.
Milton Keynes UK
UKOW06n0630020316
269437UK00009B/125/P